Forever Mame

Hollywood Legends Series

Ronald L. Davis, General Editor

Forever Mame

The Life of Rosalind Russell

Bernard F. Dick

UNIVERSITY PRESS OF MISSISSIPPI   JACKSON

www.upress.state.ms.us

The University Press of Mississippi is a member of the Association of American University Presses.

Copyright © 2006 by University Press of Mississippi
All rights reserved
Manufactured in the United States of America

First edition 2006

Library of Congress Cataloging-in-Publication Data

Dick, Bernard F.
Forever Mame : the life of Rosalind Russell / Bernard F. Dick.— 1st ed.
p. cm. — (Hollywood legends series)
Includes bibliographical references and index.
ISBN-13: 978-1-57806-890-6 (cloth : alk. paper)
ISBN-10: 1-57806-890-8 (cloth : alk. paper) 1. Russell, Rosalind.
2. Actors—United States—Biography. I. Title. II. Series.
PN2287.R86D53 2006
791.4302′8092—dc22   2005032953

British Library Cataloging-in-Publication Data available

In Memoriam
Anita Burns Platus, my Auntie Mame
Thanks for the memory.

CONTENTS

ACKNOWLEDGMENTS

First, I must thank present and former Waterburians—Anne M. Barrie, Mrs. Harry W. Bartlett, Carol Bauby, Rev. Thomas F. Bennett, Lou Gallulo, Hazel M. Keyser, Steve Morris, Peg Ruhlmann, and Doris Trianovick—with whom I corresponded or spoke by phone about Rosalind, her family, and Waterbury at the time she was growing up there. Two Waterburians, Lou and Mary D'Abramo, even went out of their way to obtain a copy of Rosalind's father's death certificate for me.

I must also acknowledge the following, without whose knowledge and expertise this book could ever have been written:

Rita Arno, director, Development Operations, Marymount College of Fordham University, for copying the college's Rosalind Russell file for me;

Jen Booth, for verifying Frederick Brisson's dates of attendance at Rossall College, now Rossall School;

Lance Brisson, for sharing his memories of his parents with me;

John E. Burke, first, for putting me in touch with Lou and Mary D'Abramo and, then, for describing for me the fate of *Mourning Becomes Electra* after its road show engagement when it had to be marketed differently for a mass audience;

Betty Comden, for a memorable phone conversation about *Wonderful Town*;

Ned Comstock, University of Southern California's archivist extraordinaire, for alerting me to collections I did not know existed;

Grover Crisp, vice president, Asset Management and Film Restoration, Sony Pictures, for providing me with tapes of *This Thing Called Love* and *Five Finger Exercise*;

Rosemary Franzen, archivist, St. Margaret's–McTernan School in Waterbury, for clarifying the sale of the Russell home to St. Margaret's for me;

George Gaynes, Rosalind's *Wonderful Town* costar, to whom Rosalind proved to be a true colleague;

Julie Graham, arts librarian for Special Collections at the University of California at Los Angeles, for granting me access to uncataloged scrapbooks that enabled me to document Rosalind's years in repertory; and her assistant, Lauren Buisson, head of operations, arts library, Special Collections, for providing such a relaxed atmosphere for research;

Tony Greco, for securing tapes of some of Rosalind's most obscure films for me;

Barbara Hall, head of Special Collections at the Margaret Herrick Library of the Fairbanks Center for Motion Picture Study, for putting at my disposal every collection that included even the slightest reference to Rosalind;

Kristine Krueger, National Film Information Service, for enabling me to continue my research in New Jersey;

Betty Lawson, director of External and Alumni Affairs at the American Academy of Dramatic Arts (AADA), for allowing me to view Rosalind's AADA file;

Dana Lucisano, reference librarian, Silas Bronson Library, Waterbury, for providing me with a copy of Rosalind's birth certificate (which Rosalind would have preferred no one saw);

The extraordinary team of Kathleen Stein-Smith and Maryann Sena of the Periodicals Division of Fairleigh Dickinson University's Weiner Library (Metropolitan Campus, Teaneck, New Jersey), for tracking down information that would have confounded a professional sleuth;

Katherine M. Restaino, my wife and partner in research, whose eye for detail, sharpened by years of reading detective fiction and working as a college administrator, has saved me from many a grammatical and syntactical pitfall, not to mention lapses in clarity;

Lawrence Roman, for explaining how Rosalind provided him with a great laugh line for his play, *Under the Yum-Yum Tree*;

Jamie Bernstein Thomas, for confirming what I had always read—that Leonard Bernstein composed the *Wonderful Town* score to suit Rosalind's limited range.

Special thanks to Harriet de Biro and the Rosalind fans who communicate via rosalindrussell@yahoogroups.com. May your tribe increase!

Forever Mame

$\mathcal{P}$reface

I started going to the movies shortly after Pearl Harbor, becoming so fascinated by the medium that, for the next three years, I kept an account of what I had seen, writing down on loose-leaf paper the names of the films and the theaters where I saw them. In looking over those still unyellowed pages in December 2004, I discovered that my first Rosalind Russell film was *Take a Letter, Darling,* which I saw on Sunday, 26 July 1942, at the West Side Theater in my hometown, Scranton, Pennsylvania. The second was also at the West Side; it was *My Sister Eileen* on Sunday, 22 November 1942.

I wish I could say that those two films turned me into a Rosalind Russell devotee. But the truth is that they left no impression, unlike some other 1942 films such as *Saboteur,* with its (then) edge-of-the-seat climax atop the Statue of Liberty; *Beyond the Blue Horizon,* in which Dorothy Lamour swam with a tiger; and *My Gal, Sal,* in which Victor Mature was tarred and feathered.

My last entry was on 15 August 1945. Perhaps the end of the war had something to do with my discontinuing the log, but, more likely, the reason was that I had become such a committed moviegoer and a reader of movie magazines—especially *Movie Story* and *Screen Romances* (later renamed *Screen Stories*), which published short-story versions of the films—that I felt no need to keep a journal. I now had a movie memory bank.

By 1946 I had seen enough pictures of Rosalind in the fan magazines to know that she was both a major star and an elegant-looking woman, even

3

though I had yet to encounter her in a film that would persuade me to add her to my pantheon, which then consisted of Bette Davis, Barbara Stanwyck, Ingrid Bergman, and Claudette Colbert. Since I was attending a Catholic grade school, staffed by Sisters of the Immaculate Heart of Mary, I was intrigued by the title of Rosalind's latest movie, *Sister Kenny* (1946). Having seen nuns on the screen before, notably Ingrid Bergman in *The Bells of St. Mary's* (1945), I expected to see Rosalind in a habit. I was surprised to discover not only that Sister Kenny was a nurse, but also that Rosalind could age so convincingly, looking nothing like the soigné woman in the movie magazines who could pass for a fashion model. Since I had a friend with polio, I felt enormous empathy with Rosalind, who, to me, was indistinguishable from Elizabeth Kenny. Rosalind had embraced Sister Kenny's crusade, and while I was too young to join it, I understood its significance. Even today, I find *Sister Kenny* an immensely spiritual film, even though religion is virtually absent from the plot.

Two years later, after seeing *The Velvet Touch* (1948), in which Rosalind looked every inch the Broadway star she was supposed to be, I added her to my pantheon, where she remains enshrined.

As I grew older and managed to see many of Rosalind's movies that I had missed during my childhood, catching them either on television or at New York revival houses—particularly in the 1970s, when such theaters existed—I was struck not so much by her range, which was far greater than the critics ever acknowledged, but by the joy of living that she exhibited in so many of them. Even before Rosalind uttered the immortal line "Life is a banquet" in *Auntie Mame*, it was evident that she had partaken of some of the courses.

I then realized why, after *Sister Kenny*, I became increasingly aware of Rosalind Russell: physically, she reminded me of my mother, who shared Rosalind's zest for life, which was unusual in our family. My grandmother, a Lithuanian immigrant, subscribed to the "life as a vale of tears" philosophy, which her daughter, my mother, gratefully did not inherit. Rather, my mother believed in life as a present from God, who would have been insulted if it were not unwrapped immediately and put to use. My mother had more in common with Mame Dennis than she did with any member of her family—except, I would like to think, for me.

I was fortunate to see Rosalind on Broadway in both *Wonderful Town* and *Auntie Mame*. Rosalind's performance in *Wonderful Town* (which I saw at a Saturday matinee in August 1953) was a revelation; although I was familiar with the score from the Decca original cast LP, I had no idea what to expect from Rosalind in a musical, knowing her primarily as a comic, and sometimes dramatic, actress. To see her in *Wonderful Town* from row C, side orchestra, at the Winter Garden remains one of the highlights of my theatergoing career, which began three years earlier in August 1950 with *Kiss Me, Kate*. I was struck by both the naturalness of her acting and the professionalism of her dancing. She was not a fashion statement; except for the dress she wore in the finale, she looked like any woman living in a Greenwich Village basement apartment in the 1930s. Her singing seemed more musical that Saturday afternoon than it did on the record. But it was her ability to hold her own with trained dancers that truly impressed me, particularly in "Swing," a pastiche of popular lyrics that has to be performed as if it were an exercise in free association. "Conga!" was not the free-for-all that I imagined from the record. The cadets handled Rosalind as if she were a package marked "fragile," either because she had another show that evening or because she had incurred too many bruises to perform the number as energetically as she did earlier in the run. Regardless, that afternoon was magic time. A sixteen-year-old from Scranton, Pennsylvania, had seen Rosalind Russell in person, and close enough to experience that privileged moment when the rest of the audience dissolves into a dark mass, so that you have the star to yourself.

Auntie Mame, which I saw twice at Broadhurst Theatre (first as a standee in December 1956; then a month later in row H, side balcony, now called the rear mezzanine), was another matter. The play corresponded more or less to my expectations: a grand entrance, a bravura performance, costumes that generated a buzz from the audience as if they were at a fashion show, some profanity (although I was not prepared for "goddamn, "son of a bitch," and "bastard" in one play, much less from Rosalind), double entendre (which, at twenty-one, I understood), repartee (less witty than I thought), and continuous laughter (which was the case at both performances). Having read the novel, I did not expect the tenderness that Rosalind displayed in her scenes with Patrick, in which she acted more like a mother than an aunt. However, as I hope to show in chapter 9, the movie was an improvement over the stage version, as was Rosalind's screen performance, which had far greater warmth.

I have tried to place Rosalind's art within the context of her career, integrating biography, film history, and criticism to create as complete a picture as possible. I am honored to be the first to write a critical biography of Rosalind, and I hope biographies will be done of such talented performers as Claudette Colbert, Susan Hayward, Ann Sheridan, and the sadly unappreciated Eleanor Parker, all of whom deserve to be more than memories.

CHAPTER 1

The Gal from Waterbury

Rosalind never told the truth about her age. Her obituary in the *New York Times* gave 1912 as her year of birth. She would have been pleased. In 1962, when Rosalind chronicled her career in the pages of the *Saturday Evening Post*, she also admitted to 1912, which would have meant that she received her high school diploma in 1930. Actually, by 1930, Rosalind had graduated from the American Academy of Dramatic Arts, done at least one season of summer stock, and was performing with a Boston repertory company.

She never altered month and day, however; that was always 4 June. The year was a moveable feast. It was variously reported as 1908, 1910, 1912 (of course), and even 1913. Rosalind would have drawn the line at 1913; that was the year of her husband's birth.

Rosalind's birth certificate tells another story. It was 4 June, all right, but the year was 1907. Rosalind had a reason for the fabrication. She belonged to an age that subscribed to Orsino's view of marriage in Shakespeare's *Twelfth Night* (2.4): "Let still the woman take / An elder than herself; so wear she to him, / So sways she level in her husband's heart." And when Rosalind accepted Frederick Brisson's offer of marriage in 1941, she knew she was marrying a man almost six years younger than herself. Rosalind also belonged to a profession in which forty was the point of no return for an actress, unless she was willing to play mothers or widows, and that's if she's lucky; otherwise, recluses and psychos. She would have agreed with Walter Huston, who reminded Joan Crawford, despondent at turning thirty, that age is only a number. Rosalind would have phrased it differently: Age is a number that is always a variable.

She was born at home—43 Chestnut Avenue in Waterbury, Connecticut, whose brass mills made it "the brass capital of the world." In 1997, two decades after her death, the Silas Bronson Library established the Waterbury Hall of Fame at the Brass Mill Center; among the first inductees were Rosalind, ball player Jimmy Piersall, and choreographer Lucia Chase. Even in 1997, the *Waterbury Observer*, which covered the ceremony, reported her date of birth as 4 June 1912. At least Waterburians were given her year of choice.

Although christened Catherine Rosalind Russell, "Catherine" was soon dropped in favor of "Rosalind," supposedly inspired by the name of a steamer, the S.S. *Rosalind*, that her parents had once taken to Nova Scotia. At least that is what her father always claimed. Rosalind came from a prominent Waterbury family. Her father, James Edward Russell, was a distinguished trial lawyer with a Yale Law School degree. Her mother, the former Clara Agnes McKnight, was a Waterbury native who taught at the same high school, Notre Dame Academy, which Rosalind later attended. Clara assumed Rosalind would also pursue a teaching career. Her daughter, however, had other plans.

Rosalind was the fourth of seven children, born when her father was forty-seven and her mother was thirty-two. Despite James Russell's age at the time of her birth, his good humor and infinite patience made him an ideal father. He was so energetic that Rosalind assumed he was in his late thirties when she was growing up. Rosalind's favorite sibling was her older sister, Clara, who became the fashion editor of *Town and Country*. Clara was a natural beauty, or as Waterbury resident Lou Gallulo put it, "What a gal!"

Rosalind's brothers—James, George, and John—followed in their father's footsteps and studied law. James never left Waterbury; after his father's death in 1926, he took over the practice. Gallulo found James very much like his father: a stylish dresser who never lost the common touch. Rosalind had two younger sisters, Josephine and Mary Jane. Mary Jane receives more space in Rosalind's autobiography, *Life Is a Banquet*, than Josephine, who became an executive secretary. Mary Jane was assistant to the dean of women at Sarah Lawrence College until she became a researcher and photographer at Time, Inc. Rosalind's siblings were proud of her, but, except for Mary Jane, she was always their sister, the movie star. It was Mary Jane who truly recognized the extent of Rosalind's talent, often expressing her admiration in heartfelt letters.

Rosalind's was a storybook childhood: elm-shaded streets, Victorian homes with white picket fences and rambling roses, clanging trolleys, gentleman callers, fluttery daughters, stern fathers, and anxious mothers. Rosalind would have added a few personal details: the tomboy who climbed trees, went horseback riding, tore ligaments, broke limbs, told fibs, clowned on the ice, frolicked in chiffon, survived the humiliation of a wayward bathing suit that slipped down to her waist during a diving competition, strung a rope between her home and a friend's next door so they could send each other messages in a basket, and discovered the transforming power of makeup at the same time as she was rolling dice and shooting pool.

Had Lou Gallulo known Rosalind, he would have said the same of her as he did of Clara. It was not until 1943 that the title of one of Rosalind's films summed her up: *What a Woman!* But in early decades of the twentieth century, "What a gal!" would have sufficed.

Shortly after Rosalind was born, the Russells moved to a thirteen-room Victorian house on upper Willow Street (now the site of the Snyder Funeral Home), which Rosalind described as benignly gothic, as if it had been designed by Charles Addams in a playful mood. In Waterbury, moving a few blocks from 43 Chestnut Avenue to 114 Willow Street was not just a matter of changing residences. Chestnut Avenue was an address; Willow

Street, a way of life. Waterburians referred to Willow Street as "Cracker Hill" because of the popular saying that it was so expensive to live there that the residents subsisted on crackers. The Russells dispelled that myth, along with another alleging that the women of Willow Street became bowlegged from all the walking they had to do. Walking posed no problem for Rosalind; but then, in her youth, few things did. Cracker Hill, however, was not "Snob Hill." Peg Ruhlman, who lived on nearby Ludlow Street, remembered the area not so much as a grid work of streets and trolley lines but as a community where, in a crisis, help was only a house away. The sight of a car parked outside someone's home was the cue to knock at the door and request a ride to the hospital for an ailing relative. "Nobody locked their doors in those days. If we ran out of bread mother would send us to the neighborhood grocery store, Sam's on Willow Street and Arch Street, close by. Sam Nejame, the grocer, would leave a pad and pencil attached to the door of the store and customers who needed bread before the store opened were allowed to take a loaf and write their names on the pad as the bread would be delivered in a box early and left in front of the store."

Peg Ruhlman's memories of Waterbury correspond to Rosalind's as recorded in the early pages of *Life Is a Banquet*, in which she described her father in his Prince Albert coat, her Willow Street home with its pear trees and rose garden, the rattle of the Willow Street trolley, and the Yalies who thronged the front porch waiting for sister Clara. If Rosalind's Waterbury evokes a Frank Capra movie, a Booth Tarkington novel, or a Currier and Ives painting, it only means that Capra, Tarkington, and Currier and Ives succeeded in capturing a way of life that, for the most part, is now lost or exists in a suburban penumbra beyond the pale of urban blight.

The Russells' move to Willow Street was not merely the need for a more spacious house and a barn to stable James Russell's horses, which his children were expected to ride; it also fitted in with the Russells' agenda. By providing their children with the comforts of life, including a home with an attic where they could set up a billiard table and improvise a bowling alley, James and Clara Russell instilled in them the importance of helping those less fortunate than themselves. Although James Russell was often encouraged to run for public office, he preferred to remain in law, where he could serve humanity.

Rosalind no sooner arrived in Hollywood than she began volunteering in hospitals, generally in pediatric wards. On 13 October 1949 she returned to Waterbury as spokesperson for the Community Chest. During her stay, she visited the children's ward at St. Mary's Hospital, pausing by the bed of Bobby Keyser, who had been placed in a body cast because of an auto accident. The glow she brought to the boy's face did not go unnoticed, particularly by his mother, Hazel, who remembered it as recently as 2003. If the Russells had humanitarian expectations for their children, Rosalind more than exceeded them. Although she received numerous awards throughout her career, the citations accompanying them often said more about the writer than the honoree. The 1975 Torch of Courage award, given to Rosalind by the Ladies Auxiliary to the Veterans of Foreign Wars the year before she died, was the exception: "The courage of this great lady, whose dramatic talents have entertained the world, lights the Torch of Service." Courage and service were words Rosalind understood: *courage* in the face of deteriorating health, beginning with two mastectomies, followed by rheumatoid arthritis that disfigured her hands, a bout of pneumonia from which she almost died, and cortisone injections that erased her cheekbones; *service* in the cause of humankind that lasted throughout her lifetime, starting in 1942 when she entertained military personnel during World War II and ending posthumously in 1977 when the Fourteenth International Congress of Rheumatology acknowledged her efforts on behalf of arthritis research. A devout Catholic to the very end, Rosalind would have agreed that she was put on earth to serve, not to be served—except in restaurants.

Inevitably, Rosalind received a Catholic education, which even extended to college, until she decided to try the theater. The Russells' parish, St. Margaret's at 289 Willow Street, like so many Catholic churches at the time, had its own grade school to which Rosalind could easily walk. She was notorious for skipping class and sneaking off to a movie (often without paying). Eager to do what the women on the screen did, although preferably on a stage, Rosalind was so taken with their makeup that she began experimenting with cosmetics. Noting her new look, St. Margaret's pastor stopped her one day and asked offhandedly, "Do you know what I would do if I were as pretty as you?" Expecting a compliment, Rosalind shook her head "no." "Wash my face," he answered. Without knowing it, the pastor had delivered a real Rosalind Russell putdown. If Rosalind remembered the incident, she would have agreed.

As a child, she was an exhibitionist. Deflecting attention from others to herself was not a bid for recognition, as it is with so many children, but a natural inclination to seek center stage, regardless of the venue. And in 1920s Waterbury, a budding actress could not afford to be particular. Anything would do: a beach, a skating rink, summer camp, or a basketball court.

When Peg Ruhlman was growing up in Waterbury, she often heard her mother, Helen, talk about the Russells. Helen became Rosalind's confidante, perhaps, Peg suspects, because Helen was six feet tall, and Rosalind knew she too was never meant to be petite. When Rosalind unburdened herself to Helen, admitting that she wanted to be an actress and rightly suspecting that her parents would disapprove, Helen encouraged her, but with one caveat: "Stop slouching!" From that day on, Rosalind maintained perfect posture.

After graduating from St. Margaret's, Rosalind went on to high school at Notre Dame Academy, also within walking distance of her home. She later a good student; her best subject was English. Her attendance record there was as spotty as it was at St. Margaret's. The lure of a live performance or a movie took precedence over her studies.

Catholic grammar school, Catholic high school, Catholic college: in 1925, Rosalind, somewhat reluctantly, was packed off to Marymount College (later part of Fordham University) in Tarrytown, New York. At first she balked at the prospect of spending time in a classroom, studying subjects for which she had no use, when all the time she only wanted to act. Then it struck her: Tarrytown in Westchester County was closer to New York than she had ever been. And the college had a theater program. Rosalind knew she could get good grades and do shows at the same time. Cast in the title role of the Jesuit saint, Francis Xavier, Rosalind noticed that one of her classmates, Anne Rogan, was having difficulty with her one and only line. Ignoring the director, Rosalind coached her friend until she delivered the line properly.

Rosalind was also a quick study. While only a freshman, Rosalind stepped into the title role of *The Bohemian Girl* when the lead came down with laryngitis two days before the opening. In *Banquet*, Rosalind mistakenly referred to *The Bohemian Girl* as *La Bohème*. While both are operas, Michael Balfe's *The Bohemian Girl*, once a favorite with British audiences, is rarely performed. Perhaps the Marymount production was Balfe's opera sans music—just the libretto with a few musical interludes. If the students actually performed the opera with Rosalind in the leading role, she would have played Arline (a count's daughter in love with a Polish nobleman disguised as a gypsy), who sings the opera's most famous aria, "I Dreamt I Dwelt in Marble Halls." The thought of nineteen-year-old Rosalind singing a staple of the soprano repertoire is tantalizing, especially since she later described herself as having "the vocal chords of a frog."

On Wednesday, 13 October 1926, Rosalind was in class. Her father, then sixty-six, walked from his Willow Street home to his Bank Street office, as he customarily did each morning. Although he had not been in good health for a year, he maintained the same schedule, making sure to be at his desk by 10:00 AM. For some reason, he left the office briefly, returning at 11:30 AM. His secretary sensed that he was ill when he moved his chair to an open window and sat by it. Suddenly he fell over, dying immediately. The cause of death was heart disease.

James Russell's funeral on 15 October was a major event. If Waterbury residents did not know it, the *Waterbury Republican* acknowledged that he was one of the city's biggest owners of prime real estate, much of it in downtown Waterbury. Not surprisingly, the mayor was one of the pallbearers; since James had been a board member of the Silas Bronson Library, the flag in front of the building flew at half-mast until the funeral was over, at which time the library reopened.

When the Russells gathered for the reading of the will, the children discovered how determined their father was that they become educated citizens. In 1938, Rosalind quoted the text of the will to a magazine reporter, omitting only the financial details: "To the above mentioned sons and daughters, I bequeath the annual sum of—thousand dollars as long as they study in any school or college or with any authorized instructor. Immediately after each of the above mentioned shall cease to study, he or she shall for the period of three years, live away from the family home and receive no income whatever. Also, at the expiration of this three-year period, each and everyone of the above mentioned sons and daughters shall receive—thousand dollars in cash."

After his children had completed their studies, James Russell expected them to work for three years before receiving the rest of their inheritance. Although Josephine kept taking courses until she was twenty-eight, Rosalind regarded school as a necessary evil, something one leaves as soon as possible. Still, the prospect of free tuition appealed to her, but not so she could graduate from Marymount. She knew even before her father's death that she would never be a member of the 1929 graduating class. She was determined to become an actress, which meant a professional theater school, not a liberal arts college. To her, there was only one such institution, the oldest in the country: the American Academy of Dramatic Arts (AADA). The main obstacle was Clara Russell, who assumed that Rosalind would become a teacher like herself. Once Rosalind convinced her mother that a diploma from the Academy would qualify her to teach speech and drama, Clara was satisfied, reminding her daughter that one of the great advantages of the profession was having summers to oneself.

These are the highlights of Rosalind's life up to 1927. By 1943, she had been in Hollywood for almost a decade and was now part of an industry where lives are refashioned by publicists who purge away the mundane, even at the expense of truth. As usual, 1912 was given as her year of birth;

Marymount College had become the elite Marymount School in Tarrytown-on-the Hudson; and Rosalind graduated with a BA from Barnard, "where she dabbled in literature, metaphysics, and theology, with a misguided attempt at Journalism, which she quickly gave up." This is the kind of background one might expect of the career women Rosalind played on the screen. Rosalind's life was quite different. She received honorary degrees in her lifetime, but never a BA.

Although Rosalind left Marymount in spring 1927, the college treated her as an alumna, and throughout her life Rosalind acted as if Marymount were her alma mater. In 1964 she was the guest speaker at the Marymount College Alumnae Association's luncheon in New York. Twelve years later, recovering from a hip replacement and moon-faced from cortisone injections to relieve her rheumatoid arthritis, Rosalind was forced to decline the college's invitation to the Alumnae Ball on 1 October 1976. On 31 August she dictated a letter to Marymount's director of Alumnae Relations: "I very much regret that I will not be able to join you that night . . . as I am just now slowly recovering from a complete hip replacement together with several serious complications. . . . Therefore I must stay very close to home throughout the rest of the year."

At the Alumnae Ball, Rosalind was scheduled to receive an honorary doctorate. Although Barbara Walters represented her that evening, no degree was awarded. However, Marymount sent her red roses, her favorite flower, and a plaque, which pleased her even more. On 25 October she dictated another letter in which she thanked the college for the roses and the plaque. Never one to dwell on her health problems, Rosalind noted that she was "making a little progress" and closed by saying, "Again, my heartfelt thanks to you all, and I hope that I will soon be able to be with you to receive that much delayed doctorate."

Rosalind died a month later on 28 November. There is no record of a posthumously awarded doctorate.

CHAPTER 2

Riding the Broadway- Hollywood Local

In fall 1927, a Marymount BA, much less an honorary doctorate, meant nothing to Rosalind, who was only interested in being admitted to the American Academy of Dramatic Arts (AADA), then the country's most prestigious drama school. It was founded as the Lyceum Theatre School of Acting in 1884 by Franklin Haven Sargeant, who, after his death in 1923, was succeeded by the formidable Charles Jehlinger. Jehlinger, a member of AADA's first graduating class, joined the AADA faculty twelve years later, ending his long career there as dean. It was Jehlinger for whom Rosalind auditioned on 23 September 1927.

Although Rosalind only devotes a few paragraphs in *Banquet* to her year and a half at the Academy, she was well aware of Jehlinger's reputation as an acting teacher. When Jehlinger died in 1952, the *New York Times* obituary (30 July 1952) listed Rosalind among his many students—such as William Powell, Lauren Bacall, Ruth Gordon, and Agnes Moorehead—who went on to successful stage and screen careers. Although Jehlinger never achieved the guru status of Stella Adler, Sanford Meisner, or Lee Strasberg, he anticipated their commitment to an acting style based on honesty rather than artifice, stressing the importance of technique but never making it an end in itself or a substitute for a paucity of talent. Jehlinger would have questioned Meisner's two principles, "Act before you think" and "An ounce of behavior is worth a pound of words." Jehlinger believed that thought, in the sense of analyzing the script and working out the characterization, is part of the acting process and that the actor's quest for truth does not mean subordinating language to behavior. To Jehlinger, an inaudible actor, no matter how expressive, was an oxymoron.

Rosalind's audition report in the Academy archives consists of information provided by herself, along with Jehlinger's evaluation of her performance. Rosalind supplied the following data: address (114 Willow Street, Waterbury, Connecticut); height (5 feet 7 inches); weight (126 pounds); nationality (English and Irish-Scotch); general education (two years of college); stage experience (amateur); age (twenty-two). For someone who spent her life subtracting from her age, this may have been the only time Rosalind added to it. In September 1927, Rosalind was twenty and had not yet made 1912 her year of birth. She may have wanted to appear older to compensate for her limited stage experience.

Jehlinger was impressed with the audition. Although he characterized her voice as "nasal" and her temperament as "mental-nervous," perhaps implying that she seemed high-strung (which later worked to her advantage in fast-moving comedies like *His Girl Friday* and *My Sister Eileen*), he found her pronunciation "good," her reading "intelligent," her pantomime "expressive," and her dramatic instinct "sound." Her audition piece was from *Camille*, presumably Matilda Heron's translation of the French classic that served as a vehicle for Ethel Barrymore, Eva LeGallienne, and Lillian Gish. In one sense it was an odd choice for someone who, even as a child, exhibited a natural flair for comedy. She had chosen a work that, even in a substandard production such as the one Willa Cather described in *My Antonia*, would leave handkerchiefs "wet through by the time that moribund woman sank for the last time into the arms of her lover." Knowing that she had mastered comedy, Rosalind fought typecasting throughout her career by pursuing roles that allowed her to explore a character's inner life, not just the shimmering facade. When an interviewer asked, "Have you ever missed out on a role you wanted?" Rosalind quickly answered, *Dark Victory.* The 1939 film was a tour de force for Bette Davis as Judith Traherne, who faced terminal illness unflinchingly. It is easy to understand Rosalind's interest in a role with such a broad emotional spectrum. But whether she could have traced the same character arc as Davis, who ran the gamut from spoiled socialite to cancer patient turned cancer victim, and from self-pitying pleasure seeker to noble wife who chooses to die alone, is problematic.

At the end of the report, Jehlinger wrote "gives promise." And so, in 1929, instead of graduating from Marymount, Rosalind graduated from the American Academy of Dramatic Arts.

Rosalind has written impressionistically about the five-year period, 1929–34, that preceded her Hollywood career, although those were her formative years as an actress. She does not deny that it was a hectic time, yet she only mentions a few of the plays in which she appeared, never even suggesting that in two of the stock companies where she performed she was not only the star but also a favorite among audiences and local critics. The state of Rosalind's health partially explains why *Life Is a Banquet* is not as inclusive as one would like. When she undertook the project a year before her death, she must have wondered if she would live to see its publication, which, tragically, she did not. In April 1975, Rosalind nearly died from pneumonia and spent ten days at Cedars of Lebanon hospital recuperating. Under the circumstances, it is amazing that Rosalind remembered what she did. That she made a montage of her past and transposed dates and events was both a vestige of her profession, in which time is elastic—prolonged (sometimes agonizingly) or collapsed (sometimes disconcertingly)—and her decision to disclose only what she wanted her readers to know.

Since Rosalind thought of herself as a writer as well as an actress, she could have written *Banquet* without a collaborator had she been in better health. In 1975, she knew she needed one; after reading Chris Chase's *How to Become a Movie Star, or a Terrible Beauty Is Born*, she decided that Chase, whose sense of humor was similar to hers, could assist her in celebrating life's banquet, including some of the unappetizing side dishes but never allowing them to spoil the feast. Chase arrived in Los Angeles in August 1975, leaving two weeks later with the tapes of their conversations, which she then edited and mailed back to Rosalind. Chase returned to Los Angeles in spring 1976, which proved to be the last time she would see Rosalind. Although Chase called Rosalind's memory "fantastic," "selective" is the better word. *Life Is a Banquet*—a title Frederick Brisson selected, although Chase preferred the simpler "Roz"—is not error free. Most of the errors were minor: Charles Jehlinger's name is misspelled ("Jellinger"), and the Russells' Willow Street residence is now the Snyder (not "Schneider") Funeral Home. Nor was train service between Waterbury and New York discontinued after the 1955 flood. One error, however, was disconcerting: Rosalind's insistence that she sang every note in the movie version of *Gypsy*, which she herself knew was untrue. Rosalind should have written that she recorded the entire score, as, indeed, she did. However, little of what was recorded ended up in the film.

Sometimes omissions are more frustrating than errors, which at least are correctable. In *Banquet*, Rosalind downplayed her pre-Hollywood stage work, implying that it was insignificant. Actually, it was quite the opposite. Perhaps she thought of herself as a screen star who had two Broadway hits, as opposed to, say, Helen Hayes, who made a handful of movies but had such a successful stage career that she was dubbed "first lady of the American theater." If Rosalind actually believed her 1929–1934 stage work was irrelevant, she was ignoring two important facts: the theater gave her the technical skills that she only had to scale down for the camera; and without stage training, she would have had nothing to scale down.

Unfortunately, Rosalind viewed her years in repertory as apprentice work, the equivalent of an author's juvenilia. She wrote the following in 1962: "Suppose we now skip lightly over my early years in the theater. The ups and downs of a young actress on the New York beat can be fascinating in retrospect only for herself and her contemporaries. I played in stock; I worked with an English company in Boston; I was with the Theatre Guild on the road—in short, I did a lot of this and that in the theater."

Until she came to Hollywood in 1934, Rosalind did a lot of one thing: stage acting. It was customary for the members of AADA's graduating class to appear in a play before an invited audience of friends, relatives, and agents on a Friday afternoon at the Lyceum Theatre, AADA's original home, on Forty-fifth Street, East of Broadway. In 1929, the Lyceum, a quarter of a century old, was regarded as far less venerable than it is today. Then, it was just another Broadway house distinguished by six Corinthian columns rising above the entrance and sporting a marble lobby with two dramatic staircases. Now the Lyceum is a Beaux Arts landmark theater, recently the home of the Pulitzer prize–winning play *I Am My Own Wife* (2003). By the time Rosalind walked onto the Lyceum stage in 1929, albeit in a student production, she had been preceded by such luminaries as William Gillette and Lionel and Ethel Barrymore; Sarah Bernhardt also played the Lyceum, not on stage but as the title character in the French-made film *Queen Elizabeth*, which premiered there on 12 July 1912. At almost twenty-two, Rosalind could hardly have been expected to care about tradition. She had been given the lead in Frederick Lonsdale's *The Last of Mrs. Cheyney* (1926), the same role that Ina Claire had created a few years earlier. In the AADA production, another AADA graduate, Agnes Moorehead, was appearing in a supporting role. Although Rosalind does not mention Moorehead in *Banquet*, the two of them turned out to be the most distinguished alumnae of the class of 1929.

If Rosalind had been given the lead over Moorehead, it was because she came closer than any of her peers to mastering the high style and projecting the aura of sophistication that had become Ina Claire's signature; otherwise, a comedy of manners like *The Last of Mrs. Cheyney*—in which the title character, supposedly a widow, throws elegant garden parties to meet affluent people whom she and her butler can then rob—would descend into farce. Mrs. Cheney is completely unregenerate, justifying her profession as a form of upward mobility—from selling stockings to stealing jewelry. When Charles, who poses as her butler (but who had mentored her in the art of thievery) laments that his protégée never went beyond filching watches and tie pins, Mrs. Cheney says apologetically: "You mustn't be angry with me, Charles. It's the decency that I'm cursed with that prevents me." Such candor does not go unrewarded, and in keeping with the gleeful amorality permeating the play, Charles goes on a trip around the world, and Mrs. Cheney ends up as the wife of a peer, whose father is a bishop.

Rosalind graduated from AADA in time for summer stock. In *Banquet*, Rosalind describes her first exposure to stock as if it were a scene from one of her movies. The stock company was in Saranac Lake, New York, and Rosalind, who had just lost out on a job with a Connecticut company when she scoffed at the $150-a-week salary she was offered, was not going to make the same mistake again. By exaggerating her experience, she demanded the same amount that she would have received in Connecticut if she had not had such an unrealistic perception of her worth.

Rosalind called the Saranac Lake engagement her first experience in stock. However, in an as yet uncataloged scrapbook in the Rosalind Russell Papers at UCLA, there is a notice of her appearance with the Adirondack Players in Saranac Lake during the summers of 1927 and 1928. This was supposedly the same company (Rosalind does not mention the name). Rosalind did not regard those summers as a part of her life, but as part of her past—a past that was not worth elaborating upon. To her, the past was neither prologue nor epilogue; it was myth, a mingled yarn of fact, invention, memory, and hype resulting in a colorful but problematic tapestry.

One would like to think that if Rosalind had trekked up to Saranac Lake immediately after leaving Marymount, she would have admitted it. It certainly would have been consistent with her decision to become an actress, in addition to conjuring up the image of a twenty-year-old Rosalind, her ambition sparked by the plays she did at Marymount, heading for the Adirondacks to begin her stage apprenticeship and returning in the fall to study at AADA.

Rosalind, however, did not return to AADA in the fall. According to her student registration card, she was expected to start classes in October

1927; she was classified as a junior, probably because she had two years of college. "Transferred to Jan. 1928 JR" was later typed on her card. Exactly what Rosalind did between 23 September 1927, when she auditioned, and January 1928, when she entered the program, is unknown. She may have returned to Saranac Lake; if she did, she would not have been performing in a tent, their summer venue, but in a more traditional space, given the climate in northern New York. Rosalind, in fact, could have done anything during the October 1927–January 1928 period; since the AADA program required an eighteen-month commitment, she could still graduate in 1929.

The scrapbook clipping only mentions one Adirondack Players production in which Rosalind appeared: Edwin Burke's *This Thing Called Love*; according to another news item, the Players were given special permission to perform Burke's play during its Broadway run. It was common for a play to try out in summer stock before proceeding to Broadway; Rose Franken's *Another Language* (1932), for example, opened in Greenwich, Connecticut, the summer before it arrived in New York in April 1933. But it was highly unusual for a play to be performed in stock and on Broadway at the same time.

This Thing Called Love premiered at the Maxine Elliott's Theatre on 17 September 1928 and ran for four months. The date of the Adirondack Players' production is unknown. Quite possibly, the news release was inaccurate, and the Players mounted its production either in summer 1927, prior to the Broadway run, or in summer 1928, after it was over.

Better documented is Rosalind's appearance in a Buffalo production of the play in 1933, when she was the leading lady of the Teck Players. *This Thing Called Love* also figured in Rosalind's movie career when it was filmed for the second time in 1940, with herself in the lead, and released to the consternation of the Legion of Decency in early 1941. The film was substantially different from the play, although the names of the main characters, Ann Marvin and Tice Collins, remained the same. In the play, Ann, disillusioned by her sister's recent divorce, agrees to an in-name-only relationship with Tice, with the understanding that he will pay her to run their household and that neither will interfere in the other's love life. Naturally, the plan fails, Ann and Tice fall in love, and marriage trumps infidelity. The film version, quite racy in its time, had Ann (Rosalind) arguing that divorce would be less prevalent if couples refrained from sex for the first three months of marriage. This plan also fails; since Ann and Tice are already married, the film cannot champion marriage, but rather its consummation—the sooner, the better. Rosalind barely mentions *This Thing Called Love* in *Banquet,* nor does she even allude to the play, which provided her with the only role she played in stock that she repeated on the screen.

The other entries in the 1927–1934 scrapbook are better documented; they contain nothing about her 1929 summer at Saranac Lake, but a good deal about her work in Boston, Worcester, and Buffalo stock companies. In fall 1929, Rosalind became a member of actor-manager E. (Edward) E. Clive's repertory company, whose home was Boston's Copley Theatre. The English-born Clive originally planned to be a doctor until he became obsessed with the stage. Clive belonged to the tradition of the actor-manager, once a staple of the British theater, in which an actor formed his own company and took it on tour. Clive's Copley Players was a real repertory company. True to his origins, Clive favored British plays, which partially explains Rosalind's accent in her 1930s films. Although Rosalind remained with the company for two years, she was not its resident star and thus was free to accept other offers. Naturally, her sights were set on Broadway.

In fall 1930, when she learned that there were parts available in a return engagement of the Theatre Guild's musical revue *The Garrick Gaieties,* she auditioned and was cast in a couple of sketches, all of which were satirical. "Rose of Arizona" had Rosalind playing a vamp; "How to Write for the Movies" poked fun at the Barrymores and the Lunts; "Panic's End," whose title was inspired by the great antiwar play *Journey's End,* took a comic view of the suicides occasioned by the Wall Street crash. Nothing was sacred in *The Garrick Gaieties.*

The revue had an impressive score by Vernon Duke and lyrics by E. Y. "Yip" Harburg. In the cast were Sterling Holloway, who moved on to

Hollywood, where he made a career out of playing rubes and naifs; the gifted comic Imogene Coca, who became a household name in the 1950s when she co-starred with Sid Caesar in NBC's *Your Show of Shows* (1950–1954); and Philip Loeb, who played Jake Goldberg in *The Goldbergs* from the time it moved from radio to television in 1949 until he became a victim of McCarthyism two years later, committing suicide in 1955.

The anonymous *New York Times* reviewer of *The Garrick Gaieties* (17 October 1930) implied that the replacements, of which Rosalind was one, did not measure up to the original cast. Of the sixteen-member company, only Holloway, Coca, and Loeb were singled out for the faintest of praise. But to Rosalind, it was Broadway, and there was a tour that paid three hundred dollars a week. Besides, the 1930–1931 season was far from over.

Nineteen thirty-one found Rosalind back on Broadway as Miss Mallory in Alma Wilson's *Company's Coming!* which had an even shorter run than *The Garrick Gaieties*: eight performances as opposed to twelve. In his *Times* review (21 April 1931), Brooks Atkinson (then J. Brooks Atkinson), who soon became the nation's most influential drama critic, resorted to culinary imagery to describe the play as "a thick stew of random laughs and indigestible dullness." Again, there was no mention of Rosalind, only of her character: "a Southern belle introduced because her exaggerated drawl may sound funny." Perhaps it was better that she went unnamed.

Then it was back to Boston, but not for long. Once movies found a voice, repertory houses began losing the popularity they enjoyed during the silent era. Believing he might have a future in Hollywood, Clive took off for the West Coast, returning periodically to New York and working steadily in film and theater until his sudden death from a heart attack in June 1940. In *Banquet*, Rosalind does not mention (or perhaps had forgotten) that Clive played the minor role of a tour guide in the film version of Emlyn Williams's *Night Must Fall* (1937), in which she costarred with Robert Montgomery.

Nor does Rosalind allude to her engagements with the Worcester, Massachusetts Civic Repertory Company or Buffalo's Teck Players, both of which provided her with starring roles and brought her accolades from the local press, as the scrapbook entries attest. One critic wrote of her performance in Philip Barry's *Paris Bound* (1927), which she did in Worcester in early January 1933: "The first act was about to fall to pieces of its own inertia until a young woman named Rosalind Russell walked on stage."

If Rosalind enlivened the Worcester production of *Paris Bound*, she must have been playing Fanny, who mistakenly greets a divorced woman by her former name, Mrs. Hutton, only to be corrected: "Mrs. White, it is now." Not to be undone, Fanny delivers the kind of rejoinder for which Rosalind became famous: "Of course. Trust me to forget it, though." Her performance in the Teck Players' production of *Goodbye Again* (1932) was deemed "a personal triumph," and Rosalind was praised for having "a nice critical feeling for farce." Soon she had become "our Miss Russell, leading lady of the Teck Players." Wearing the latest fashions, she attended chamber of commerce luncheons, charming the business community. In fact, Rosalind had become so indispensable to the Teck Players that the company disbanded shortly after she left.

By late fall 1933, Rosalind realized she had gone as far as she could with the Teck Players or any stock company. Her 1933 credits reflect the versatility actors acquired in stock, where they discovered their strengths and weaknesses by exposure to a wide range of plays. If Rosalind had any weaknesses, they were not apparent. Her strengths were evident: comedy of every type (drawing room, farce, romantic) and psychological melodrama. That she did more of the former than the latter was indicative of the way the public perceived her: a class act with a wardrobe to match. Still, in 1934 there were not that many actresses destined for Hollywood stardom whose resumes included such plays as these:

Philip Barry's *Paris Bound* (1927), Civic Repertory
A wife who originally took a "sensible" view of extramarital sex thinks differently when her husband commits adultery but accepts his indiscretion, realizing it is insufficient grounds for divorce.

Robert E. Sherwood's *The Queen's Husband* (1928), Civic Repertory
While the queen of a mythical island kingdom is away in America, the
   king staves off a coup and enables his daughter to marry the man she
   loves, even though he is not royalty.

Allan Scott and George Haight's *Goodbye Again* (1932), Teck Players
A novelist on a lecture tour encounters a woman from his past and nearly
   loses the secretary who loves him.

J. B. Priestley's *Dangerous Corner* (1932), Teck Players
This is a classic melodrama about a dinner party that ends in tragedy.

Frederick Lonsdale's *The High Road* (1928), Teck Players
An actress discovers, after two abortive affairs, that her true love is the theater.

Rose Franken's *Another Language* (1932), Teck Players
A popular comedy with serious overtones about the Hallams—a family
   that resonated with theatergoers but never achieved the popularity of
   the Days in *Life with Father*—includes a spirited wife, her domineering
   mother-in-law, and her less than supportive husband.

Philip Barry's *Holiday* (1928), Teck Players
Love and alcoholism among the wealthy who are portrayed with Barry's
   unique blend of criticism and compassion.

Rachel Crothers's *When Ladies Meet* (1932), Teck Players
This is perhaps the most atypical and insightful *ménage à trois* ever written
   for the stage. A mistress and a wife, neither knowing who the other is,
   discuss the man they have in common, only to discover each other's
   identity. Rather than sever the bond that formed between them, the
   wife leaves her husband, and the mistress realizes the consequences of
   being "the other woman."

Hugh Buckler's *The Barker* (1927), Teck Players
In this drama about tent show life, Rosalind played the same role that
   Claudette Colbert had on Broadway.

Ring Lardner and George S. Kaufman's *June Moon* (1929), Teck Players
The authors take an affectionately satirical look at song writers and their
   obsession with rhyme.

Edwin Burke's *This Thing Called Love* (1928), Teck Players
A marriage conceived as a business proposition leads to the real thing.

Lynn Starling's *Meet the Wife* (1923), Teck Players
A celebrity-obsessed wife discovers that her first husband, whom she
   thought had died in the San Francisco earthquake, is really alive.

Although Rosalind fought against being typecast, and often succeeded,
by 1933 it was obvious from her resume that her métier was romantic comedy, the more sophisticated the better. She had mastered the ability to pick
up cues as quickly as they were tossed to her, and, in the absence of dialogue,
delivered a putdown with a deflating glance or a slow turn of the head. The
Worcester and Buffalo press may have marveled at her technique, and she
may have been the toast of Buffalo, but in New York she was just another
member of Actors Equity looking for a job. Still, she knew she had acquired
enough training in repertory to qualify as a Broadway actress, if not yet a
Broadway star. Even more important, she had found her specialty: sophisticated comedy, which did not rule out melodramas like *Dangerous Corner* or
comedies with serious overtones like *Holiday*. The same was true of her film
career. Although Rosalind could play drama, moviegoers preferred her in
comedies. It was the opposite with Bette Davis. Davis's forays into comedy
with *The Bride Came C.O.D* (1941) and *June Bride* (1948) found as little favor
with the public as Rosalind's attempts at serious drama in *Sister Kenny* (1946)
and especially *Mourning Becomes Electra* (1947). Ironically, both Rosalind
and Davis starred in films about the stage that proved commercially and
critically successful: Rosalind in *The Velvet Touch* (1948) and Davis in *All
about Eve* (1950); the former, a thriller in which Rosalind murders her producer and ex-lover; the latter, Joseph L. Mankiewicz's take on the theater
with Davis as an aging actress who behaves more like a Hollywood diva
than a Broadway star.

Shortly after leaving the Teck Players, Rosalind was cast in *Talent*, a new play by Rachel Crothers, America's best-known and most prolific female playwright before Lillian Hellman arrived on the scene. Since Crothers's last three plays had been hits—*Let Us Be Gay* (1929), *As Husbands Go* (1931), and *When Ladies Meet* (1932)—Rosalind assumed *Talent* would be, too. At least it should run for more than a week. The choice of theater also augured well: the Royale (renamed the Jacobs in 2005) on West Forty-fifth Street, where Crothers's last play, *When Ladies Meet*, enjoyed a run of 173 performances. Nineteen thirty-three was a banner year for Crothers. *As Husbands Go* returned to Broadway in January 1933. Two months after *When Ladies Meet* closed in New York on 4 March, the Chicago company went into the Royale on 15 May, but was forced to end its run after 18 performances because of a union dispute. Even so, the Royale seemed the right venue for another Crothers success.

Talent, which tried out at the Cape Playhouse in Massachusetts in early September, was scheduled to open at the Royale on 2 January 1934, with Mady Christians and Brian Donlevy in the lead roles. Rosalind was cast in the supporting role of Mazie Myrtle. At first the mood was upbeat. By 18 December the programs had been printed. The 31 December *New York Herald Tribune* carried Al Hirschfeld's caricature of the entire cast, including Rosalind. When previews began a week before the opening, Christians came down with acute laryngitis, missing several performances. Finally, a decision was made to cancel the opening, and a notice to that effect appeared in the *Herald Tribune* on 1 January. There was no attempt to mount another production, and the play is not even mentioned in Lois C. Gottlieb's *Rachel Crothers* [Twayne: Boston, 1979], the standard book on the playwright.

If Broadway was not beckoning, the subway circuit was. At least there Rosalind could play leads and not have to worry about a show closing before it even opened. The term "subway circuit" was a misnomer. Originally, it referred to plays that toured the other boroughs of New York or nearby cities in New Jersey, such as Newark, that were accessible by subway or bus. Soon, the subway circuit extended as far south as Philadelphia and Washington,

D.C., and as far east as Hartford, Connecticut. In 1934, Rosalind was on the Newark spur of the circuit, alternating between Frank Vosper's *Murder on the Second Floor* (1929) and S. N. Behrman's brilliant comedy of manners, *The Second Man* (1927). In the former, her costar was Cesar Romero, who, like Rosalind, would soon be heading to Hollywood. The play is remembered for Laurence Olivier's New York debut, although it barely lasted six weeks. Romero played Olivier's role—Hugh Bromilow, a neophyte dramatist struggling to write a typical British whodunit. Since there was only one significant female role in *Murder*, Rosalind was probably Sylvia Armitage, who challenges Bromilow to restrict the setting of his play to the boardinghouse where he lives (and which her mother owns), the characters to the residents, and the plot to a murder, with everyone a suspect. In the denouement, the audience discovers that Bromilow succeeded in writing his whodunit, which is the play they have just seen.

However, it was not *Murder on the Second Floor* but *The Second Man* (1927) that brought Rosalind to Hollywood. In *The Second Man*, her co-star was Bert Lytell, a fairly successful actor during the silent era, with considerable stage experience as well. Lytell and Rosalind were cast in roles created by Alfred Lunt and Lynn Fontanne: Lytell as Clark Storey, an irreverently witty writer of unlimited charm, and Rosalind as Mrs. Kendall Frayne, a rich widow who is captivated by him, although she knows he is as interested in her money as he is in her. Storey, however, finds Monica Grey more appealing; Monica, however, is as "poor as a church mouse" and courted by Austin Lowe, a millionaire scientist. The second act climaxes with Monica's disclosure that she is pregnant with Storey's child; although she later denies it, Kendall is not convinced. No doubt some members of the audience would have preferred that Storey "do the right thing," but Behrman understood that marriage between the self-absorbed Storey and the ingenuous Monica would have been disastrous. Instead, Monica accepts Austin's proposal, leaving Storey on the phone with Kendall, struggling to get back in her good graces, which, given his charisma, should not be difficult.

Lytell's was the showier part, but Rosalind's was the more complex. Physically, she was the incarnation of Kendall, as Behrman described her at the rise of the curtain, when she is trying to phone Storey: "She is a tall, handsome, beautifully dressed woman. . . . She might be described as 'majestic'; she has a fine face; her voice is beautifully modulated and restrained even when she speaks under stress or deep feeling." Kendall has to express her irritation at Storey's cavalier attitude to convention while at the same time suggesting that she finds it endearing—so much so that, for the final scene to work, the audience has to believe that even if Storey were the father of Monica's child, Kendall would be willing to take him back.

In 1934, Rosalind, like so many actresses who envisioned careers in the theater, took a dim view of the movies. Then, there was a distinction between the "legitimate theater" and its bastard offspring, film, once (and perhaps even in 1934) laughingly dismissed as the "flickers."

Rosalind would have agreed with Terry Randall, the heroine of George S. Kaufman and Edna Ferber's *Stage Door* (1936), filmed in 1938 with Katharine Hepburn in the lead and performed live by Rosalind in 1939 on *Lux Radio Theatre*. When a playwright succumbs to the lure of Hollywood, insisting that he will write "garbage" for the studio during the day and work on his plays at night, Terry is skeptical: "But will you?" she asks. Similarly, would a stage actress, offered the customary seven-year contract and a higher salary than she could ever make on Broadway, take the money and rush back to the theater when her contract is up? And how would the same actress, who had appeared in enough plays that tweaked conventional morality, react to an enforced Production Code that would never have allowed *The Second Man* to be filmed as Behrman had written it? As it happened, *The Second Man* never reached the screen. If it had, Storey would have ended up "doing the right thing," and Kendall would have encouraged him.

All Rosalind knew in early 1934 was that a Universal Pictures talent scout had seen her in *The Second Man* and wanted to sign her. If she did not seem flattered, it was not surprising. Despite her indifference to film, she knew that, with the coming of sound, the studios were desperate to hire talent from the stage with voices that suited the characters. Silent actors, on the other hand, only had to resemble the characters physically, leaving their voices to the audience's imagination. However, with the arrival of the talkies, the failure of voice and appearance to complement each other could spell the end of a career.

Rosalind could not have known that Universal was refurbishing its image under Carl Laemmle Jr., who took over production in 1930. Although Carl Sr. founded the studio that evolved into Universal Pictures, he always thought of it in terms of its original name: the Universal Film Manufacturing Company, which evoked the image of a factory where movies rolled off the assembly line and into the theaters.

Carl Jr. knew that, to compete in the sound era, Universal had to shed its second-tier image. Of the eight major studios of the 1930s and 1940s, Universal was never one of the Big Five (MGM, Paramount, Warner Bros., Twentieth Century-Fox, RKO); it was one of the Little Three, the others being Columbia and United Artists—the latter really a distribution company. Still, Carl Jr., who had far better taste than his father, forged ahead, authorizing a budget of almost $900,000 for *All Quiet on the Western Front* (1930), which eventually cost $1.45 million. To Carl Jr., it was not too high a price to pay for the recognition the film brought Universal: Oscars for best picture and best director, Lewis Milestone.

Carl Jr., who frequented the theater regularly when he was growing up on New York's Upper West Side, was particularly interested in making the movie versions of such Broadway successes as Elmer Rice's *Counsellor at Law*, Preston Sturges's *Strictly Dishonorable*, and the Jerome Kern and Edna Ferber musical *Show Boat*, none of which would have been possible without such stage actors as John Barrymore (*Counsellor*, in the role created by Paul Muni); Paul Lukas (*Strictly Dishonorable*); and Irene Dunne, Helen Morgan, and Paul Robeson (*Show Boat*). Like his father in his heyday, Carl Jr. thought nothing of raiding the theater to recruit talent on the order of

Edward G. Robinson, Margaret Sullavan, Diana Wynard, Bette Davis, and Charles Laughton, none of whom became Universal regulars. Nor did Rosalind, even though she represented everything Carl Jr. was seeking in an actress: someone who was stage trained, poised, attractive, and versatile. Universal, however, was not what Rosalind was seeking.

In early 1934, Rosalind had three options: to continue on the subway circuit, wait around for a Broadway show, or accept Universal's offer of $300 a week, the same salary she received four years earlier when she toured in *The Garrick Gaieties*. Unlike Margaret Sullavan, who was hired by Universal after appearing in the Broadway hit *Dinner at Eight* (1933), Rosalind had only been in two Broadway shows, each of which ran a week. She may have been the leading lady of the Teck Players and a star on the subway circuit, but to theater producers she was supporting-cast material. The movies seemed to be her best bet.

Rosalind had encountered enough actors with Hollywood connections to know that $300 a week was unacceptable for someone with her experience, even though most of it was in stock. Her price was $750 or nothing; after some haggling, $750 is what she received, along with $100 for every screen test she made.

Rosalind did not make the five-day train trip to the West Coast without having some idea of what to expect. Bert Lytell must have prepared her for the culture shock that awaited her, as did her friend Charlotte Wynters, whom she had met in stock and who was now living in Hollywood with her actor husband, Barton McLane, while unsuccessfully pursuing a movie career herself. But nothing could have prepared her for the screen-test ritual. After being ignored by Universal's casting director, makeup department, and even director John Stahl, whose idea of a screen test was having an actress feed lines to the actor auditioning to play opposite Claudette Colbert in *Imitation of Life* (1934), Rosalind was desperate to leave the studio. Then Wynters reminded her that, according to her contract, Universal had a seven-year option on her services. Rosalind was devastated, especially after Wynters had encouraged her to test at MGM for a new film, which turned out to be *Evelyn Prentice*. The MGM test went well; it was the Universal contract that was the problem.

With help from Wynters, Rosalind worked out a scenario for her meeting with Carl Jr. that would free her from seven years of servitude. Rosalind Russell, the actress he wanted to sign, turned out to be a plain woman with carelessly applied makeup, wearing a shapeless outfit with dirty shoes, and speaking in a nasal voice. The ruse was so successful that when Rosalind asked to be released from her contract, citing her unhappiness with Hollywood, Carl Jr. was more than willing to comply.

Rosalind returned to Universal for two pictures—one in 1940 and another in 1967. By 1940 she was a star; by 1967 she was a legend. In 1934, she was just an actress about to join a studio that boasted of having "more stars than there are in the heavens."

CHAPTER 3

The Lady and the Lion

Universal's logo at least had something to do with the studio's name. At first, the logo was a globe encircled by "Universal Pictures"; in the 1930s, it was a globe encircled by an airplane. MGM, on the other hand, the "Tiffany of Studios," had a logo with a lion.

MGM was the result of the merger of Metro Pictures, Goldwyn Pictures Corporation, and Louis B. Mayer Productions. Of the three, only Goldwyn's company had a distinctive trademark, a lion with a celluloid nimbus bearing the Latin phrase *Ars Gratia Artis* (art for art's sake). Art was the furthest thing from Goldwyn's mind—and MGM's, for that matter—but the logo was eye catching. Its creator was then a junior publicist, Howard Dietz, who became a distinguished Broadway lyricist. Dietz claimed that his inspiration was a Columbia University student magazine with a lion on the cover and a professor of classical languages who was fond of quoting "*Ars Gratia Artis.*"

With the formation of MGM in 1924, the Goldwyn logo with the lion, the celluloid motif, and the Latin maxim was retained. But another image was added: an African mask. The final version of the logo appeared four years later; below "Metro Goldwyn Mayer," there was a lion inside a circle that was clearly made of film with perforations on either side and inscribed with *Ars Gratia Artis*. To the right and left of the unclosed circle, ribbons of film unspooled, as if they were waiting to be tied together. The circle was left slightly open so that a primitive mask could be placed beneath the lion, providing both balance and contrast, as well as creating a macrocosm-microcosm relationship between the lion above and the mask below. Since the first lion used for the Goldwyn logo came from Sudan, the mask might have been added to suggest its origins. In contrast to the encircled lion, the mask was decked out with a fernlike headpiece that looked like an inverted U with extensions on either side, complemented by the same frondlike motif below and drawing attention to the strips of film streaming out of the circle. The symbolism was far less obvious than Universal's globe; the MGM logo said nothing about the studio but a great deal about the nature of film: without that transparent material with perforations along the edges, movies could not exist. This magnificently subtle touch turned the MGM logo into an homage to the art of film as well as to the studio that (arguably) made the best films in Hollywood—or at least the studio that once claimed the lion's share of the screen.

Even those who could not deconstruct the logo, regarding it as more of a celebration of Africa than Hollywood, could not deny that it was vastly different from the literal Universal globe, Paramount's star-spangled mountain, Fox's crisscrossing spotlights, Warner Bros.' heraldic shield, RKO's tower spelling out "RKO Radio Pictures" in code, and Columbia's evocation of Lady Liberty. MGM may have made its share of jungle movies (*Trader Horn* [1931] and some of the first Tarzan films), but the reputation MGM acquired for its galaxy of stars and distinctive musicals justified its position as Hollywood's premier studio, which Rosalind had now joined.

The symbolism of the MGM logo was the least of Rosalind's discoveries. Far more useful was learning how Louis Mayer handled an actor or actress who balked at appearing in a film to which he or she had been assigned. He simply threatened to replace the star with another contract player. There was always an understudy waiting in the wings, Mayer warned those who questioned his wisdom. He bluntly informed Judy Garland that if she stepped out of line, June Allyson would inherit her roles, as if the latter, talented as she was, could possibly stand in for Garland. After seeing Rosalind in a few films, Mayer realized that she had some of the same qualities as Myrna Loy—an air of elegance that did not rule out vulnerability and a down-to-earth personality with which audiences could identify. Thus Rosalind was earmarked as the next Myrna Loy and actually replaced her in *Rendezvous* (1935). And when Rosalind garnered the best reviews in *The Women* (1939), Mayer thought it was time to groom her successor, deciding on Ruth Hussey, who had played a minor role in the film but did not go unnoticed. As it happened, Rosalind decided to leave MGM in 1941 and freelance. Ruth Hussey, who became a star but not an icon because she was too good a character actress, stepped out of Rosalind's shadow and into her own spotlight, not as encompassing as Rosalind's, but wide enough for a career in film, theater, and television. Mayer did not have to groom Ruth Hussey to succeed Rosalind; she also left MGM to freelance shortly after Rosalind did. Like Rosalind, Hussey went back to the stage, but a decade earlier. By the time Rosalind took Broadway by storm in *Wonderful Town* (1953), Hussey had already co-starred with Ralph Bellamy in *State of the Union* (1945–1947) and replaced Madeleine Carroll in *Goodbye, My Fancy* (1948–1949).

In spring 1934, Rosalind knew nothing of the Mayer Doctrine or Ruth Hussey, who had yet to arrive at MGM. Rosalind only knew that she would be making her film debut in *Evelyn Prentice* with two of MGM's biggest stars, William Powell and Myrna Loy. The rest she left to Providence.

Even the most naive Hollywood newcomer would not have considered the role of Nancy Harrison in *Evelyn Prentice* a career maker. The opening credits identified the stars as William Powell and Myrna Loy, "with Una Merkel"; Rosalind's name appeared in the cast of characters just before the beginning of the film—a practice relatively common in the movies of the 1930s—and sometimes repeated at the end as well. Rosalind had fourth billing, between

Una Merkel and Isabel Jewell, the latter having a far more important role. Nancy Harrison was the proverbial merry widow—wealthy, glamorous, and available—particularly to any lawyer who could get her acquitted of vehicular homicide. She appears almost immediately, looking like a true 1930s grande dame in a smart hat and a coat with a fur collar. Nancy Harrison, who has only three scenes, is a plot peg: unable to seduce her dashing lawyer, John Prentice (William Powell), Nancy retaliates by planting evidence that she did, causing Prentice's wife, Evelyn of the title (Myrna Loy), to have an affair herself. In the 1930s, "affair" was a generic term covering everything from a flirtation to a liaison. Evelyn's affair with Larry, a smooth-talking parasite who courts rich women, ends in murder—his.

Nancy's vindictiveness sets off a chain reaction, climaxing in a courtroom where Prentice convinces a jury that "vermin" like Larry deserve to die, thereby getting his killer (who is not Evelyn) acquitted. Rosalind did what she could with the part, although femmes fatales were never her métier. Fresh from the theater and knowing that in film less is more, she gave a minimalist performance, devoid of bravura, and delivered her lines in a soft yet theatrical voice that sounded faintly British (a vestige of her repertory days) and corresponded to what audiences regarded as an upper-class accent.

The dialogue gave Rosalind little to suggest that Nancy was a socialite on the make. When Prentice bolsters her spirits by reminding her that "a jury in doubt is a jury in the bag," Rosalind moves aggressively toward him and is about to plant a kiss on his lips when director William K. Howard prudishly cuts to a nightclub, allowing the audience's imagination to complete the scene. After her acquittal, Nancy, learning that Prentice is Boston bound, boards the same train, booking a compartment across from his to show her "gratitude." At that point Nancy disappears from the plot, but not before taking revenge on Prentice, who had apparently rebuffed her. She sends a watch inscribed "Nancy from John" to Evelyn, with a note that it had been left in Prentice's compartment.

Disillusioned, Evelyn succumbs to Larry's blandishments—or perhaps to Larry, to whom she writes *billets-doux* that can easily be interpreted as love letters. When Larry decides to blackmail Evelyn with the letters, she threatens to kill him. Howard then cuts to a shot of Larry's mistress, Judith (Isabel Jewell in the film's best performance), arriving at the apartment; hearing a shot, Judith enters through the kitchen just in time for Evelyn to depart without being seen. After Judith is accused of the murder, the conscience-stricken Evelyn prevails upon her husband to defend Judith. However, during the trial, Evelyn, no longer able to remain silent, bolts from her seat and blurts out the truth. Although her confession almost exceeds the flexible bounds of courtroom melodrama, Loy is so moving, and Powell so stunned yet composed, that the scene actually works. Larry, it seemed, became abusive and struck Evelyn, causing the gun to go off accidentally. Evelyn fled the apartment, assuming Larry had been killed, not knowing that he was only wounded. It was Judith who fired the fatal bullet.

Despite Judith's confession, Prentice convinces the jury that the Larrys of the world deserve to die and that their victims, the Judiths (and, by extension, the Evelyns), do not even merit the mildest of sentences. Although Prentice's speech is both logically and morally flawed, Powell delivered it so persuasively that some viewers would have agreed that predatory and abusive males, whether their victims are working girls or Park Avenue matrons, forfeit their right to life even if their worst offence is a slap across the face or an extortion attempt. None of the critics seemed concerned about the skewed morality, perhaps because Hollywood preferred happy endings to retributive justice, particularly in the 1930s—for example, *A Free Soul* (1931) and *The Trial of Vivienne Ware* (1932), which operated on the principle that when honorable folk dispose of "vermin," it is not so much an act of homicide as the elimination of a social menace.

Evelyn Prentice started production on 20 August 1934. After shooting her few scenes, Rosalind was loaned out to Paramount for *The President Vanishes* (1934), which began production on 30 September. Despite being billed thirteenth in the cast of characters, Rosalind had a much larger role than she did in *Evelyn Prentice*. *The President Vanishes* was Paramount's second response to the far-from-remote possibility in depression America that the country could turn to fascism as Italy and Germany had, and as Spain was about to do.

The first was *This Day and Age* (1933), Cecil B. DeMille's nightmarish vision of mob violence, in which right-wing adolescents resort to vigilantism to rid their community of a lawbreaker. It does not matter that the students have no respect for the law, either; politically, they are on the side of the angels. Anyone seeking a DeMille film reflecting the director's rightist views (which became more evident during the Hollywood blacklist, when, as president of the Screen Directors Guild, he tried to push through a loyalty oath) had to look no further than *This Day and Age*.

Paramount's second contribution to Great Depression paranoia was *The President Vanishes*, another cinematic curiosity which, like *This Day and Age*, is remembered for its director, William Wellman, as well as for its assistant director, Dorothy Arzner, who was one of the few female directors in a male-dominated industry and who would soon provide Rosalind with her first starring vehicle, *Craig's Wife* (1936). Arzner probably realized Rosalind would make an ideal Harriet Craig on the basis of her fleeting appearance as an imperious lobbyist's wife in *The President Vanishes*, in which the title character is an isolationist president unwilling to involve America in a war that has already erupted in Europe. The president, a composite of Woodrow Wilson and Franklin D. Roosevelt, must contend with a quintet of influential profiteers who embark on a "Save America's Honor" campaign to mobilize support for the country's entry into the conflict, the nature of which is, naturally, unspecified.

While the film reflected the nation's 1930s isolationist mood, it also implied that, except for a handful of decent souls, Americans were so obsessed with their country's image that they equated neutrality with cowardice. The president allows himself to be kidnapped and held in the headquarters of a right-wing paramilitary group, the Grey Shirts, modeled after Italy's Black Shirts, Hitler's Brown Shirts, and William Pelley's Silver Shirts—the last being America's contribution to color-coordinated fascism. Suspense is minimal, since the FBI agent-hero (Paul Kelly) knows the president's whereabouts, making his death unlikely. Thus, when the Grey Shirts guru (Edward Ellis) with the emblematic name of Lincoln Lee is about to kill the president, the agent intervenes, making short shrift of Lee and leaving the president free to preach the gospel of non-intervention.

How exactly, one might ask, did Rosalind's character figure in this political farrago? She played the impeccably attired wife of a Washington lobbyist (fellow stage actor Sidney Blackmer). The wife has grown so cynical about her husband's lack of principles that she expresses her disdain for the five war mongers at a dinner party. First, she warmly acknowledges each of them, as if she were presiding at an awards banquet; then, ever so subtly she assesses each man's moral worth—or, more accurately, lack of it. At the end, she compares the quintet to a flock of encircling birds. When one of guests naively inquires about the species of bird, Rosalind pauses and delivers her exit line as she would have on stage: "Eagles." The scene was a testament to her stagecraft, which first required her to deliver a monologue both flattering and critical, which Wellman nearly sabotaged with an aerial shot of menacing birds.

All the scene really needed was Rosalind's grand exit, which she provided with her customary flair. Her role, however, was expository; she was the equivalent of a protatic character (except that she had two scenes), created to introduce each of the five "war gods," thus saving the writers the trouble of finding a more imaginative way of revealing their background.

After shooting her two scenes in *The President Vanishes*, Rosalind was back at her home studio for *Forsaking All Others* (1935). Nancy Harrison was at least a plot peg, but Eleanor in *Forsaking All Others* was so inconsequential that her omission would never have been felt. The character was a madcap, a type at which Rosalind later excelled, although one would never have known it from her performance, which consisted of a few scenes in which she either tossed off wisecracks (the best being "I'm tired of being a bridesmaid. I wish I could get married so I could wear a decent hat") or, in the absence of dialogue, adopted expressions ranging from deadpan to bemused. Given Eleanor's insignificance, Rosalind was lucky to get fourth billing—this time, under the title and as the last member of the supporting cast—the others (Billie Burke, Charles Butterworth, and Frances Drake) at least being essential to the plot.

Forsaking All Others revolves around a trio of childhood friends who grow up to discover that friendship has yielded to desire. The three—Robert Montgomery (Dill), Joan Crawford (Mary), and Clark Gable (Jeff)—are first seen during the main title as mature adults, merrily walking arm and arm. At first, Mary is drawn to Dill, who, on their wedding day, abandons her for Connie (Frances Drake) in a radical departure from the conventions of romantic comedy, in which the bride is the one who jilts the groom (*It Happened One Night* [1934], *It Had to Be You* [1947]). That twist, however, is only one of several, making *Forsaking All Others* a delightfully amoral film, not as irreverent as *Design for Living* (1933), but close. Although left in the lurch, Mary still carries a torch; but so does Dill—for Mary. The course of true love is not only rough but also circuitous. Mary and Dill are not the only torchbearers; Jeff carries one, too—for Mary. Despite his marriage to Connie, whose lacquered looks and spangled wardrobe evoke bargain basement boutique, Dill resumes his relationship with Mary, which is far from platonic. Just as the film began with a marriage, in which Rosalind's character was a member of the bridal party, it also ends with one; however, by that time, the character has long disappeared from the plot. Again, the groom is to be Dill, until Mary sees the light and elopes with Jeff. The denouement is so swift that only a moralist would ponder the implications of an unmarried couple boarding a ship for Spain, where civil war would break out a year later. Most 1935 moviegoers sensed that, to cite a familiar movie cliché, Jeff and Mary were made for each other.

Forsaking All Others originated as a 1933 stage play by Edward Roberts and Frank Cavett, starring Tallulah Bankhead in the Joan Crawford role. Although the play had a modest run of 110 performances, it allowed Bankhead to reveal her flair for sophisticated comedy, which was shown to even greater advantage in Thornton Wilder's *The Skin of Our Teeth* (1941) and the acclaimed 1948 revival of Noël Coward's *Private Lives*, in which she also toured. Looking at *Forsaking All Others* from the vantage point of Rosalind's entire body of work, one can see that she would have been a more convincing Mary than Crawford. Eleanor, Rosalind's role, had been played on stage by Ilka Chase, a character actress who could do everything Rosalind did (dead pan delivery, double takes, double entendre) but without her star power and glamour. Chase looked great in suits, as did Rosalind. But Rosalind also looked sexy, while Chase just looked professional. Little did Rosalind know that five years later she would play the same role in *The Women* that Ilka Chase had originated on Broadway.

Crawford's approach to comedy, a form for which she was ill suited, was the opposite of Rosalind's. Whenever Crawford was given comedic lines, her delivery was hard-edged, caustic without being witty; it was a case of one-upmanship rather than repartee. Instead of froth, there was foam spilling over the rim and leaving a residue. Rosalind knew that lines that were devastating or ego-puncturing needed a light touch—an airy deftness that kept the one-liner or the zinger afloat so that it wouldn't land with a thud. Such lines had to deflate, like a tire gradually losing air. For example, in the stage version of *Auntie Mame*, when the bigoted Upsons extolled their "restricted" Connecticut community to the ultra-liberal Mame, Rosalind paused and then replied dryly, "I'll have a blood test."

Crawford's acting style seemed to have been inspired by art deco—streamlined and sleek, paneled rather than layered, metallic instead of earthy. Later on, Russell would play women who found themselves in similar situations—attracted to one man but really meant for another, or confronted with an overdressed rival who needed a lesson in true class. The role of Mary required the kind of breeziness that Rosalind brought to romantic comedy, a sophistication that kept it from veering off into screwball, which has its own conventions. Thus, one is left with the feeling inspired by the trio's favorite song: "Row, row, row your boat / gently down the stream / merrily, merrily, merrily, merrily / life is but a dream." The best romantic comedies subject lovers to such a downstream journey, suggesting that the right couples will sail upstream, pair off, and awaken to reality.

Within a year, Rosalind was an MGM contract player, supporting cast only, whose character types were "ditzy," "sophisticated-raucous," "sophisticated–high toned," or "Brit plus" ("milady," if necessary, or else a finishing school product). Since *West Point of the Air* (1935) required an amorous socialite, the role naturally went to Rosalind, even though it was a high-testosterone aviation movie prefiguring such military preparedness films as *In Old Monterey* (1939) and *Flight Command* (1940) that were released prior to America's entry into World War II. There was little difference between *Evelyn Prentice*'s Nancy Harrison and *West Point of the Air*'s Mrs. Dare Marshall, except that as the latter Rosalind had more scenes, despite being given eighth billing; and, as a wealthy widow or divorcée (the script does not specify), she had a more extensive wardrobe. She spoke in the same attenuated voice that she used in *Evelyn Prentice*, condescendingly aristocratic but without the hauteur of a Park Avenue hostess. Rosalind did what she could to humanize the character—another lady on the make—this time for Robert Young, as a second lieutenant straight out of West Point. She had to compete with the wholesome Maureen O'Sullivan, on a short hiatus from the Tarzan series, for Young's affections, which initially were directed toward Rosalind, certainly the more glamorous of the two women. However, there was little likelihood that a movie conceived as a paean to army flyers would end with Young's succumbing to Rosalind's allure.

The real star of the film was Wallace Beery, billed above the title, as Young's father, a master sergeant at the same training base as his lieutenant son. Father and son are "Big Mike" and "Little Mike." The difference is not one of size or even age, but of responsibility. Beery is determined to make his joker son into a real army man, even if it means socking him in the jaw—an action that gets Big Mike court-martialed, but not for long. A happy ending is in the offing, as Rosalind realizes that the sound of planes overhead sets Young's face aglow, which she does not. Young gets Sullivan, Beery gets reinstated, and Rosalind gets five more pictures, bringing her 1935 total to a phenomenal seven.

The same year saw Rosalind playing the other woman to the ultimate platinum blonde, Jean Harlow, in *China Seas* (1935) and *Reckless* (1935). In both films, Rosalind not only had to contend with Harlow's blinding persona—a combination of hair that looked like spun silver and front lit into luminosity and a manner so aggressively unsubtle that it was impossible for any rival, especially the genteel types that Rosalind played, to compete with it—but also had to hold her own with such notorious scene stealers as Wallace Beery, C. Aubrey Smith, and Lewis Stone in *China Seas* and the great character actress May Robson in *Reckless*. Even Harlow's leading men, Clark Gable in *China Seas* and William Powell in *Reckless*, had all they could do not to be eclipsed by the platinum earth mother whose artificial trappings could not conceal the carnal force within.

Of the two, *China Seas* was the better film, largely because of Tay Garnett's direction. With the action limited to a ship sailing from Hong Kong to Singapore, Garnett provided some breathtaking tracking shots at the beginning, as the camera swept across the dock, recording the frenetic activity preceding a sailing. Garnett also balanced the romantic subplot, in which the skipper (Gable) discreetly courts a British widow (Rosalind) while being pursued by "China Doll" (Harlow), the proverbial lady with a past—uncouth and untrustworthy, but also a one-man woman, capable of turning against the one man if she feels slighted. Believing Gable has passed her up for Rosalind, Harlow starts playing up to Wallace Beery, even after she discovers he is in league with pirates planning to take over the ship. Rebuffed by Gable, she gives Beery the key to the arsenal, enabling him to arm the pirates.

Although China Doll's treachery should have been enough to damn her in Gable's eyes, he eventually realizes that she acted out of jealousy. He also must have had an enormous capacity for forgiveness, since he nearly loses his mobility after the pirates subject him to the "Malay boot," in which his foot is encased in a viselike instrument that is gradually tightened until he reveals the location of the gold shipment. Fortunately, an officer (Lewis Stone in a grand performance), shunned as a coward, redeems himself by locating some grenades and saving the ship—but not himself.

Will Gable exit with Rosalind, whom he met in London (don't ask if Gable is supposed to be a Brit) when she was married? Everything seems to be pointing that way, until Gable confesses that he would never be comfortable as a landlubber in Britain; and Rosalind, taught to sheath her emotions, accepts the inevitable by arching her eyelids to keep the tears from spilling out. Ladies only cry in private.

Once Beery commits suicide, Gable realizes that China Doll was only playing the spurned lover, even though her role in the abortive piracy could have left him with a disability. He even downplays the possibility of a jail sentence, despite the deaths she caused by her vindictiveness. But what does it matter? When a police officer escorts Harlow off the ship, her triumphant wave to Gable is nothing less than a metaphor for a happy ending.

In *Reckless*, Rosalind at least had a chance to create a character instead of an elocutionist. Ironically, she had fifth billing, followed by the teenage Mickey Rooney in an inconsequential role. Rosalind's character, the well-bred Josephine "Jo" Mercer, does not appear until after the first hour of the 108-minute film. The main plot is another romantic triangle: musical comedy star Mona Leslie (Jean Harlow) is pursued by playboy millionaire Robert Harrison (Franchot Tone) while her agent, Ned Riley (William Powell), is forced to stand by and watch his discovery marry into a class that nearly destroys her.

Jo is first seen fishing on the Harrison estate, as Mona comes by. Rosalind handled the reel naturally, as if she were accustomed to fly fishing—as, indeed, she was, from her Waterbury childhood. She adopted a jaunty walk and an insouciant air—her armor against a press that portrayed her as the rejected fiancée after Harrison abandoned her for Mona. When Jo marries a stage actor (Allan Jones) on the rebound, Harrison berates her, implying that she should have remained single and waited until he tired of Mona and recovered his self-respect—never, of course, indicating when that might be. Jo stoically conceals her pain; Harrison cannot and shoots himself.

Although Jo was an impossible role, Rosalind had one jaw-dropping moment that had more to do with costuming than character. While Harlow wore her share of Adrian's provocative costumes, it was Rosalind who elicited sighs from female moviegoers in the bridal scene. Rosalind was resplendent in a gown of white satin fitted to the contours of her body, the veil from her pearl-encrusted headpiece trailing like gossamer as she descended the stairs. An Adrian creation, however, was not enough to justify another supporting role requiring a cultivated voice and a soulful smile. Jo was a better role than Sibyl in *China Seas*, but it was not enough.

Harlow is indisputably the star of *Reckless*, even though her singing voice was dubbed and her dance numbers were handled by a professional. All Harlow had to do was raise her shoulders in a devil-may-care shrug and shuffle along, as if she were about to go into her dance. Margaret Booth's artful editing created the illusion that Harlow was doing her own dancing, making the long shots with her double look so authentic that it is almost impossible to tell the difference. All Harlow did was sashay around, tilting her jaw to the side and rolling her eyes dreamily. Even when she sang, particularly the haunting title song by Jerome Kern and Oscar Hammerstein, she lip-synched so perfectly that she seemed to be doing her own singing.

No actress stood a chance playing opposite Harlow unless the screenplay allowed her to compete with, or at least complement, this study in luminosity. Loretta Young succeeded in Frank Capra's *Platinum Blonde* (1933) because Robert Riskin's script reduced Harlow's role to a vamp, so that Young's character and the real lead, a newspaper reporter (Robert Williams, whose career was tragically short-lived), would emerge as a duo.

Reckless was another matter. The screenplay, from a story by Oliver Jeffries (a pseudonym for David Selznick, who was also the producer), was intended to capitalize on the suicide of Harlow's husband, MGM producer Paul Bern, who committed suicide under circumstances suggesting that he was sexually unable to satisfy his wife. Harrison shoots himself not because he is impotent but because he cannot decide between the ultra-refined Jo and the déclassé Mona.

The bluebloods hold Mona responsible for Harrison's suicide and appear en masse at her Broadway return to boo her off the stage. Harlow played the final scene with great feeling, as if she personally identified with her character, determined to justify her own image as a "bombshell" to those who felt her talent lay in her platinum mane and uncorseted body. Even singing with another's voice, Harlow conveyed the longing of someone yearning for acceptance. One is supposed to think of the outcry against Mae West that was partially responsible for the enforcement of the Production Code in 1934 and the creation of the Legion of Decency. Historically, Mae cleaned up her act (not that there was much to purge) but was never the same; Mona got an ovation (and a proposal from Riley). Harlow and Powell, then lovers, never knew the kind of happiness that the finale of *Reckless* implied. Harlow died the following year.

If there is any film that illustrates the vicissitudes of a 1930s MGM contract player, it is *The Night Is Young* (1935), a Sigmund Romberg operetta in which Rosalind, billed in eighth place, played an important part, but only in terms of the plot, in which she was the betrothed of an Austrian archduke (Ramon Navarro). The stars were the incandescent Evelyn Laye (who sang Romberg's "When I Grow Too Old to Dream" exquisitely), as the ballerina in love with the archduke, and Navarro, who acted like a stolid Valentino. Since MGM had just embarked on an operetta cycle with Jeanette MacDonald and Nelson Eddy, *The Night Is Young*, despite Laye's charm, was nothing more than a footnote to that series.

Having worked in repertory, Rosalind knew that a leading role one week could be followed by a virtual walk-on the next. And a walk-on is exactly what the Countess Rafay was. But with a screenplay clearly indebted to Romberg's *The Student Prince* (which MGM had filmed in 1927 with Navarro in the title role), the archduke and the ballerina had about as much of a chance of marrying as Prince Karl and Kathie had in *The Student Prince*. Since Rosalind had a grand total of three scenes, one of which only required her to look up from her orchestra seat at Navarro in a box, the audience probably forgot at the end that Navarro would end up with her, and not Evelyn Laye.

Terence Rattigan chose a similar plot for his play *The Sleeping Prince*, remembered chiefly for the movie version, *The Prince and the Show Girl*

(1957), with the unlikely pairing of Laurence Olivier and Marilyn Monroe. However, Marilyn stole the movie from Olivier, as did Laye from Navarro. Given the size of her role in *The Night Is Young*, Rosalind had no opportunity to create a character, much less steal the film from anyone.

Philo Vance, the series detective created by S. S. Van Dine, proved so popular with moviegoers that he went on solving crimes in fourteen movies between 1929 and 1947. Unlike the Thin Man series, which was exclusively MGM's, the Philo Vance series was produced by several studios—first at Paramount, then at Warners and MGM, and finally at Poverty Row's PRC, where the series ended in 1947.

William Powell is the actor most associated with Philo, having appeared in four Philo Vance movies—Paramount's *Canary Murder Case* and *The Greene Murder Case* (both 1929), *Benson Murder Case* (1930), and *The Kennel Murder Case* (1933). However, when MGM decided to have a go at Philo, Powell had already been tapped for *The Thin Man* (1934); casting him as another detective would have been at odds with MGM's concept of a series, which meant keeping the same leads whenever possible (the *Thin Man* movies only with Powell and Loy; the *Tarzan* ones with Johnny Weissmuller and Maureen O'Sullivan; later, the *Andy Hardy* series with Mickey Rooney, Lewis Stone, and Ann Rutherford; and *Dr. Kildare* with Lew Ayres and Lionel Barrymore), using different leads with similar acting styles (the *Fasts*), or surrounding the series character with different co-stars (the *Mazies* with Ann Sothern as the title character).

Since MGM could not use Powell in *Casino Murder Case* (1935), Paul Lukas was recruited for the part. Lucas was an excellent actor when given the right material, such as *Watch on the Rhine* (1943), for which he won an Oscar; however, he was out of his element in *Casino Murder Case*. Although Van Dine's Philo possessed the most arcane sort of knowledge, Lukas's Philo was a tiresome polymath in need of deflation, which made Rosalind his ideal co-star.

However, her billing did not give her such status. Her name appeared fourth after Lukas's, Alison Skipworth's, and Donald Cook's. She was the secretary to the Skipworth character, an imperious dowager with a house-hold of neurotics including an alcoholic daughter (Isabell Jewell); a murder-ous son (Cook) whose wife keeps threatening to return to the theater, whereupon she is promptly poisoned; an omniscient butler (Leo G. Carroll); and a snoopy maid (the scene-stealing Louise Fazenda), all of whom could easily be suspects. But then, this is a movie in which everyone, except Rosalind, behaves suspiciously. Being a sleuth does not necessarily preclude an encyclopedic knowledge of chemicals, except in Philo's case. Thus Philo can not only solve the murder but also explain the motive for Skipworth's suicide.

Rosalind was a good sport, sliding down a coal chute and nearly get-ting shot; still, it was as if she were trying to keep the fizz in champagne that has gone flat. Although that same year Rosalind co-starred in the fullest sense of the word with William Powell, had she played opposite him in *Casino Murder Case*, the result would have been an entertaining whodunit, as opposed to an intricately plotted exercise with enough red herrings to keep the audience from noticing the vacuum at the core.

Rendezvous (1935) is usually considered Rosalind's first starring vehi-cle. The credits indicate as much. William Powell's name appears above the title, with Rosalind's below it. Even in the cast of characters preceding the film, Rosalind's name comes under Powell's; and under hers, Binnie Barnes as a glamorous Russian-born, pro-German World War I spy. Rosalind's role, a socialite trailing after code breaker Powell, who prefers active duty to tracking down German spies, is almost negligible. Myrna Loy, who refused to play the role that went to Rosalind by default, made the right choice. Barnes had the better part—and the better outfits. On the first day of shoot-ing, Rosalind apologized to Powell for appearing opposite him in a role that had been slated for Loy; Powell assured her that apologies were unneces-sary. In *Banquet*, Rosalind treats *Rendezvous* as just another MGM movie, which it certainly is. The title, which has nothing to do with a romantic tryst, denotes the meeting place for ships. But the film is very much a romantic melodrama, in which Rosalind's character has enough clout to get

Powell transferred to Washington, where he can serve his country as a code breaker, thus ensuring a happy ending for both of them.

Rosalind's first leading role occurred the following year, not at MGM but at Columbia. Of the four films Rosalind made in 1936, three were loanouts, the best being *Craig's Wife*. When Columbia decided to make the film version of George Kelly's Pulitzer prize–winning play, *Craig's Wife* (1926), Harry Cohn, the studio's president as well as head of production, realized he had no contract player for the title character, a woman whose obsession with security alienates everyone, including her husband, who finally leaves her. Impressed with the way Rosalind played *grandes dames*, Cohn knew she would be perfect for Harriet Craig, who required the same kind of regal detachment. And so did the director, Dorothy Arzner, and for the same reason, having seen Rosalind in action in *The President Vanishes*. The difference, however, was that Harriet's glacial exterior was her armor against the male sex, which she viewed as the enemy, personified by her improvident father who abandoned his family, leaving his wife with a mortgage, a broken heart, and a shortened life. Harriet vows that she will never experience her mother's fate. She may lack marketable skills, as she explains to her niece, but she had "one skill" that she acquired from her impoverished childhood: the skill of achieving independence through marriage.

When Harriet's niece is puzzled by what seems to be a paradox, Harriet explains that only with a house can a woman be independent, once she realizes that if the marriage fails, the house is hers. Thus Harriet turns her house into a shrine, as coldly elegant as herself and equally unwelcoming. Her husband, Walter (John Boles), is too fascinated by his trophy wife to realize she has alienated his friends, who prefer a real home to a stage set.

Rosalind must have known such women (or at least sympathized with them), who made certain that when—not if—their husbands left them, they would at least have a place to live. Her Harriet was not a monster, like Joan Crawford's in the remake, *Harriet Craig* (1950). Rosalind's Harriet was marmoreal yet feminine; Crawford's, with her mannish hairdo and manacle-like bracelets, seemed hewn out of granite.

In *Banquet*, Rosalind barely mentions *Craig's Wife*, for which she received three thousand dollars, and does not even acknowledge the director, Dorothy Arzner, the best-known female filmmaker in 1930s Hollywood. Unfortunately, there is no way of knowing how the two women got along. But from Arzner's direction, it is clear that she and Rosalind understood Harriet, without necessarily condoning her philosophy of marriage.

Like the play, the film has the air of a Greek tragedy as it moves inexorably toward its resolution, in which Harriet is left completely alone. Except for Walter, everyone leaves Harriet in pairs: Elsie the maid and her boyfriend; the housekeeper and Walter's aunt; Claire and her professor fiancé; and, finally, Walter, who literally walks out the door after informing Harriet that the house is hers. The last thrust of the knife is the shattering news that Harriet's sister has died. Arzner gave Rosalind a series of memorable close-ups in the final scene. Left alone, her eyes glistening with tears that cannot flow liberally because the wellsprings of emotion have long dried up, Rosalind stands in the hallway, alternately wary and frightened. The house suddenly becomes unfamiliar, as it if were a mausoleum. For the first time, she must climb the stairs to rooms that are now empty. The final scene was a tour de force for Rosalind, as was the entire film, and established her credentials as a serious actress. In a year MGM would offer her another opportunity to appear in an adaptation of a famous play, Emlyn Williams's *Night Must Fall*. But first came two loan-outs to Twentieth Century–Fox; and an atypical MGM melodrama about a suicide club.

Rosalind's 1936 MGM film, *Trouble for Two*, saw her billed above the title alongside Robert Montgomery, although it would have made no difference if her name appeared at the head of the supporting cast, given the nature of her part. *Trouble for Two* was inspired by Robert Louis Stevenson's "The Suicide Club," which would have been difficult, if not impossible, to film in its original form, since all of the principals were male. Instead, the screenwriters, E. E. Paramore and Manuel Seff, were familiar enough with Stevenson's works to know that there was a Lady Vandeleur in two related stories, "The Rajah's Diamond" and "The Adventure of Prince Florizel and a

Detective." The writers used only the character's name and raised her to the rank of princess; she is now Princess Brenda of Irania, who, after refusing to marry Florizel (Robert Montgomery), the crown prince of Bohemia, rushes off to London, where she assumes the name of "Miss Vandeleur." Like the princess, Florizel is so distraught at the prospect of an arranged marriage that he joins a suicide club, only to discover that Miss Vandeleur is also a member, presumably for the same reason. Each member is dealt a card; whoever draws the ace of clubs dispatches whomever draws the ace of spades. When Florizel's card turns out to be the ace of spades, and Miss Vandeleur's, the ace of clubs, she confesses that, although she had drawn the same card on another occasion, she could no more bring herself to commit the deed then as now. When Florizel and Vandeleur realize they have something in common, she discloses her identity, not knowing Florizel was to have been her betrothed. Once Florizel learns about his bride-to-be, he has no problem with the marriage; nor, in fact, does she. After Florizel disposes of the club's president in a duel, the king of Bohemia announces their forthcoming union.

The script was a strange mix of romantic melodrama and the macabre, requiring the high style—artifice, not art. Rosalind could program herself into the high mode, except that here the high mode only required her to look mysterious at the beginning, conflicted in the middle, and radiant at the end. On the other hand, Montgomery's range was limited to looking droll and amused, then droll and serious, and finally just droll. He would do much better work the following year as Danny in MGM's *Night Must Fall* (1937).

Of Rosalind's two films for Fox in 1936, the first, *It Had to Happen*, has the kind of a title that tempts one to ask, Why? Fox's implausible pairing of an immigrant (George Raft) and a blueblood (Rosalind) may have been in the 1930s tradition of uniting the classes, but that formula works better in a screwball comedy with a suave leading man like Clark Gable or William Powell, not "tough guy" George Raft. *Under Two Flags* (1936), Rosalind's second—and better—Fox film that year, found her in North Africa. This time she was truly a lady, Lady Venetia, who falls in love with Victor (Ronald Colman), a French legionnaire with a past, thus becoming the rival of a cafe owner known only as Cigarette (Claudette Colbert). The Paris-born Colbert had the showier role. She played Cigarette with gusto, reveling in the occasion to speak some French and play the cocotte, but never the camp follower that the script implied she was. Her love for Victor is so genuine that in enlisting aid for Victor's beleaguered battalion, she dies in the process— but in her beloved's arms. For her loyalty to the Legion, she is awarded the Medal of Honor posthumously, as Lady Venetia and Victor look on solemnly.

It was inevitable that Lady Venetia would end up with Victor, particularly after we learn that Victor is an Oxford graduate and his dying brother cleared him of the charges that prompted him to flee England and join the Legion. But we still root for Cigarette, even though it is obvious that Victor cannot return her love. Lady Venetia was just another member of the privileged class whom Rosalind had to humanize, which she did by flirting decorously with Colman and evidencing a genuine delight at being introduced to an alien culture.

After Colbert's, the second most satisfying performance was purely visual; it was the work of the second unit director, Otto Brower, who staged the climactic attack in waves, with Arabs on horseback streaming through the sand and churning it into a powdery haze. One marvels at the skill with which extras fell from their horses on cue without getting trampled. Brower's ability to coordinate the disparate elements of the attack—the legionnaires leading the charge with Cigarette riding alongside them, the remnants of the battalion that is no match for the enemy, and the Arabs themselves riding down the dunes with terrifying majesty—is a testament to the years he spent directing westerns with Tim McCoy, Harry Carey, and Hoot Gibson. Little did Brower suspect that such potboilers as *Stairs of Sand* (1929) and *Fighting for Justice* (1932) would prepare him to create such an impressive finale for a not especially impressive film.

After *Trouble for Two*, MGM thought of Rosalind and Robert Montgomery as a team that could handle romantic comedy as well as psychological melodrama. They were paired again in John Van Druten's adaptation of Emlyn Williams's classic play, *Night Must Fall* (1937). As a playwright himself, Van Druten admired Williams's sense of structure; thus he retained the basic plot and much of the dialogue. Nor did he tinker with the character of Danny (Montgomery), a psychopath with a seductive voice and a penchant for murder and decapitation, thereby making it possible for audiences to understand and perhaps feel some compassion for someone whose ambivalence toward women had its origins in childhood. Both Williams and Van Druten are intentionally vague about Danny's background, some of which is imaginary; what is real is Danny's early exposure to the ways of his prostitute mother, who alternately repelled and fascinated him. Yet even for audiences that either could not or failed to make the connection between Danny's past and his attraction-repulsion to women, the character remained fascinating in his complexity; and Montgomery's creepy charm lightened, however slightly, Danny's dark places.

Rosalind's Olivia was another matter. Van Druten retained the outlines of her character: the niece-companion of an invalid (May Witty), on whom she is financially dependent and whose abuse she must endure. Rosalind kept her body taut, as if a combination of repression and resentment left it in knots, awaiting the right circumstances, the right person, or both, to loosen it. Like Danny, Olivia revels in morbidity; when she learns of a woman's disappearance and the possibility that her body may be lying in the nearby woods, she imagines the last day of the woman's life, as if it were unfolding before her eyes.

What Van Druten denied Olivia, however, is a growing attraction to Danny that becomes so strong that, in the play, she is willing to shield him from the authorities, even after she discovers that he has murdered her aunt. All Van Druten can do is hint at an incipient bond between them, as Olivia's resentment of Danny, whom she finds transparent, turns to curiosity, and finally to intercession. When a police inspector discovers a locked hat box in Danny's room, Danny is thrown off guard, becoming speechless. Since Olivia suspects the box contains the murdered woman's head, she casually asks the inspector what he is doing with *her* hat box. There was no reason for Olivia to come to Danny's aid, except to protect him, thereby becoming his mirror image. Yet Van Druten never develops their growing relationship, even though both Rosalind and Montgomery played their scenes together as if such an attraction existed. The film, however, ends quite differently from the play—with Olivia virtually betraying Danny to the police. Rosalind was obviously familiar with the original, in which Olivia was so drawn to Danny that she looks at him longingly as he is taken away in handcuffs. One has to imagine how Rosalind would have done the final scene on the stage, or even on the screen if Williams's ending had been retained.

Any Olivia would have had difficulty holding her own with a Danny like Montgomery, who picked up an Oscar nomination for his performance. Even so, Rosalind fleshed out the character admirably until Van Druten turned Olivia's relationship with Danny into the equivalent of a bad dream, from which she awakened just in time to be rescued by a stuffy suitor. However, only Van Druten (and MGM) thought Olivia needed rescuing, assuming that audiences that could accept a male psychopath would feel differently about a woman romantically drawn to one.

Rosalind and Montgomery co-starred again in *Live, Love, and Learn* (1938), which was responsible for her loan-out to Warners two years later for *No Time for Comedy* (1940). Both films featured a woman whose husband is seduced into channeling his creativity into a medium for which he is unsuited. In *Live*, the husband is an artist (Montgomery), whom a well-connected socialite (Helen Vinson) tries to turn into a portrait painter of the idle rich and their race horses. In *Comedy*, the husband (James Stewart) is a playwright with a knack for comedy, persuaded by the proverbial other woman to switch to social consciousness, for which he has no gift. In *Comedy*, Rosalind was the playwright's supportive wife; in *Live*, the artist's.

However, in 1938, *Live* was just another assignment that may have given Rosalind co-star billing with Robert Montgomery but demanded little of her. MGM was not the kind of studio to condescend to screwball comedy; on the few occasions that it went slumming, MGM came up with a pastiche of screwball, slapstick, and romance—which is exactly what *Live* turned out to be. First, there was the "meet cute," a staple of both romantic comedy and screwball. Rosalind makes her entrance during a fox hunt when her horse gallops over a stone wall, throwing her into Robert Montgomery's canvas. Montgomery no sooner delivers a diatribe against the privileged class, to which Rosalind belongs, than the two of them are joined in matrimony.

Despite her blue-chip upbringing, Rosalind adapts to her husband's bohemian lifestyle because it is so alien to anything she has ever known. MGM made it easier for her with its mythical depiction of Greenwich Village as a haven for eccentrics, one of whom (Robert Benchley) becomes a permanent member of their household. All that Rosalind had to do was look amused, marveling at the quaintness of it all.

The script had become a comic grab bag in which people are humiliated and objects destroyed—all in the name of fun. Rosalind must register delight at the antics of Montgomery and Benchley as they snip off men's ties, including the tie of an important gallery owner (Monty Woolley), whom they mistake for an imposter. Since neither Montgomery nor Benchley was adept at physical comedy, their antics were annoyingly sophomoric. Rosalind was spared; she only had to laugh.

Frank Capra's 1930s films, which codified the conventions of screwball comedy, must have influenced the writers, who added a dash of social consciousness to *Live*. Although one expects Montgomery to free himself from Helen Vinson's clutches and return to Rosalind, his decision to speak to a class of aspiring art students comes as a surprise, since he had earlier declined the invitation. Yet when Montgomery addresses the group in the final scene, he delivers a Capraesque speech about the importance of artistic integrity and the folly of easy money.

Because Rosalind's frame called for gowns that seemed to flow down her body, she was usually given a wardrobe that guaranteed her a place on somebody's "best-dressed" list. In *Man-Proof* (1938) her bridal gown was even more elaborate than the one in *Reckless*: it sported a train that trailed down an entire staircase, as befits a woman of wealth. Although Rosalind had replaced Myrna Loy in *Rendezvous*, she now found herself cast in a secondary role in *Man-Proof*, playing Loy's competition for the affections of Walter Pidgeon.

Rosalind was fortunate in not being the female lead. Loy had the thankless role of Pidgeon's former inamorata who still carries the torch after Pidgeon marries wealthy Rosalind. When Rosalind discovers that her husband has renewed his relationship with Loy, she confronts the two of them, delivering an unusually long monologue, in which she admits that Pidgeon, whom she characterizes as an "ordinary" man, only married her for her money. She delivers the lines reflectively in a voice slightly tinged with ruefulness but without any trace of self-pity. The speech is such a model of civility that, after Rosalind exits, Loy can only express her admiration: "There goes a general in any woman's army." The resolution is predictable: Pidgeon, chastened, returns to Rosalind; and Loy, to Franchot Tone, whose love she finally acknowledges.

Four's a Crowd (1938), Rosalind's first loan-out to Warner Bros., was the studio's attempt to capitalize on the Errol Flynn–Olivia de Havilland success, *The Adventures of Robin Hood*, released four months earlier. Flynn and de Havilland had become a popular screen couple ever since they appeared together in *Captain Blood* (1935), the first of six films in which they co-starred. The other two making up the "crowd" are Rosalind and Patrick Knowles—the latter as the publisher of the newspaper where Rosalind is an ace reporter and where Errol Flynn had once been managing editor before he discovered that there was more money in public relations.

Rosalind's Jean Christy was the precursor of Hildy Johnson in *His Girl Friday*, breezing into the newsroom with the bouncy self-confidence that only a true professional can exude. It might have taken a while for audiences to get used to Rosalind in a tailored suit, although she did get a few classy outfits. Still, it was refreshing to see her as a member of the working class for a change.

The plot itself was a romantic mix-up with Knowles originally in love with de Havilland, who finds Flynn more to her taste. But then so does Rosalind. However, with two sets of lovers, the pairing off was not what moviegoers expected—certainly not those who remembered Flynn and de Havilland as the romantic duo of *Captain Blood* and *The Charge of the Light*

Brigade (1936). *Crowd* concludes with a double wedding before a daffy justice of the peace (the delightful Hugh Herbert), but not until there is a change of partners: Rosalind and Flynn, and de Havilland and Knowles.

Except for Rosalind, the other principals seemed uneasy in their roles, which called for actors equally at home in sophisticated comedy and farce. Rosalind had the comic timing and deftness for both, but on the few occasions de Havilland attempted comedy (e.g., *Princess O'Rourke* [1943], *The Well-Groomed Bride* [1946]), she was unconvincing, perhaps because there was so little humor in the material. Flynn was saddled with the impossible role of a well-paid publicist who returns to the ailing newspaper to mount a hate campaign against de Havilland's anti-philanthropic grandfather (Walter Connolly) with the emblematic name of John P. Dillingworth.

The "Hate Dillingworth" crusade was a sop to depression audiences, who enjoyed seeing the "rich rich" acquire a social conscience after being held up to ridicule. Flynn convinces Dillingworth to become the anonymous benefactor of a clinic specializing in infantile paralysis, which was a critical health issue in the 1930s. The plan almost backfires, and the film nearly does, too, in its attempt to grapple with the ethical dilemma of printing the news and suppressing a story that could sabotage a worthy cause. However, there are enough sight gags involving butter, yapping dogs, and a troublesome terrier to deflect attention from the weightier issues that are raised but never explored.

By 1937, Rosalind was on MGM's short list of bankable talent. She now had a mobile dressing room in blue and white with a divan, a vanity, a radio, and a refrigerator. The color scheme matched her home on Elm Drive in Beverly Hills: a white brick Spanish colonial with leaded glass windows; a bar in gold and white; a blue, white, and coral dining room; and a living room with blue and white Venetian glass vases on the mantel. She also had Greta Garbo's former maid, Hazel Washington. "Top of the world," it seemed. But there was still a void in her life: "I live alone and hate it," she told the *Boston Sunday Globe* (11 February 1940). The following year, her status would change.

The Citadel (1938) paired Rosalind with another actor who, like Montgomery, garnered an Oscar nomination for a role that overshadowed hers: Robert Donat. There was little Rosalind could do in King Vidor's production of A. J. Cronin's best-seller but play second fiddle to Donat, around whose character the film revolved, as did the novel. Rosalind was the wife of a highly regarded Welsh doctor (Donat) until resentment erupts among the ignorant because of his "unorthodox" methods of scientific research, including the use of guinea pigs. Disillusioned, the couple sets out for London, where Donat becomes a consultant, earning big bucks for little work. It is Rosalind's job to revive his commitment to the underprivileged, which takes some doing once Donat has had a taste of the good life. Her gentle prodding and the death of his friend Denny (beautifully underplayed by Ralph Richardson) at the hands of an inept surgeon return him to his roots. Denny, a specialist in lung disease, was dismissed as a quack because he lacked a medical degree, even though he was an expert pulmonologist. In his climactic speech, Donat vindicates his friend at a public hearing, winning accolades for his oratory. Rosalind basked in the reflected glory, and audiences, one hopes, thought twice before entrusting themselves to degreeless physicians, realizing that Denny was an exception as well as a fictitious character.

Oddly, Rosalind was not on King Vidor's short list for Donat's wife. Vidor's first choice was Margaret Sullavan, followed by Virginia Bruce and Margaret Lindsay. One would never have known it from Vidor's panegyric to Rosalind when they appeared on WJZ (soon to be NBC) radio on 8 January 1939, speaking on behalf of the film, which the New York Film Critics had voted one of the ten best of 1938. Vidor implied that Rosalind's performance was largely responsible for the award, which was patently untrue. Still, it was further proof of her ascendancy in Hollywood, which, for those who were unaware, became evident in September 1939, when she made the cover of *Life*.

Of the two films Rosalind made that year, one was *Fast and Loose*, the final pairing of Rosalind and Robert Montgomery. The success of the *Thin Man* films, coupled with complaints from exhibitors that they appeared too infrequently, prompted MGM to create a spin-off with the same premise, but a different gimmick: a husband and wife team of amateur sleuths, with the husband as a rare books dealer who moves in a world of first editions and priceless manuscripts. The "Fast" series—so called because "Fast" appeared in each title (*Fast Company, Fast and Loose*, and *Fast and Furious*)— lacked the production values of the *Thin Man* films as well as the star power of William Powell and Myrna Loy; the *Fast* films were the equivalent of B movies, and not especially memorable ones at that. Unlike the *Thin Man* series, in which William Powell and Myrna Loy played Nick and Nora Charles in all six films, each of the *Fast* films had different co-stars: Melvyn Douglas and Florence Rice in *Fast Company* (1938), Robert Montgomery and Rosalind in *Fast and Loose* (1939), and Franchot Tone and Ann Sothern in *Fast and Furious* (1939).

What the series needed, and got, was sophistication—never to the degree to which Powell and Loy supplied it, but in a diluted form. *Fast and Loose* belonged to Robert Montomery, who triumphed over an intricately plotted script about the theft of a Shakespeare manuscript. Although he solves the case by using Sherlockian deduction, Rosalind ends up accidentally shooting him in the butt while he is fighting it out with the murderer. Although Rosalind played the quick-with-a-quip heroine gamely, she was given little to do, particularly in the film's midsection, during which she virtually disappeared.

Her second 1939 film, *The Women*, was quite the opposite. When Rosalind learned that MGM had bought the rights to Clare Boothe's *The Women* (1936), which ran on Broadway for 657 performances, she immediately began campaigning for the role of the gossip Sylvia Fowler, which Ilka Chase had originated. It is difficult to explain Rosalind's attraction to the part—a woman who is married to a philanderer and assumes the same about her friends. Rosalind may well have known women like Sylvia, who spend their days in beauty parlors and reducing salons, garnering bits of gossip that they weave into scenarios of infidelity. When Sylvia learns that the husband of Mary Haines (Norma Shearer) has become infatuated with Crystal Allen

(Joan Crawford), she sets the rumor machine in motion. Mary, however, can only play the noble wife until nobility gives way to pride, and pride to a Reno divorce. Meanwhile, when Sylvia's unseen husband—there are no men in the film, in keeping with the title—takes up with a chorus girl, Miriam Aarons (Paulette Goddard), Sylvia heads for Reno as well.

If Rosalind walked off with the film, as some critics claimed, it was not just because hers was the showiest role. With Norma Shearer underplaying Mary, and Rosalind doing everything in her power to avoid turning Sylvia into a grotesque, Rosalind achieved the impossible: by substituting humor for malice, she found favor with women who, if they knew Sylvias in real life, would have shunned them. Rosalind's Sylvia Fowler was a compulsive gossipmonger, unable to control herself because, as we learn at the end, Howard Fowler is even a bigger philanderer than Stephen Haines. There is a way to play a woman who thrives on Schadenfreude and a woman who does not know what it means. And if Sylvia had learned that it meant joy at another's misfortune, she would have denied she meant any harm, only that she was alerting a "friend" to a situation she may not have known existed. That Sylvia can associate with a woman like Crystal, after Crystal becomes Mrs. Stephen Haines, is not surprising. Sylvia can remain on good terms with a woman who broke up her friend's marriage, but not with the woman who broke up her own. Sylvia gets her comeuppance when she must acknowledge her husband's infidelity with Miriam, but only after she takes on her rival in an uncommonly realistic fight scene.

However, it is Norma Shearer who deserves the laurels for under-playing the part. As Mary, she has to run the gamut from perfect home-maker to betrayed wife, whose only alternative is divorce; yet when her husband seeks reconciliation, she is magnanimous enough to take him back. Shearer's finest moment occurs when a manicurist starts blabbing about Crystal's affair with Stephen Haines, assuming that, as one of Sylvia's friends, Mary is interested in dirt. Unable to hear any more, Mary starts to leave. When the manicurist asks her name, Shearer replies with great dignity, "Mrs. Haines."

The Women got Rosalind on the 4 September 1939 cover of *Life* magazine, where she looked anything but glamorous in a striped shirt with her arms crossed. That may have been the point: Rosalind as one of the girls, not one of the "women." The cover was a lead-in to a two-page spread on *The Women, Life*'s Movie of the Week. Rosalind may have made the cover of *Life*, but the text was chiefly a comparison between the beauty treatments depicted in the film and those available at Elizabeth Arden's and Helena Rubinstein's. The timing was unfortunate. *Life* hit the newsstands three days after World War II broke out, and a day after England and France declared war on Germany. At the time, Rosalind's sister Mary Jane was working as a researcher at Time, Inc., *Life's* publisher. The editors were furious that a movie star appeared on the cover at the beginning of World War II. Naturally, Mary Jane did not reveal her relationship to the star.

No matter how Rosalind rationalized it, Sylvia Fowler was not a leading role, the kind that she felt she now merited. The industry realized it, too. The situation changed when she was loaned out to Warners the following year for the film version of S. N. Behrman's play *No Time for Comedy* (1940), an odd choice for a studio that was not known for sophisticated comedy. Rosalind was the logical choice for Julia Page, a stage star appearing in a Minnesota journalist's first play. The journalist-turned-playwright was another contract player from Metro, also on loan—James Stewart. Rosalind's performance in Behrman's *The Second Man* brought her to Hollywood, and by 1940 her flair for drawing-room comedy far exceeded what it was in 1934. Although the film was faithful to Behrman's plot—in which a dramatist decides to abandon comedy, at which he excels, for social realism, at which he is inept—the style and tone had to be completely altered, not so much for Rosalind as for Stewart in the role that Laurence Olivier had originated. The star of the play was Katharine Cornell, one of the most accomplished stage actresses of her generation. With James Stewart, fresh from *Mr. Smith Goes to Washington* (1939) as the playwright from the boondocks, it was as if the actor were doing "Mr. Smith Goes to Broadway"; like Jefferson Smith, who takes a tour of Washington before proceeding to his office, the playwright stops off at the Grand Canyon, Santa Fe, and New Orleans before arriving for rehearsals—much to the annoyance of the director and producer, but not the star, who finds him refreshingly sincere, compared to the types that inhabit the theater world.

Because Stewart is so cartoonish, Rosalind underplays Julia, changing from a stage diva to a woman so disarmed by the playwright's integrity that she proposes to him on a park bench. Even when Stewart falls under the influence of Genevieve Tobin, who persuades him to abandon comedy for serious drama, Rosalind refuses to play either the jealous or the noble wife, choosing instead to wait for him to realize his mistake, as he does when "The Way of the World," a piece of 1930s agitprop and a far cry from William Wycherley's Restoration comedy of the same name, fails abysmally.

At the end of the film, Stewart is alone in the theater—or so he thinks—after the opening night fiasco. Rosalind is also there; standing in the aisle, she calls, "Author! Author!" It is an eloquent moment in which the husband realizes his wife's worth; and the wife, her husband's vulnerability.

Nineteen forty was Rosalind's loan-out year: *His Girl Friday* (Columbia), which will be discussed in the next chapter; *No Time for Comedy* (Warners); and *Hired Wife* (Universal). She obviously relished arriving on the Universal lot from which she fled six years earlier. However, no one there probably remembered her, since the Laemmle era ended in 1937. *Hired Wife* was the first of Rosalind's four films with Brian Aherne, whose understated virility made him a perfect co-star. Rosalind played the executive secretary of a cement manufacturer (Aherne), enamored of a model (Virginia Bruce) whom he wants for an ad campaign. Knowing that Aherne needs her (and hoping he will realize how much), Rosalind agrees to be his wife in name only so that the company's assets would be in her name, thereby averting a hostile takeover. When a Latin American playboy (John Carroll) enters the plot, it is only a matter of time before he takes up with the model, leaving Aherne and Rosalind free to legitimize their mock marriage. Even so, the Legion of Decency gave *Hired Wife* a B rating ("Morally Objectionable in Part for All") because of its "light treatment of marriage."

The role demanded little of Rosalind, who wore designer clothes but had only one scene requiring her to act. Before she and Aherne go through the motions of marriage, Rosalind witnesses a real ceremony as a justice of the peace marries a young couple whose mutual love is obvious from the way they look at each other. Director William A. Seiter gave Rosalind a close-up, revealing a woman who, despite her formidable professionalism, was a romantic at heart, even to the point of whispering "I do" as the couple exchange vows.

In 1940, Rosalind knew she was a star. But she also knew that star billing—in the sense of one's name appearing not just above the title, but in first place as well—reflected the actor's importance to the studio or his or her popularity, but not necessarily the film's quality. In *The Feminine Touch* (1941), Rosalind's name was above the title, followed by those of her co-stars, Don Ameche and Kay Francis. It was also one of her least impressive performances.

The Feminine Touch was not exactly panned, yet it illustrated some of the excesses to which Rosalind was prone unless a tough-minded director managed to curb them, which W. S. "Woody" Van Dyke did not. As the wife of a psychology professor (Ameche) who abandons Academe for commercial publishing, Rosalind adopted a voice that either she or Van Dyke believed was characteristic of a woman whose mother ran a boardinghouse. Rosalind could sound tough—and did—in *Gypsy*, yet her voice was never irritating as it was in *The Feminine Touch*.

When the couple arrive in New York, the professor falls under the spell of a literary agent's assistant (Kay Francis) while Rosalind finds herself courted by the agency's owner (Van Heflin). Jealousy, the subject of the professor's book, extends to the plot, with Rosalind becoming suspicious of Ameche's involvement with Francis, while Ameche remains coolly indifferent to Heflin's blatant attempts to seduce his wife. When Ameche discards academic civility and starts throwing punches at Heflin, the result is a painfully extended scene, revealing the limitations of both actors, neither of whom was adept at physical comedy. If MGM did not realize that Helfin's forte was drama, it became apparent the following year when he was voted best supporting actor for *Johnny Eager* (1942). In *The Feminine Touch*, however, Heflin bellowed his lines in accordance with Van Dyke's idea of repartee. Heflin was not the only offender; he was part of a trio of shouters, comprised of Rosalind, Ameche, and, to some extent, Francis, who alone endowed the film with an aura of sophistication—something Rosalind might have provided if the film had been recast with William Powell as the professor, Myrna Loy as his wife, and Rosalind as the assistant. She would not have had star billing, but she would have had a better part.

To be brutally frank, Rosalind was badly directed. She tended at times to nasalize her *a*'s. "Man" was always a problem with her. Sometimes she would flatten the vowel, as if it were on the verge of becoming disyllabic. In *Touch*, Rosalind was trying to adopt the voice of lower-middle-class woman married to a college professor whom she met when he was a student living at her mother's boardinghouse. Neither the director nor the trio of writers, which included Ogden Nash, served Rosalind well; someone must have thought that a hair-pulling fight between Rosalind and Kay Francis would evoke memories of *The Women*. Donald Meek intervenes, positioning himself between Rosalind and Francis, presumably to double the laughs. Mercifully, the scene is brief, as the three fall down, and the shot fades out—and not a moment too soon.

Rosalind was also billed first in *Design for Scandal*, released in December 1941, a month after *The Feminine Touch*. Since she was playing a professional once more, a judge by the name of C. C. Potter, she was able to reclaim her cultivated voice that had turned shrill in the previous film. Rosalind's co-star was Walter Pidgeon, playing a reporter whose urbanity matched hers and whose gentlemanly decorum and unthreatening masculinity were exactly what was needed to bring out the woman concealed beneath the judge's robes. Pidgeon's plan, at first, is to help out his boss (Edward Arnold), against whom Judge Potter ruled in a divorce suit, in which Arnold's ex-wife was awarded a sizeable settlement. The reporter eventually succeeds in ingratiating himself with the judge, who grows increasingly feminine as he becomes more interested in her than in looking for evidence to discredit her. It was a joy to watch Rosalind blossom under Pidgeon's courtship, which slowly moves from calculated seduction to intimations of love. Rosalind knew how to be discreetly amorous, allowing a certain amount of physical closeness between herself and Pidgeon, softening her voice until it acquired a hint of sensuousness, and letting the rest of the scene play itself out in the audience's imagination. One of the most charming moments in the film occurs when Rosalind and Pidgeon are bicycling together, singing "A Bicycle Built for Two," as if they were teenagers pedaling down Main Street, U.S.A.

Even after Rosalind discovers the truth, Pidgeon does not have to convince her of his love; his sincerity speaks for itself, thus dispensing with the need for an elaborate explanation. One reason Rosalind seemed so relaxed in the role, and so responsive to Pidgeon's attempt to woo her, is that during the shoot she was engaged to marry Frederick Brisson, which she did on 25 October 1941, about six weeks before the film's release. Like Pidgeon, Brisson was suave without being unctuous, exuding a natural self-confidence and a subdued masculinity that was neither aggressive nor overwhelming. Both Pidgeon and Brisson were comfortable about who they were and showed it. When Rosalind starred with an actor who made her feel at ease (which Ameche did not), she would not so much act as react to his line readings, particularly in moments of intimacy. If an actor like Pidgeon lowered his voice to an audible whisper, she would, too, intrigued and delighted at the attention he was lavishing on her. There were other actors—especially Cary Grant, Brian Aherne, and Melvyn Douglas—with whom she felt a similar rapport.

Of Rosalind's three 1941 MGM films, only one could be called a real stretch: *They Met in Bombay* (1941), in which she and Clark Gable played a pair of jewel thieves planning to steal the same necklace. As a phony baroness, Rosalind meets her match with Gable, an ex-British officer (sans accent) turned soldier of fortune and more adept at theft than she. The theft succeeds, but their mutual greed interferes, resulting in a detour that would have turned *They Met in Bombay* into a "couple on the lam" movie had it not been for clear signs of Japanese aggression in the Far East. Although MGM was never in the vanguard of political or social consciousness, it seized the opportunity to bring the film's improbable plot into the present by having Gable return to his old profession just as Japan invaded China. The script would have us believe that the invasion had just occurred, although Japan's agenda was evident in 1931 with the takeover of Manchuria. However, by June 1941, when the film was released, the "rape of Nanking" had already occurred, Shanghai had fallen, and Pearl Harbor was six months away. Thus the Sino-Japanese War, which seems to have come as a surprise to the British, was a decade old.

The new plot twist served both Gable and Rosalind well. Playing his new role to the hilt, Gable lobs grenades at the Japanese, getting wounded in the process, but also receiving the Victoria Cross. The writers threw verisimilitude to the winds: when Scotland Yard insists on prosecuting the recipient of Britain's highest honor, Gable hands over the necklace and returns to the army, presumably to fight in a war that America has yet to enter. Since Gable was playing a former British captain, it would have been the war that began in September 1939.

Gable was the chief attraction in *They Met in Bombay*, but Rosalind was the one to make the transition—specifically, from thief to patriot, or, in terms of costume, from haute couture to clothes off the rack. But the sudden shift from romantic melodrama to combat film with Japanese stereotypes gave the film a curious relevance. Until 7 December 1941, Hollywood was reluctant to endorse a war that, historically, began in Europe with the invasion of Poland on 1 September 1939 when the United States was still isolationist. Yet the studios could not ignore the rumblings of war that were reverberating throughout Europe and Asia. The solution was simple: history became a subtext with enough detail for the knowledgeable moviegoer to view the film within a contemporary context. Anyone who realized the importance of the Burma Road as a strategic supply route would have derived far more from MGM's *A Yank on the Burma Road* (1941) or Universal's *Burma Convoy* (1941) than a moviegoer only interested in an action adventure. MGM dealt more daringly with Japanese militarism in *They Met in Bombay* than it did with Nazism in *The Mortal Storm* and *Escape* (both 1940). Since there was a smaller percentage of Japanese moviegoers than German ones, alienating the former would not have as much of an effect on the box office as antagonizing the latter, many of whom were pro-Hitler, not to mention anti-Semitic. Furthermore, in 1941, "yellow peril" caricatures would not have been considered grossly offensive—and certainly not politically incorrect. Thus, portraying the Chinese as victims of Japanese aggression would inspire far less criticism than portraying German Jews as victims of a pogrom that would soon escalate into the Holocaust.

In MGM's *The Mortal Storm* (1940), "Jew" was not spoken, "non-Aryan" being the preferred designation; the closest the film came to identifying the professor interned in a concentration camp was the "J" on his arm band. In *Escape*, the country where enemies of the state are carted off to a concentration camp is never identified, nor is the camp, although given the film's Bavarian setting, it was probably Dachau. Although "deconstruction" had yet to be coined, there were a number of pre–Pearl Harbor films that, when the veneer was peeled away, revealed another level of meaning. *They Met in Bombay* was one of them.

The film by no means minimized the plight of the Chinese at the hands of their aggressors. However, once it switched directions and moved into the combat zone, the invasion of China became the yardstick for evaluating the main characters' actions, making their past irrelevant. Neither Gable nor Rosalind could reclaim the screen, which had now ceded to the grim realities of the present. Brief forays into the world of the caper and adventure film provided enough plot points to move the action along until the writers (or studio) decided it was impossible to end the movie in Hong Kong without acknowledging the Sino-Japanese War. While Gable is always Gable, whether he is a thief or an officer, Rosalind evolves; once she abandons her profession (to which she is unsuited), she evidences a genuine concern for the Chinese whose evacuation is being blocked by a Japanese regiment—until Gable takes a stand, which, predictably, saves the day. The way Gable played the role, his character was more concerned with defying the Japanese than with evacuating the village; Rosalind, on the other hand, found the woman beneath the wardrobe, but only after she began looking like one; it was as natural for Rosalind to wear a simple suit or a skirt and blouse as it was to wear a tailored outfit topped with a turbanlike hat. However, when Gable traded in a suit for a uniform, it was simply a change of costume.

Nineteen forty-one marked the end of Rosalind's MGM tenure. Rather than renegotiate another seven-year contract, she preferred to freelance. She received her first leading role in a Columbia movie, and when the studio offered her a multipicture deal, she accepted. The lion's roar would no longer introduce any of her films.

CHAPTER 4

The Lady and the Mogul

Columbia Pictures originated as the CBC Film Sales Company, the creation of two Cohns, Harry and Jack; and a Brandt, Joe. Once the corporate name became Columbia Pictures in 1924, only one of the founders would emerge as studio head: Harry Cohn, who became both president and head of production. Of all the moguls, Cohn was considered the arch vulgarian. Nicknamed "White Fang," he had been at various times a pool hall hustler, trolley car conductor, song plugger, and traveling exhibitor; playwright Garson Kanin used him as the model for the millionaire junk dealer, Harry Brock, in his comedy, *Born Yesterday*.

There were two Harry Cohns: the womanizer and tyrant and the studio head who read scripts carefully, respected writers, and treated a select number of actresses as ladies and the rest as dames. Like all of Hollywood, Rosalind was aware of the dichotomy. Her Harry Cohn was a man of "innate taste, quite remarkable taste." She also knew about Cohn's office and what it held for women who wanted the shortest route to stardom, which they rarely achieved. Even so, they did not leave empty-handed. The office was a study in white. Cohn's desk was on an eight-inch riser that enabled him to look down at his visitors, so that he appeared to be taller than he actually was. Behind the desk were Columbia's Oscars, theatrically spotlighted as if they were his trophies. Behind the statuettes was another row of shelves, stacked with nylons (a luxury during World War II) and French perfume.

When Rosalind decided in 1941 that she would only sign a multi-picture contract with Columbia if a bottle of Arpège were part of the deal, Harry balked, knowing he would get nothing in return—at least not what he normally received from women willing to accommodate him on the white couch in his office. But he finally yielded, having never considered Rosalind a potential conquest. Cohn divided women into two categories: ladies and broads. Rosalind was one of the former. Cohn was never less than courteous to her, watching his language and behavior, even when she got the better of him, as she did in October 1943, a few months after her son, Lance, was born.

Rosalind was about to resume her tour of army camps. Despite her limitations as a singer, she was a born entertainer, and service men and women were so taken with her down-to-earth manner that they paid no attention to her voice, which *New York Times* drama critic Brooks Atkinson compared to "the Ambrose Lightship calling for its mate." Rosalind's 1942 tour was so popular that she was named an honorary major by the Aviation Cadet Corps, a second lieutenant by the Army Nurses Corp, and mess sergeant in the U.S. Army by the Cook and Mess Sergeants School at Camp Wallace, Texas. There would be further honors and citations throughout the war years. After the war ended, she was given the War Agencies of the United States Government plaque for outstanding service on the War Activities Committee and commissioned "Honorary Colonel for Lifetime" by Hollywood Post 43 of the American Legion.

For her 1943 tour, Rosalind needed a wardrobe that was both glamorous and utilitarian. Knowing that Columbia allowed its stars to purchase their costumes at half price, Rosalind approached Cohn, who informed her that he had suspended the policy for the duration, claiming that fabrics were either too expensive or unavailable. She could, however, purchase the ones she wanted at cost, which came to $3,400. Rosalind agreed and made out a check for that amount. But there was a third act in the "Rosalind Gets Her Dresses" scenario. Just when Cohn thought he had trumped Rosalind, she casually remarked that she had purchased a coat from the same furrier as his second wife, the former actress Joan Perry. Cohn shrugged. Rosalind then reminded him that she wore the coat—her own, not the studio's—as part of her wardrobe during the twenty-seven-day shoot of *This Thing Called Love*. When she inquired about the cost of renting the coat for the same amount of time, the furrier replied, "a hundred dollars a day." Since she had saved Columbia $2,700 by wearing her own coat, Rosalind told Cohn to write out a check to her for that amount. Thus she only paid $700 for the dresses.

It may have been a minor victory, but it only confirmed what was common knowledge in Hollywood: Rosalind Russell was a shrewd business woman who may have been uncommonly generous, but who also knew the difference between contributing to a charity and to a corporation.

Despite his irascibility and tight-fistedness, Rosalind found Cohn— whom she always addressed as "Harry," as opposed to Louis Mayer, who was always "Mr. Mayer"—endearing. Rosalind was grateful to him for providing her with her first starring role in *Craig's Wife*. She was even more grateful in September 1939, when he recommended her for the female lead in Howard Hawks's production of *His Girl Friday*, a remake of *The Front Page*, that was substantially different from the Ben Hecht–Charles MacArthur play and the faithful 1931 movie version. Fidelity was not upmost in the minds of Ben Hecht and Joseph Lederer when they were writing the screenplay. The writers were following Hawks's mandate to convert the original into a screwball comedy, a genre that Hawks helped perfect and that had become a Columbia specialty after the release of Hawks's *Twentieth Century* (1934) and Frank Capra's *It Happened One Night* (1934), both of which were Columbia films, the latter winning five Oscars as well. By 1939, Columbia had produced a number of screwballs, including *Mr. Deeds Goes to Town* (1936), *Theodora Goes Wild* (1936), *The Awful Truth* (1937), *Holiday* (1938), and *You Can't Take It with You* (1938). However, transforming a play—in which managing editor Walter Burns goes to extreme lengths to keep his star reporter, Hildebrand "Hildy" Johnson, from marrying and leaving the newspaper business—into a screwball comedy could only work if Hildebrand became Hildegarde, so that the character could still be called Hildy Johnson, but would now be female. And so, a battle of wits becomes a battle of the sexes, with Burns's machinations remaining the same, except that (a) he and Hildy were once married and are now divorced; (b) Hildy is about to remarry, give up journalism, and move to Albany with her insurance salesman fiancé the very day she informs Walter of her decision; and (c) Walter realizes that if Hildy leaves, he has no one to interview Earl Williams, an anarchist who has been given the death penalty for killing a policeman and is due to be hanged the next morning. Walter has little time to sabotage Hildy's marital prospects, get the interview, and reclaim Hildy for himself and the paper, without resorting to the *Front Page*'s denouement, which would never have worked in *His Girl Friday.* In the play, Hildy is about to leave Chicago with his bride-to-be, Peggy, and relocate in New York, where he plans to go into advertising. Pretending to wish Hildy well, Walter even offers him his gold watch as a memento. After Hildy leaves to catch his train, Walter has a wire sent to the chief of police at the next stop, demanding that Hildy be arrested and brought back to Chicago. Walter's explanation is one of the most famous curtain lines in the theater: "The son of a bitch stole my watch!" As memorable as the line was, it could only work in a faithful screen adaptation of *The Front Page*. Otherwise, there had to be a different ending.

When the actresses considered for Hildy—Carole Lombard, Irene Dunne, and Jean Arthur, all of whom had done screwball comedy—passed on the role, Cohn recommended Rosalind and arranged to borrow her from MGM. Meanwhile, Rosalind happened to reading the *New York Times,* where she learned she would be playing a part that others had rejected. Furious at not being consulted, she vented her anger not at Cohn—at whom she knew she couldn't—but at Hawks, who, she assumed, never wanted her in the first place, which was true. But it was zero hour, and Rosalind was Hawks's

Hildy Johnson by default. After listening to her tirade, Hawks told her to get fitted for a striped suit, which, along with a hat, would be the extent of her wardrobe. Rosalind knew that she had no choice, since MGM had agreed to the loan-out. Besides, Hawks was a major director, and her co-star was Cary Grant.

His Girl Friday was not *The Women*, nor was Hildy Sylvia one-note. More important, Rosalind was not a member of the supporting cast, as she had been in *The Women*. She was Cary Grant's co-star. Hildy and Walter were complex roles; in fact, Hildy was the most difficult part Rosalind had been handed since Harriet Craig. She had to portray a conflicted woman, torn between staying in the only profession she knew or becoming the spouse of a dullard with a mother fixation. Similarly, Grant had to play the Machiavel, subverting Hildy's marriage plans for reasons ranging from love to self-interest, making it possible for her to rediscover herself, regain her professionalism, and abandon the pipe dream of being an Albany homemaker. A Walter Burns without charm would have been an oily manipulator; a defeminized Hildy, who admits to being a "newspaper man" without looking like one, would have been a female parody. Despite her suit, Rosalind never lost her femininity; and Grant wove a web of deception with the cunning of a nonlethal spider who only wants the best for the entrapped.

Rosalind had to establish Hildy's character immediately. The camera tracks her as she breezes into the newspaper office, acknowledging her former colleagues, who respond warmly to her. Hildy, after all, is one of them. She even looks like one in her pin-striped suit. A newspaper man, not a female journalist, is how she perceives herself—and still does, despite her divorce from Walter. Ostensibly, she has returned to tell her former managing editor and ex-husband that despite his attempts to woo her back (including phone calls and telegrams), she is about to leave for Albany with her fiancé, Bruce Baldwin (Ralph Bellamy), and his mother. But she has also brought Bruce along, presumably to convince Walter she is capable of a starting a new life. Walter knows she is not, and, unconsciously (or perhaps even consciously), so does she.

The opening sequence is a masterpiece of repartee, in which Rosalind and Grant pick up their cues without seeming to take a breath or sacrifice clarity and nuance for speed. Hawks wanted rapid-fire delivery to convey the ambience of a newsroom with fast-talking reporters, which meant that five pages of script would be shot in the time it would take to shoot four, forcing the actors to speak twenty times faster than usual and still be understood.

It is immediately obvious that "the lady doth protest too much." Rosalind's Hildy is a born reporter, hoping perhaps that Walter can rescue her from her impending marriage to an oedipal male so that she can return to the business she loves and the man who is her mirror image. Otherwise, why does she bother to bid adieu to Walter in person, much less bring Bruce along? By introducing Bruce to Walter, Hildy becomes an accomplice in her fiancé's trial by ordeal, as Walter, first, agrees to buy an insurance policy from Bruce, if Hildy writes up the Earl Williams story. To get Bruce out of the way so Hildy can do her job, Walter then subjects him to a series of humiliations, including having his pocket picked and getting him jailed on a trumped up theft charge. Meanwhile, the more involved Hildy becomes in the Williams case, the less aware she is of Bruce's absence.

Rosalind's Hildy seems to have been born in a newsroom. She knows how to land a difficult interview: she merely drops a twenty-dollar bill in front of the guard—a nonverbal bribe, if there ever was one. Hildy speaks slowly to Williams, as if he were a child, which, politically, he is. Like the other reporters, Hildy is a smoker; in fact, in *His Girl Friday*, cigarettes distinguish those in the newspaper world from the outsiders. Hildy offers a cigarette to Williams, who declines, which immediately establishes him as "other." (Bruce is a non-smoker, too, and would only be comfortable in a smoke-free environment.)

The interview is one of Rosalind's finest moments. She adopts a sympathetic, almost soothing voice, as she patiently tries to extract information from Williams for a lead. Knowing that he is familiar with the radical left's jargon, Hildy plays around with the phrase "production for use," which left a deep impression on Williams when he heard it at some left-wing rally denouncing capitalism. The context is unimportant; all Williams hears is "production for use." The logic is simple: Whatever is manufactured is intended for use; a gun is manufactured; therefore, a gun is intended for use. And Williams put one to use.

Another memorable scene only requires Rosalind to speak four words. When her male colleagues ridicule Williams's only friend, the prostitute Mollie Malloy, Hildy must stand by, even though, from the look on her face, she would like to intervene. As a "newspaper man," Hildy cannot censure her own in the presence of an outsider, although her natural inclination is to come to the defense of a victim of harassment, which, one suspects, Hildy also was at the beginning of her career. On the other hand, Hildy knows she must comment, however obliquely, on the men's sexism. The men themselves sense that they have behaved badly, especially in Hildy's presence, and Hildy has no intention of letting them off. "Gentlemen of the press," she says quietly, in a voice steeped in disappointment.

Earl Williams and Mollie Malloy are only characters in a subplot; we do not have to wait for the denouement to discover that Williams will not be hanged, and that Malloy, even after jumping out of a window, has not died from the fall. What matters in this kind of a comedy is the restoration of relationships. Bruce finally realizes he has been a scapegoat and returns to Albany with his mother, leaving Hildy free to practice a profession at which she excels and, perhaps, even another—as a managing editor's wife, at which she may also excel, but probably not until she retires from her full-time job. It is only at the end of the film that one realizes that the action was almost continuous. Hildy is near exhaustion; a day that began with her announcement of a new life ends with a return to the old one. That she is on the verge of tears is understandable. Hers are tears of emotional release, a delayed reaction to twelve hours in the fiery furnace of cutthroat journalism, from which she emerges intact as well as transfigured; perhaps they are also tears of guilt for the indignities that Bruce has endured on her account. But there is no time for tears or guilt; there is a strike that has to be covered in, of all places, Albany.

By 1940, Rosalind had become so identified with Hildy Johnson that writers struggled—and, in some cases, strained—to create Hildy spin-offs with a more varied and glamorous wardrobe. They were so successful that Rosalind found it difficult to shed the career woman image with which she had been saddled.

Harry Cohn thought otherwise. He was so delighted with the success of *His Girl Friday*, despite its failure to win a single Oscar nomination, that he negotiated another loan-out for Rosalind for *This Thing Called Love* (1941), hoping she would consider joining Columbia after the expiration of her MGM contract. Rosalind did, but not as a Columbia regular like Rita Hayworth, Glenn Ford, and Evelyn Keyes. She returned to Columbia for a series of "career woman" comedies—or rather, comedies in which the careerist heeds the siren call of marriage and "fulfillment," often leaving her career in limbo.

As early as 1936, Cohn was interested in making *This Thing Called Love*, which Pathé had attempted without much success in 1929. Once Rosalind arrived on the Columbia lot for *Craig's Wife*, he knew he had his star. However, Joe Breen, who headed what was once called the Hays Office (the industry's attempt at self-censorship, still called by that name, although Breen was now in charge), was shocked that this "travesty of marriage" might return to the screen. Breen reminded Cohn that the 1929 version encountered "enormous protest" from the state censors, some of whom demanded so many cuts that the film was "slashed to pieces." By 1940, Breen still found the script unacceptable, but Cohn, who had a way of humoring him and then going his own way, agreed to his demands.

Finally, Breen approved the script, and casting began. Cohn realized there was no one at the studio who could play Ann Marvin in *This Thing Called Love*, just as five years earlier there was no one for Harriet Craig in *Craig's Wife*. Again, the answer was Rosalind, who could be alternately coy, determined, flirtatious, and sensuous, without making it seem that the character had a multiple personality disorder. It was loan-out time, and for the second year in a row, Rosalind was back at Columbia.

Rosalind had played Ann at least once in stock and could give the role the combination of breeziness and vulnerability that it needed. Although the George Seaton–Ken Englund screenplay took substantial liberties with the original, the film remained a bedroom comedy with Ann as a numbers cruncher in an insurance firm; she is so alarmed by the rising divorce rate that she concludes it would drop if couples practiced celibacy for the first three months of marriage. Tice (Melvyn Douglas), Ann's husband, balks at the idea, looking for ways to convince his wife of her folly. When Ann grows amorous and decides to abandon her theory, she and Tice find themselves in compromising situations, each suspecting the other of infidelity, until, at the end, they retire to do what they should have done three months earlier.

Cohn was right. Rosalind was the perfect choice for Ann. The part allowed her to display a sensuality that, in the past, she could only suggest. But when Rosalind appears in one of Jean Louis's provocatively sheer negligees, one knows it is only a matter of time before Ann realizes that abstinence is no basis for a lasting marriage.

Melvyn Douglas is an excellent foil as Tice, who keeps undermining Ann's determination, watching it dissolve into playfulness as the audience awaits a "will they or won't they?" resolution. There are some delightful set pieces in the film, including a dinner party that spirals out of control when Tice invites a Peruvian investor (Lee J. Cobb) and his wife to dinner, hoping for a $1 million loan and unaware that Ann has guests of her own. As the father of eight children, the investor is so obsessed with parenthood that, to ensure the loan, Tice leads him to believe that Ann is pregnant. The Peruvian couple immediately become solicitous, advising Ann to drink milk with dinner and avoid exertion. When the subject turns to Ann's three-month plan, the insiders start proposing toasts to keep the conversation from going any further. When that fails, Tice leads the guests in singing "America the Beautiful."

A statue of the Mexican deity Quetzalcoatl, mistakenly called a fertility god, is cleverly worked into the plot. At first, it is simply an artifact that Tice has brought home from his travels; then it becomes a plot point. At the end, Ann signals to Tice that she is ready to consummate their marriage. *This Thing Called Love* may not be a female empowerment film, but at least Ann is the one who calls an end to marital celibacy, admitting that her theory is unworkable. To the unsubtle strains of "There'll Be a Hot Time in the Old Town Tonight," Ann marches up the stairs to Tice's bedroom, opens the door, and places the figurine on the table. Overjoyed, Tice leaves his room for hers, and Quetzalcoatl's closed eyes suddenly pop open.

The National Legion of Decency's eyes opened too after the film was screened for its members. Scheduled to premiere at Radio City Music Hall on 13 February 1941, the film was condemned by the Legion a week earlier because it was contrary to the "Christian concept of marriage." Since Radio City had already signed a contract with Columbia, the film could not be withdrawn. It opened with a C (Condemned) rating, although it had received the approval of the Motion Picture Producers Association (MPPA). Breen was furious; he was one of the Legion's founders and head of the Production Code Administration (PCA), which was created by the MPPA.

Although the Legion was never officially an organ of the Catholic Church, and its movie ratings were nonbinding, many Catholics were still guided by the Legion's classifications. In 1941, the Legion was sufficiently powerful to demand cuts. Columbia knew that few exhibitors would risk showing a C-rated movie; and with state censorship boards still in existence, cuts were inevitable. Within a week, fifteen lines of dialogue were deleted, and the film was given a B (Objectionable in Part) rating. The ratings booklet published by the National Legion of Decency included a signed letter from Columbia's executive vice president, Jack Cohn: "In accordance with your request, this Company has made all the changes . . . requested by the Legion of Decency." The branch offices had been notified, and Cohn assured the Legion that only the revised version would be distributed. Even so, *This Thing Called Love* was banned in Ireland, Australia, and British Columbia.

Rosalind was pleased with her treatment at Columbia. To tempt her to join the studio as a contract player, Cohn had her dressing room redecorated to resemble the one she had at MGM. Although Rosalind was determined to become a freelancer, she negotiated a contract allowing her to accept offers from other studios, as long as she fulfilled her Columbia commitments. On 23 October 1941, two days before her wedding to Frederick Brisson, Rosalind agreed to appear in ten pictures with budgets no less than $500,000, for which she would receive $100,000 for each of the first six and $125,000 for each of the next four. If location shooting was required, she and her maid, Hazel Washington, would travel first class. Rosalind also had the right to select her own wardrobe, subject to the director's approval. No time frame was specified, except that her first Columbia film, *My Sister Eileen*, would start on 15 February 1942, four weeks after she had completed *Take a Letter, Darling* (1942) for Paramount.

Although initial contracts are often more ideal than real—renegotiated, bought out, or significantly altered—Rosalind actually made ten pictures for Columbia, but over two decades: *My Sister Eileen* (1942), *What a Woman!* (1943), *She Wouldn't Say Yes* (1945), *The Guilt of Janet Ames* (1947), *Tell It to the Judge* (1949), *A Woman of Distinction* (1950), *Picnic* (1955), *Five Finger Exercise* (1962), *The Trouble with Angels* (1966), and *Where Angels Go . . . Trouble Follows* (1968). The first six were part of the 1941 contract. The last four were negotiated separately. For *Picnic*, which Rosalind made after her Broadway triumph in *Wonderful Town*, $125,000 would have been insulting, even though Rosalind was playing her first supporting role since *The Women*. Columbia only distributed *Exercise*, a Sonnis production from Frederick Brisson's company; and the two *Angels* were produced for Columbia by William Frye. However, in 1941, Rosalind's Columbia contract was more than satisfactory.

Before starting *My Sister Eileen*, Rosalind stopped off at nearby Paramount for *Take a Letter, Darling*, which was never intended for her. When Claudette Colbert, who had an arrangement with Paramount similar to Rosalind's at Columbia, relinquished the part of an advertising wiz in *Take a Letter, Darling* (1942) for a much better role in Preston Sturges's *The Palm Beach Story* (1942), director-producer Mitchell Leisen paged Rosalind, who was now on the verge of becoming the screen's quintessential career woman.

Darling conforms to the popular notion of the career woman as "a brain without a pulse," as she is described in the film, whose arctic exterior any high- or medium-testosterone male could melt. Love must triumph, and the resolution should be sufficiently open-ended to suggest that boss lady is not so much relinquishing her career as taking a vacation from it—a vacation sometimes known as marriage.

In *Darling*, Rosalind plays the head of a public relations firm who hires a male secretary (Fred MacMurray) to accompany her to supper clubs, where he is expected to distract the client's wife while she charms the husband into signing with her agency. MacMurray is so successful that the sister (Constance Moore) of a tobacco tycoon falls for him, while the tycoon (Macdonald Carey) becomes so enamored of Rosalind that he proposes marriage. When MacMurray tries to sabotage their relationship by retouching a painting of a provocatively dressed woman so that it bears a resemblance to Rosalind, Carey is even more eager for marriage, believing that the sensuous figure in the painting is the real Rosalind. Appalled by the tycoon's unwillingness to accept the truth, Rosalind storms out of his mansion and heads for the train station. But before she can get there, MacMurray, on his way to Mexico, intercepts her and drags her into his car. Since Leisen used an extreme long shot for the final scene, it is impossible to see Rosalind's reaction to what looks like an abduction. Since *Darling* is a romantic comedy, audiences would assume that she is not averse to being manhandled by someone who apparently knows her mind better than she does. How anxious Rosalind is to accompany MacMurray as he drives around Mexico, looking for subjects to paint, is another matter. That would be a movie in itself.

It was not Rosalind's finest hour. Even fewer sparks flew between Rosalind and MacMurray than did between herself and Don Ameche in *The Feminine Touch*. MacMurray had a way with a wisecrack and a flirty leer that worked beautifully in his first scene with Barbara Stanwyck in *Double Indemnity* (1944), in which the two of them no sooner meet than they start trading double entendres. But MacMurray never projected an air of intelligence, while Rosalind could pass for a Vassar summa cum laude.

Only once in the film was there even the hint of a connection between them—when they revealed their secret aspirations: his to paint, hers to write poetry. But that was it. The real star of the film was Mitchell Leisen, who began his film career by designing costumes for Cecil B. DeMille's films. (Leisen designed Constance Moore's in *Take a Letter, Darling*, leaving Irene to handle Rosalind's). The physical production was elegant, particularly the tobacco heirs' museum-like estate. However, the film's take on career versus marriage was retro even by 1940s standards. The problem was the last shot; one would like to think that some women winced at the sight of Rosalind Russell being yanked into a car by Fred MacMurray.

Rosalind's best Columbia film of the 1940s was *My Sister Eileen*, the film version of the 1940 Broadway success by Joseph Fields and Jerome Chodorov, who also wrote the screenplay. The original was an adaptation of some *New Yorker* stories by Ruth McKenney that were, for the most part, autobiographical and recounted the adventures of two sisters, Ruth and Eileen Sherwood, who left Ohio to pursue careers in New York—Ruth as a writer and Eileen as an actress. As Ruth, Rosalind was playing the role that Shirley Booth had originated on stage. Although Booth excelled in both comedy and drama, she is chiefly remembered as a comic actress, particularly for the long-running sitcom *Hazel*. What Booth brought to the character was a self-deprecating sense of humor and a healthy cynicism that made it possible for her to live in the shadow of her sister Eileen, everyone's favorite, although, intellectually, not on a par with Ruth. Rosalind brought the same qualities to the role, but added another: an air of sophistication that even a plain blouse and skirt could not conceal. Since Ruth refuses to wire home for money, she and Eileen must succeed on their own; Ruth does, while Eileen charms soda fountain managers, who oblige her with free lunches. Even when she lands in jail, the police wait on Eileen as if she were their houseguest.

My Sister Eileen brought Rosalind her first Oscar nomination. Although she knew she had no chance of winning, just to be nominated in the company of Greer Garson (*Mrs. Miniver*), who, in 1958, would replace her on

Broadway in *Auntie Mame*; Bette Davis (*Now, Voyager*); Katharine Hepburn (*Woman of the Year*); and Teresa Wright (*Pride of the Yankees*) was honor enough. With World War II underway and patriotism on the rise after a decade of isolationism, Greer Garson was a shoe-in for best actress for her portrayal of Kay Miniver, a model of home-front courage who weathered the Blitz as if it were a summer storm. That Rosalind was even nominated indicates that the Academy of Motion Picture Arts and Sciences acknowledged her brand of comedy, which lay somewhere between the drawing room, the bedroom, and—in *Eileen*—a basement apartment (the layout varied). After *Eileen*, Rosalind never had a vehicle where she could exercise her true comedic talent until she returned to the stage in a touring version of John Van Druten's *Bell, Book and Candle* in late 1951. Meanwhile, she tread water in *What a Woman!*, *She Wouldn't Say Yes*, *Tell It to the Judge*, and *A Woman of Distinction*, until she was rescued by *Bell, Book and Candle*, which allowed her to make selective use of her impressive repertory of facial expressions, double takes, throwaway lines, deadpan expressions, and camera-ready eyes that moved from left to right as if they were executing a pan shot.

Eileen required Rosalind to play the comic scapegoat, garnering laughs from moviegoers who would have been furious had they been in the same situation: living in a basement apartment over a subway construction site. However, if an actress alienates the audience by overplaying the character to the point of exaggeration, the audience will laugh at the character's predicament because they feel she has gotten what she deserves. The prospect of two sisters from Ohio duped into paying a month's rent on a Greenwich Village basement apartment with a barred window can be comic. But comedy works from the "up the ante" principle. Living below street level with a window into which drunks can bend down and ogle the sisters in their pajamas can be comic. But what about the sisters' discovering that work is underway on a new subway line? We may laugh whenever the blasting sends tremors throughout the apartment, but we also know that we would never tolerate such a situation in real life. How Ruth reacts to the blasting and other inconveniences will determine how successful a comic scapegoat she is. Eileen can pout, but she also has a host of moonstruck men who cater to her. Ruth, on the other hand, has to stay in the apartment, writing her stories. If Ruth loses her sense of humor, the audience will become apathetic, the laughter will dwindle, and the critics will wonder how a hit Broadway comedy became such a humorless film.

Fortunately, this never happens. Rosalind underplays, reacting to her predicament like a veteran ironist, as if every misfortune is one more manifestation of life's slings and arrows. When "Wreck" from upstairs is ironing Ruth's skirt for her (the sisters let him stay with them while his wife's mother is visiting), he asks Ruth how she wants the pleats turned. Rosalind delivers the two-word reply with her signature drollness: "Toward Mecca." Rosalind did not turn Ruth into a caricature; if she had, there would have been no Oscar nomination. Unlike the effervescent Eileen, who knows how to charm men, Ruth operates on a different level. Her femininity does not elicit head-turning or free lunches. Ruth's femininity lies at the opposite end of the spectrum, where the colors are muted and subtle, until deepened by love. For a potential author like Ruth, that love must embody respect, which comes from an editor (Brian Aherne) who believes in her talent and jeopardizes his job to get her published.

My Sister Eileen came to the screen relatively intact, except for a few changes necessitated by the Production Code: Violet, the apartment's former tenant, is no longer a prostitute, but a psychic; Wreck and Helen, the couple upstairs who were living together in the play, are now married. The play ended with Ruth's getting her first story, appropriate entitled "My Sister Eileen," in the *Manhatter*—obviously a stand-in for the *New Yorker*—thanks to editor Aherne, who defied his boss and published it, losing his job in the bargain. Since *Eileen* is a comedy, the boss relents, the editor is reinstated, and Ruth at least gets a husband who respects her talent. The final scene is identical to the play's, with the exception of a gratuitous sight gag. After Ruth's success, the sisters extend their lease on the apartment, once they are assured that the blasting has ended. Suddenly, the apartment shakes. The landlord explains that while the blasting has stopped, the drilling has started. Then, breaking through the floor are the Three Stooges—Moe, Larry, and

Curly—in hard hats. Since the *Three Stooges* was Columbia's most successful short, someone at the studio must have thought that including the trio in the coda would add a touch of the zany, not to mention self-promotion, to a film whose enlightened approach to the career and/or marriage dilemma might have been too liberal for traditionalists.

As a freelancer, Rosalind was able to fit in a film at RKO before starting her second Columbia comedy, *What a Woman! Take a Letter, Darling*, which did excellent business at the box office despite its primitive view of the male-female relationship, had turned Rosalind and Fred MacMurray into a marketable team; or so thought RKO, where someone—probably RKO board chairman Floyd Odlum, whose wife was the famous flier Jacqueline Cochran—believed they would be perfect for *Flight for Freedom* (1943). The film was a thinly disguised biopic about Ameila Earhart's last solo flight in 1937, combined with enough details about Cochran to suggest that Rosalind's character, Tonie Carter, was an amalgam of the two women. Rosalind was interested. She wanted a vacation from comedy, and once she realized there would be no schedule conflict, she signed on.

Rosalind's reunion with MacMurray was more of a stretch for her than for him. She was an aspiring "lady aviator," eager to win her wings while laboring in the shadow of an aircraft designer (Herbert Marshall) and an ace pilot (MacMurray), each of whom falls in love with her. The script was the reverse of *Darling*; it was a modified version of *A Star Is Born*, with Rosalind as the neophyte and MacMurray as the pro she surpasses. If *A Star Is Born* is the paradigm, "the new kid on the block scenario" should end with the self-willed death of the old icon to make way for his successor. In *Flight for Freedom*, it is the reverse; Tonie, the novice-turned-celebrity, performs what appears to be a sacrificial gesture, an act that, barring divine intervention, will result in her death. Was it suicide? The Legion of Decency, which relegated the film to the "Morally Objectionable in Part" category, apparently thought so.

Whether Tonie's sacrifice can be considered suicide or patriotism is problematic. With America's entry into World War II, screenwriters—including the *Flight for Freedom* team—concocted various scenarios implying that while America was taking refuge in isolationism, Japan was preparing for all-out war. Because of her international reputation, Tonie is recruited as a government spy—a role she accepts, perhaps because, as a woman who has triumphed in a man's profession, she is eager to move to the next level: espionage, traditionally another male fiefdom. As an admiral spells out the details to a peculiarly pliant Tonie, the two stand against a wall map that literally dwarfs them, suggesting that world affairs take precedence over individual concerns. Tonie is instructed to resume her solo flight, which was aborted in Hawaii because of a malfunction deliberately arranged by the government, by flying to New Guinea and then to an island in the mid Pacific where the Japanese were believed to be setting up military installations.

At this point, 1943 moviegoers would have sensed a parallel between Tonie Carter and Amelia Earhart, who disappeared in the central Pacific with her navigator, Frederick Noonan, renamed Randy Britton (MacMurray) in the film. As with most films whose characters are loosely based on historical figures, *Flight for Freedom* deviates from the Earhart biography as often as it runs parallel to it. The controversial flight that resulted in the disappearance of both Earhart and Noonan occurred in July 1937, when their plane, scheduled to land on Howland Island (Gull Island in the film) for refueling, never arrived, presumably because it ran out of gas and fell into the ocean. That explanation soon gave way to another more intriguing one, namely, that Earhart and Noonan were on a secret mission to look for signs of impending warfare (e.g., airfields and bunkers) in the Marshall Islands, over which the Japanese claimed sovereignty. Although there has never been proof of such military activity, that did not stop Hollywood from assuming it existed.

In *Flight for Freedom*, Tonie, now convinced that the Japanese are preparing for a war against the United States, agrees to land on Gull, which she and Noonan are expected to photograph in detail. Since the landing will interrupt her round-the-world flight, she will issue a distress call, claiming that her plane is running out of fuel. Because she is a famous American, the public will demand a rescue, which the navy will provide, after which Tonie will resume her solo flight—without Britton.

Because the film went into production five years after Earhart's disappearance and about a year after Pearl Harbor, a nose dive into the Pacific not only would constitute an act of patriotism (or suicide disguised as patriotism), but, for audiences equating Tonie with Earhart (and RKO assumed most would), would also dispel the popular myth that Earhart was taken prisoner by the Japanese after landing on Howland. To make the film truly topical, the disappearance date was advanced from 1937 to shortly before Pearl Harbor. Even more topical (and illogical) was the prologue claiming that the dive bomber, "America's answer to December 7," came about because of a female aviator's (Earhart's, presumably) achievements in flight, although the two are completely unrelated.

In the radio version of *Flight for Freedom*, presented on *Lux Radio Theatre* on 20 September 1943—with Rosalind again as Tonie, and George Brent and Chester Morris in the parts played originally by Herbert Marshall and Fred MacMurray, respectively—the host, Cecil B. DeMille, made the same point in less politically correct terms, proclaiming that the film "delivers a screaming message of death to the Japs."

Since Japan-bashing was a common feature of World War II movies, the writers implicated Japan in Tonie's disappearance. On the evening before Tonie is scheduled to resume her flight from Lae, New Guinea, the Japanese proprietor of her hotel—a "yellow peril" stereotype with rimless glasses that made his eyes bulge ominously—informs Tonie that he knows who she and Randy are. In their attempt to find a plausible way for Tonie to fly alone, the writers violated one of the cardinal principles of espionage: an enemy agent like the proprietor does not divulge what he knows. Rather than involve Randy, with whom she is in love, or inform Washington that her cover was blown (to do so would suggest cowardice), Tonie departs earlier than planned. Realizing her fate if she lands, Tonie stays airborne until she loses consciousness, and the plane, running out of fuel, plunges into the Pacific.

Tonie has chosen to perform an act resulting in her death, in a sense willing it. However, since the lack of oxygen has left Tonie unconscious, one can also argue that she was oblivious to what was happening before the plane went into a tailspin, although the only way she could have prevented it would have been by landing on one of the islands. Suicide? Patriotism? Or patriotic suicide? The working title was "Stand By to Die," a downer if there ever was one, but more accurate than *Flight for Freedom*. Anyone who saw enough World War II movies knew that operatives carried L-tablets or suicide pills that they were expected to take if captured, with expediency replacing traditional morality for the duration. Thus, only the morally inflexible would carp at Tonie's choice; most 1943 moviegoers would have found it noble. The Legion of Decency, however, did not. Like so many of Rosalind's 1940s films, *Flight for Freedom* was slapped with a B rating (Morally Objectionable in Part for All) because "the suicide of the leading character is presented as noble and justifiable." If anything, Tonie's act illustrates the principle of double effect, in which an action is performed that has two results. Landing on Gull would lead to Tonie's becoming a Japanese prisoner who, under interrogation or torture, could compromise American intelligence. The alternative is remaining airborne, even though it will cost her her life. Morally, it is a matter of priorities. She does not will her death; she simply puts her country before her life. One would have thought the Legion understood the difference.

When Rosalind wasn't saddled with a wig that made her hair look like a helmet with earmuffs (the result of saucer-like buns on either side of her face), she delivered a convincing performance. However, she must have sensed that the script was an excuse for another RKO flag-waver. In fact, many of the movies RKO released that year were war related; some revealed the presence of Nazi agents where one would least expect them (*Tarzan Triumphs, Tarzan's Desert Mystery, The Fallen Sparrow*), others documented enemy atrocities (*The North Star, Hitler's Children, Behind the Rising Sun*), and a few idealized home-front America (*Tender Comrade, Gangway for Tomorrow, So This Is Washington*). Compared to *Behind the Rising Sun,* in which the Japanese bayoneted Chinese babies, raped women, and tortured an American journalist by inserting bamboo shoots under her fingernails, *Flight for Freedom* was subtle.

After completing *Flight for Freedom,* Rosalind rushed back to Columbia for *What a Woman!* (1943), which reunited her, for the third time, with Brian Aherne. In *What a Woman!* Rosalind plays Carol Ainsley, the daughter of a famous senator and equally famous actress—the latter spending so much time touring that Carol learns early in life that success takes precedence over everything. Realizing she has to achieve celebrity in her own way, Carol becomes a formidable literary agent who snags the rights to a steamy best-seller and sells them to Hollywood. When difficulties arise in casting the male lead, Carol discovers that the author (Willard Parker) is an English professor who wrote the novel under a pseudonym. Once she sees what a hunk Parker is, she cajoles him into deserting higher education for the silver screen—even if it means planting doubts in the dean's mind that one of his faculty has written a decidedly unscholarly but widely popular novel. World War II audiences were not about to quibble over academic freedom, and those who knew something about it probably never saw the movie.

Carol is so determined to turn the author into a star that she makes him her protégé without realizing that he has misinterpreted their client-agent relationship and regards her as a potential mate. The situation is complicated when a journalist (Aherne), assigned to write a feature on Carol, becomes attracted to her himself and waits for her to fall into his arms out of sheer frustration with the professor's newly developed machismo. When the professor-turned-screen-star informs the press that he and Carol plan to marry, Carol can no longer tolerate his presumptuousness. She is, after all, his agent; she represents him, not vice versa.

In the final scene, the principals end up in the Washington mansion of Carol's father, as if it were the modern equivalent of a garden, the traditional stage setting for doffing masks, rectifying mistakes, and restoring order. The scene had personal significance for Rosalind. No longer able to endure being made to feel subservient to a man whom she had single-handedly transformed into a celebrity, Carol rushes into the hall, awakening everyone. In a quavering voice, and eyes coated with a film of tears, Carol bluntly informs her client that she will not marry him, stating that when it comes to marriage, "a woman decides that for herself." After Rosalind delivered the same speech in the *Lux Radio Theatre* version on 14 March 1949, the audience burst into applause.

After delivering her manifesto, Carol storms down the hall, but before she gets to her room, the journalist grabs her by the arm and pulls her into his, which suggests that the writer, the director, or both had seen Cary Grant drag Rosalind out the door and off to Albany at the end of *His Girl Friday*; and Fred MacMurray behave similarly in *Take a Letter, Darling*. Admittedly, their behavior was not gentlemanly, but then, neither purported to be a gentleman. But in *What a Woman!* the "me Tarzan, you Jane" bit is only a sight gag. "What a woman!" Aherne exclaims in admiration, when the two of them are alone. The concluding dialogue makes it clear that Carol is nobody's chattel. She has no intention of giving up being a "ten percenter," as agents are known in the business, nor does Aherne expect that of her. They agree that marriage is also based on the percentage principle, but it's fifty-fifty. The fade out has the two of them shaking hands, leaving viewers with the impression that Carol's ten percent from her clients will be separate from the fifty-fifty arrangement with her husband.

What a Woman! which proved that it was possible for a woman to have a career without swearing an oath of allegiance to her husband, was as feminist as Hollywood got in 1943. By 1945, empowerment was over, and Rosalind's next round of comedies subjected her characters to even greater manipulation by men, including fathers.

Columbia's *She Wouldn't Say Yes* (1945), *Tell It to the Judge* (1949), *A Woman of Distinction* (1950), and, later, RKO's *Never Wave at a WAC* (1952)—discussed in chapter 6—introduced a new character to the Rosalind scenario: the omniscient father/grandfather whose daughter/granddaughter is (1) too wedded to her career to consider marriage (*She Wouldn't Say Yes, A Woman of Distinction*), (2) contemplating remarriage when she should be concentrating on her career (*Tell It to the Judge*), or (3) planning to marry another when she should be remarrying her ex (*Never Wave at a WAC*). In the true style of patriarchal Hollywood, father/grandfather knows best, the exception being *Tell It to the Judge*, which, if taken seriously, would have caused women in the professions to abandon their jobs and become homemakers.

In *She Wouldn't Say Yes*, Rosalind as a psychiatrist is especially convincing in the opening scenes as she converses with veterans suffering from postwar trauma. Perhaps because she encountered such cases while doing volunteer work in hospitals, she speaks as compassionately with the trauma patients as Hildy Johnson did with Earl Williams. Rosalind's father (Charles Winniger), a physician whose office adjoins hers, frets about his daughter's indifference to romance, which seems to preclude any possibility of marriage. For a film that was produced and co-written by the only female executive producer in the business at the time, Columbia's Virginia Van Upp, the film is so antifeminist that it probably made male moviegoers howl with glee as Rosalind's ironclad persona was dismantled piecemeal, revealing a unfulfilled woman who would rather have a man in her bed than a patient on her couch. Although father and daughter both have medical degrees, Winninger is not beyond engineering a fake marriage between his daughter and a cartoonist (Lee Bowman) who has created an impish character, the "Nixie," that encourages people to yield to their impulses, provided they are harmless enough. Since Rosalind has dismissed the whistling Nixie as socially irresponsible and potentially dangerous, it is only a matter of time before she changes, which is exactly what 1945 audiences expected.

The possibility of a plausible denouement is slim. A psychiatrist should not be as easily duped as Rosalind is when she fails to see that a word like "marry" is ambivalent. And that is precisely the trap that Van Upp and her co-writers have devised for her. There is an enormous difference between two people marrying and one person (e.g., a member of the clergy or a judge) marrying two people—a difference that Rosalind does not grasp; or, rather, the script does not allow her to grasp.

Beginning with a "meet cute," in which Rosalind and Bowman collide at the office of a travel agent, who plays Cupid and assigns them the same upper berth on a Chicago-bound train, the film is awash in double entendre. Bowman, sensing that Rosalind's steely professionalism is merely protective coloration, wangles a seat for her in a crowded club car by passing her off as his pregnant wife, which leads to a series of gag lines, including a concerned passenger's ordering a glass of milk for her (Van Upp was clearly familiar with *This Thing Called Love*) and the conductor's puzzlement at her refusal to share the berth with Bowman. Naturally, Bowman sleeps elsewhere on the train, but that does not stop him from pursuing Rosalind when they arrive in Chicago.

Once Winninger meets Bowman, he knows the cartoonist is the right match for his daughter. The trick is to get them married. But first it is innuendo time, as Bowman recounts their train experiences and Rosalind's "motherhood," prompting an uncomprehending Winninger to inquire if his daughter became a mother before or after marriage. When Bowman replies that there was never a marriage, Winninger simply shrugs. Asked what he does for a living, Bowman replies, "I do a strip," which must have elicited guffaws in 1945. Now Winninger does a double take, raising his eyebrows but making no comment. Anything to see his daughter married.

If any members of the medical profession saw *She Wouldn't Say Yes*, they would have attributed the plot to Hollywood's ignorance of doctor-patient and father-daughter relationships—the latter being a special case since father and daughter are both MDs. To rid herself of Bowman, Rosalind tries to pawn him off on the voluptuous Allura (Adele Jergens). When that fails, Bowman and Winninger conspire to arrange a ceremony in which Bowman can marry Rosalind without her knowing it. They convince a judge that Rosalind is a bit daft. She thinks the same about the judge, who persistently talks about "marrying" her—meaning, of course, to Bowman. Believing the judge is obsessed with the idea of marrying people (especially when she hears that he "has to get up in the middle of the night to do it"), Rosalind takes him on as a patient. To humor him, she agrees to the "marriage," but here the plot pegs start sagging. When Bowman arrives at the judge's home, Rosalind thinks he is still pursuing her, not knowing that he is the bridegroom. An early version of the script had the ceremony taking place on screen, which infuriated Joe Breen, who insisted it be dropped. What was neither dropped nor questioned was the dubious therapy Rosalind devised for the judge. Hoping to cure him of his marriage mania, she agrees to play bride to Bowman's groom on the assumption that the ceremony is just play acting.

After Rosalind discovers the truth about her "marriage," she is not all that disappointed. However, there is one final complication. When Bowman learns about Allura, he stalks off, Rosalind's eyes tear up, and the audience is left wondering how long it will be before the denouement. Actually, there is not so much a denouement as a deus ex machina, in the form of wily Winninger, who, for reasons that are never explained, has himself, Rosalind, and Bowman booked on the same train to San Francisco. The three are in the same Pullman. Bowman assumes he will be occupying the upper berth; and Winninger, the lower. The upper, however, has an occupant: Rosalind, who pops her head out to remind Bowman that she loves him, but, to marry, "you have to know what's happening." Winninger announces that they can be married in Nevada; and Rosalind, although she has been, like Shakespeare's Malvolio, "notoriously abused," asks Bowman with a sincerity that only a true actress could bring off, "Will you marry me?" Since a romantic embrace is impossible in a Pullman, the scene fades out as Rosalind's hand reaches down to his.

The original ending was even more cockeyed. Rosalind has a nervous breakdown and has to be analyzed herself. The analyst administers a drug that induces a surrealistic dream in which the Nixie is whistling advice in her ear while Allura metamorphoses into a spider, and Bowman into an aspirin bottle. When Rosalind inquires about the nature of her neurosis, the analyst replies, "Some call it love," which was the film's working title.

Cured, Rosalind discovers that Bowman is leaving for the West Coast by train. When he climbs into his berth, he finds Rosalind there, insisting that they are married. The conductor, on the other hand, insists she get off the train. Bowman persuades him to let them stay on until they reach Nevada, where they can have a "real" wedding; and the film was to end with the train whistle mimicking the sound of the Nixie.

Neither ending was plausible, although the first was more imaginative. But plausibility was never an issue in *She Wouldn't Say Yes*. If it were, the American Psychiatric Association would have denounced it.

The issue, at least for the Legion of Decency, should have been the dialogue. No 1940s film, not even *This Thing Called Love*, abounded in so much double entendre, which even today can elicit a chuckle if one dissociates it from the pervasive sexism. Although Breen found the final script acceptable, the Legion threatened a C (Condemned) rating, not because of the dialogue, but because of the film's "irreverent view of marriage." The Legion insisted on at least one line of dialogue in which Rosalind states that consent is necessary for a valid marriage; hence, "You have to know what's happening." The matter was resolved by early fall 1945. The November issue of *Screen Romances* (later renamed *Screen Stories*), which synopsized the latest films in short-story form, included a fairly accurate version of *She Wouldn't Say Yes*. Since the magazine hit the newsstands in mid October and film went into release in late November, the change must have been made by the end of September 1945.

Personally, Rosalind was unconcerned. Her films had run afoul of the Legion before and would continue to raise sanctimonious hackles. Besides, as an actress she knew that deception has always been an integral part of comedy: disguised females attracting unsuspecting males, wives dressing up as their maids to trick their philandering mates, and men adopting outrageous disguises to test their fiancée's fidelity. *She Wouldn't Say Yes* pulled out all the stops: the chance meeting, the mix-up in the Pullman, the steady stream of double entendre, verbal misunderstandings, the lovers' quarrel, and finally reconciliation. Although "offend and mend" was the comic credo, the Legion's idea of mending was adding a line of dialogue. Yet one wonders how many moviegoers, including Catholics, paid any attention. Rosalind was the attraction; as a bonus there was the usual Jean Louis fashion show, racy dialogue, a swift-moving "will she or won't she" plot, and a happy ending.

The cycle of breezy comedies that Rosalind made at Columbia in the 1940s came to an end with two films similar in their philosophy that professional women are incomplete unless they marry. But given the way Rosalind played a prospective federal judge (*Tell It to the Judge*) and a college dean (*A Woman of Distinction*), it is hard to imagine either character sacrificing a career for domesticity. Those familiar with the Rosalind Russell persona would reshoot the ending in their imagination, so that the character would have a marriage *and* a career, like Rosalind herself.

Buddy Adler's production of *Tell It to the Judge*, for all its sophisticated trappings, was low farce jacked up a few notches to screwball without the accompanying wit. Rosalind seemed so disinterested in the film that she went on autopilot, relying on technique alone, since there was no character to develop. *Tell It to the Judge* was a B movie with an A cast; besides Rosalind, there were Robert Cummings, Gig Young, Marie McDonald, and the venerable character actor Harry Davenport as her grandfather. Rosalind is a federal judge nominee whose appointment is imperiled by her recent divorce from lawyer Robert Cummings, whose relationship with a sexy client (Marie McDonald) Rosalind has misinterpreted, as is generally the case in comedies of misunderstanding. The only way a movie like *Tell It to the Judge* could justify its ninety minutes was to keep the action moving at such a clip that audiences would never know they had experienced the filmic equivalent of cotton candy—sugary but lacking in nutrition. And when the plot pegs buckled, sight gags propped them up, such as Cummings hitting his head against whatever object was in the way. Although Cummings became a television celebrity, he always seemed uncomfortable in a secondary role—and that was what he had in *Tell It to the Judge*. Cummings's shtick was corny, not clever. When Harry Davenport discovers that Rosalind has remarried Cummings, thus further endangering her chances for the appointment, he has Cummings, who has been accidentally drugged in the call of duty (don't ask how), put on a train bound for Philadelphia. Cummings awakens in a berth with a suitcase filled with women's clothes. He throws a satin robe with a fluffy collar over his underwear and stalks through the train, eliciting laughter from the passengers and probably the audience.

Screenwriter Ned Avery spun a web of deception around the characters, but loosely enough so that Rosalind and Cummings could break through it and find each other, which was not easy. She and Cummings concealed their lack of chemistry by going over the top whenever they could. How many times could Rosalind make Cummings jealous by joining Gig Young in a dance that was more exhibitionistic than erotic? In *Tell It to the Judge*, sex was only a possibility—and not even an intriguing one.

Tell It to the Judge is a film of set pieces, the best of which is a quick getaway in a rowboat after a raid on waterfront casino. As Rosalind thrashes about in the water in a strapless gown with a train, Cummings tries to lift her onto the boat—pushing, pulling, and even resorting to what Joseph Breen suspected were "goosing actions." Rosalind had shed her dignity before, but never for so unworthy a cause.

Rosalind and Cummings manage to reach a lighthouse, where their former love is rekindled, until it is temporarily extinguished after Gig Young and McDonald reappear, causing Rosalind to assume Cummings and McDonald are still an item; and Cummings, the same about Rosalind and Young. *Tell It to the Judge* is all talk, with a few effective comedy sequences and a stunningly costumed Rosalind, who, even in the drab clothes the lighthouse keeper loans her, looks glamorous—courtesy of the necklace that she has no intention of removing, despite its inappropriateness.

Again, Rosalind subjected herself to male dominance as well as to the popular belief that women are only complete in marriage. When Rosalind chooses to return to Cummings, Davenport reminds her that her appointment went through and that her job is in Washington. Always faithful to the script, Rosalind replies, "Tell them I'm off to my job as a wife."

The line was totally inconsistent with the character, but not with Rosalind. A year after she died, Frederick Brisson wrote the following about his wife:

> Rosalind's ability to play a career woman who eventually succumbed to true love was consistent with her own life. She was a successful actress and an exemplary wife and mother.
>
> Her Catholicism saved her from the marriage vs. career dilemma that often results in divorce when it cannot be resolved. That she married a producer did not hurt.

But as a comic actress (and that was essentially how the industry and the public perceived her) Rosalind had become the sum of her plot points and characters, along with their mannerisms, vocal inflections, double takes, and melting glances at men with whom she had little in common but with whom she had to cohabit by the fadeout. *A Woman of Distinction*, also a Buddy Adler production, was a rehash of *Tell It to the Judge*, with Rosalind as a college dean who has admitted publicly that there is no room in her life for romance. The script turns her confession into an act of hubris for which, the audience knows, she will pay. And pay she does, when a British astronomy professor (Ray Milland) enters her life, bringing a locket that a dying French resistance fighter has given him. During World War II, Rosalind's character was a WAC (hint: her next comedy) stationed in France, where she met the resistance fighter and may well have become his lover. Confronted with the locket, Rosalind dismisses the matter, implying that she was motivated by pity. When Milland informs her of the resistance fighter's internment in a concentration camp and his death shortly after being liberated, she is completely unmoved.

Structurally, the locket bit is shaky. Originally, the locket may have figured in a subplot that never reached the screen and involved Rosalind, the resistance fighter, and a female child. In the film, Rosalind claims that the girl is a war orphan whom she adopted. Others, including Rosalind's father (Edmund Gwenn), wonder if the child is actually her daughter. It is a throwback to the "did they or didn't they" scenario that allowed audiences to take their pick, depending on how far their imaginations would lead them. Since there was no World War II flashback, even a hyperactive imagination would reach a dead end. The main point is not Rosalind's eventual thawing out, which is a given; but rather how often she can be humiliated for being so unfeeling.

Since a water gimmick worked in *Judge*, it is repeated in *Woman*. Unable to locate her house keys, Rosalind steps up on an outdoor faucet so she can crawl through a window. Unaware that a hose is attached to the faucet, she accidentally turns it on and gets sprayed. At a beauty parlor, she overhears a conversation in the next cubicle. Eager for details, she climbs up on a table to peer over the divide, catching the sheet she has draped around herself in an electric fan. Rosalind looked better in a Jean Louis gown than in a slip.

Unlike the grandfather in *Tell It to the Judge*, Gwenn, who hopes that his daughter will abandon higher education in favor of marriage and motherhood, encourages Milland to court her, using such homely aphorisms as "when an icicle melts, it becomes warm water"—which is as suggestive as the dialogue gets. But Rosalind is not ready to melt. To avoid encountering Milland at a prom, she persuades a student to drive her home, only to find herself in a jalopy with a drag racer. When a police officer stops them, the student has no license; and Rosalind, no explanation.

The board, however, demands one. Tired of being interrogated and having the legitimacy of her daughter questioned, Rosalind arches her back and delivers her exit line: "You don't have to ask for my resignation. You've got it." She then rushes to the railroad station just as Milland is about to board a train. Suddenly becoming docile, she reminds Milland that wherever he goes, she goes. The icicle has melted in record time, but so has the plot. Audiences, however, had now become so accustomed to Rosalind's sudden conversion from career woman to helpmeet that it probably never occurred to them that if Milland is headed back to the United Kingdom, so is she.

Rosalind's Columbia films of the 1940s were all comedies, with one exception: *The Guilt of Janet Ames* (1947), which in mid-production Rosalind realized was a mistake. In the 1940s, particularly after World War II, filmmakers began exploring the dark side of consciousness. Traumatized vets needed a woman for their recovery (*I'll Be Seeing You* [1944], *Daisy Kenyon* [1947]), so did amnesiacs who shut themselves off from a past they would rather forget (*Spellbound* [1945]). Even career women require therapy—e.g., Liza Elliott (Ginger Rogers) in *Lady in the Dark* (1944), who cannot remember the lyrics to a childhood song because she associates it with her loveless father.

The Guilt of Janet Ames offered a new take on the postwar neurotic, who was generally male. Janet Ames (Rosalind), the wife of a Congressional

Medal of Honor winner, is unable to walk as the result of a minor traffic accident that, she insists, has left her paralyzed. With the aid of a once successful journalist (Melvyn Douglas), now an alcoholic, Janet learns that her neurosis is the result of her inability to forgive the five men whose lives her husband saved when he fell on a grenade that otherwise would have killed all of them. The journalist acquaints her with Peter Ibbetson, the hero of George du Maurier's novel, who refused to let prison bars keep him from escaping into the world of his imagination, where time and space dissolve into a continuum so that he can visit any era he wishes. Through an artful combination of hypnosis and therapy, the journalist transports Janet to a parallel world, as he conjures up four of the men (he happens to be the fifth, as she infers) so that she can see them not as they were but as they might be—that is, as their best.

The fantasy sequences, with their silhouettes and expressionistic lighting, were obviously inspired by the dream sequence in Hitchcock's *Spellbound* (1945). When director Henry Levin was not waxing expressionistic, he ventured into surrealism, with desert landscapes and phantasmagoric restaurants that serve oyster cocktails consisting solely of pearls.

Rosalind and Douglas, who fared better in *This Thing Called Love*, did what they could with the material, which was not so much a mistake as a mélange of so many warring elements (realism, expressionism, surrealism, romantic melodrama, reductive psychology) as to render any resolution implausible. With the ads reading "Don't Condemn Janet Ames until You've Seen the Picture," the audience is prepared for a revelation, which occurs in the last ten minutes but is hardly what they have been led to expect. Janet confesses her guilt, which derives from (1) insisting her husband remain in his routine job because she craved security and (2) talking her husband out of starting a family and building a house until he returned from the war. Now it is equal time: the journalist reveals that he was Ames's commanding officer and ordered him to intercept the grenade, which Ames did, thereby saving everyone's life, including his CO's. But now that Janet has been restored to normalcy (or what passed for it in 1947), she sheds her guilt, reminding the journalist (and the audience) that her husband probably never heard the order and thus sacrificed his life willingly. How Janet knows this is never explained, but after eighty minutes of angst, some kind of closure is necessary so that the two principals can embrace at the fade out.

The muddled script was bad enough; worse was the waste of Sid Caesar's comic genius. In *Janet Ames*, Caesar's second—and last—Columbia film (the first was *Tars and Spars* the previous year), he appeared in one of the fantasy sequences, delivering a satiric monologue lamenting Hollywood's current obsession with Freudianism, which has taken the "fun" out of movies. If the monologue was intended as a parodistic gloss on *Janet Ames*, Caesar's frenetic delivery defeated the purpose. It was obvious that *Janet Ames* was anything but fun, but neither was Caesar's monologue. Sid Caesar was meant for better things, which was evident after *Your Show of Shows* premiered on NBC Television in February 1950, validating his credentials as one of America's finest comedians.

Within the context of Rosalind's career, *Janet Ames* may seem atypical, but not within the context of 1944, when Rosalind was determined to alter her image and prove she could do more than look glamorous and sound witty. Although *Craig's Wife* and *Night Must Fall* established Rosalind's credentials as a dramatic actress, every film she had made since 1939, except for *They Met in Bombay* and *Flight for Freedom*, was a comedy. She wanted a respite from boss lady movies and got one in Warner's *Roughly Speaking* (1945) and RKO's *Sister Kenny* (1946) and *Mourning Becomes Electra* (1947).

CHAPTER 5

Losing to Loretta

Since 1934, Rosalind had been averaging around two films a year; in 1941, she made four. Even after her marriage to Frederick Brisson in 1941, she showed no sign of slowing down: two each in 1942 and 1943, but nothing in 1944. In his preface to *Banquet,* Frederick wrote that Rosalind suffered a nervous breakdown in 1943. More likely, it was 1944. Even after she became a mother in May 1943, Rosalind was still active. That September, she was in front of the microphone, reprising her Tonie Carter in Lux Radio Theatre's version of *Flight for Freedom.* A month later, she was off touring army camps. The breakdown must have occurred in fall 1944. It had to be brief. Columbia wanted her for *She Wouldn't Say Yes;* Warners, for *Roughly Speaking* (1945), which was delayed until Rosalind recovered. The dizzying round of films, motherhood at thirty-six, army camp tours, and an Oscar nomination that made her determined to win the coveted statuette: these had all taken their toll. In the preface, Frederick also refers to the deaths of Rosalind's older brother and sister, John and Clara, in the same context as her breakdown. Since Frederick wrote that they died in the early years of his marriage to Rosalind, readers might assume that there was some connection between her breakdown and the loss of her brother and sister. Actually, John, born in 1905 and thus two years older than Rosalind, died on 21 October 1961 of a coronary occlusion resulting from arteriosclerosis; and Clara, "the duchess," died on 4 October 1963 of a cerebral hemorrhage.

Perhaps Frederick's despondency over Rosalind's death caused the juxtaposition of the two incidents. Still, there was enough tension in Rosalind's life to precipitate a collapse in 1944.

The breakdown caused Rosalind to modify her schedule for the rest of the decade, but only slightly: two films in 1945, one in 1946, two in 1947, and one each in 1948, 1949, and 1950. Slowing down was her only concession to mental health. Once Rosalind recovered, she reported for work on *Roughly Speaking,* which required her to age over a period of twenty years. When Warner Bros. purchased the rights to Louise Randall Pierson's autobiography, *Roughly Speaking,* there was no one at the studio who could have played the author, except perhaps Bette Davis. Davis could age convincingly—and did, in *Mr. Skeffington* (1944), for example. But she would have brought more brittleness than resilience to the role of Louise, the daughter of an improvident father whose sudden death leaves his family in financial distress. Although the film begins in 1902 (with Ann E. Todd playing Louise as a child) and covers a forty-year period, Rosalind does not appear until Louise is in her late teens, about to enter a women's college, which is little more than a secretarial school. Raised to be grateful for a comfortable existence as well as to aid those less fortunate than herself, Rosalind had no trouble playing a woman forced to make a living as a typist without suggesting that clerical work was beneath her. Rosalind's Louise is a working-class grand dame, determined to "swim upstream" regardless of the current, as if she is equipped with a life jacket that reads "Survivor." That Louise is; she survives a marriage to a Yalie (Donald Woods), who dumps her for another woman, and turns her second husband, a shiftless charmer (Jack Carson), into a go-getter as they move from one enterprise to another, hitting the big time with a parking concession at the 1939 World's Fair.

Although Louise Randall Pierson seemed to represent a departure from the career women that Rosalind had been playing, the character differed only in degree from her other roles: Louise did not have a career so much as a series of jobs. Yet whether she was taking dictation or growing roses, Louise approached her work as a professional. Rosalind was that kind of woman herself, able to take charge of her household because she first took charge of her life. That she demanded and received expensive perfume from Harry Cohn suggests a fearlessness that only someone with supreme self-confidence could bring off. Nor did she appreciate a male actor's attempts at familiarity, which she repeatedly discouraged. Although she never mentions the lothario's name in *Banquet,* she strode into his dressing room and excoriated him for his ungentlemanly behavior. Rosalind never played a lady in distress for one reason: she would not have been convincing.

When Rosalind arrived in Los Angeles in spring 1934, she immediately began doing volunteer work in hospitals—the result of her father's mandate to serve humanity. She preferred the pediatric ward, perhaps because, as an adventuresome and sports-minded child, she fractured so many bones that she was more familiar with orthopedists than internists. Inevitably, she became aware of Elizabeth Kenny, the Australian nurse, better known as Sister Kenny, who developed an unorthodox treatment for polio victims that incurred the wrath of physicians.

Elizabeth Kenny could have been a hospital nurse, yet chose to be a bush nurse, traveling long distances on horseback (or in a buggy) to serve those without access to medical help. The more Rosalind learned about Elizabeth Kenny, the more determined she was to play her on the screen. However, her other film commitments delayed the project, which was still in the planning stages, consisting merely of a desire—but lacking a script, co-stars, and, most important, studio backing.

Rosalind's breakdown caused another delay; yet even during that period of enforced rest, she continued to devise a strategy to get the film made. Once she recovered and started work on *Roughly Speaking,* in which Louise's daughter develops polio, she knew that film was the dress rehearsal for *Sister Kenny* (1946), in which she would have to age over a longer period, with an accompanying weight gain that, for an actress with Rosalind's willowy frame, meant realistic padding.

Like Louise Randall Pierson, Elizabeth Kenny (1880–1952) was a historical figure. In the mid 1940s, the average American was acutely aware of infantile paralysis—or polio, as it was usually called—for which there was still no cure. Some may have also known about Elizabeth Kenny, who was awarded the title of "Sister" for serving on hospital ships during World War I; they may also have read that she treated polio patients by wrapping their limbs in heated strips of cloth and massaging (or, as she would have said, "reeducating") their muscles. To her credit, Sister Kenny never claimed she had effected a cure, which, she insisted, was only possible with a vaccine. Unfortunately, she died two years before the Salk vaccine became available in 1954. She always considered her treatment, which she carefully distinguished from a cure, as an alternative to the immobilizing braces and splints that produced no improvement. The medical establishment, at the time a formidable patriarchy, felt otherwise and seized every opportunity it could to denounce her then-controversial therapy.

Rosalind first met Sister Kenny in 1940, when she came to the United States, hoping that American doctors would be more impressed by her success rate and less concerned about her lack of a medical degree. Upon her arrival in Los Angeles, Sister Kenny became Rosalind's houseguest. Rosalind knew then that Sister Kenny's life had to be portrayed on the screen with herself as star. The studios, however, were cool to the idea. Finally, Rosalind's RKO connection paid off. In 1945 RKO agreed to make the film, as part of a four-picture deal—the studio's way of indulging Rosalind in order to get more pictures from her, as RKO did with *Mourning Becomes Electra* (1947), *The Velvet Touch* (1948), and *Never Wave at a WAC* (1952).

Although Rosalind knew that *Sister Kenny*'s appeal would be limited, she identified so strongly with the character, particularly her unwavering belief in her treatment, that she was determined to be as authentic an Elizabeth Kenny as possible. By observing Sister Kenny in operation, Rosalind learned to massage children's limbs so realistically that she could have passed for a physical therapist. A gray streak in the hair may have been sufficient for the middle-aged Louise Randall Pierson, but for Elizabeth Kenny, whose life spanned two world wars, Rosalind needed a silver wig and considerable padding for a woman in her sixties, as Sister Kenny was in 1945, the year in which the film ends. When Sister Kenny must confront her nemesis, an arrogant doctor who has done everything in his power to discredit her, Rosalind, figureless but defiant, holds her ground like a champion orator, determined to worst her opponent—but to no avail. Sister Kenny's American visit did not produce the results for which she had hoped, nor could the film claim otherwise. Although she was welcomed at Rochester's Mayo Clinic and the University of Minnesota, the National Foundation of Infantile Paralysis refused to endorse the Kenny method. Just when it seems that *Sister Kenny* will end on a note of defeat, the children, whose muscles have been "reeducated" and whose mobility has been restored, greet her with a rendition of "Happy Birthday," so that the camera can dolly out on a misty-eyed but radiant Rosalind.

Sister Kenny, more than any other film thus far in her career, made the greatest demands on her as an actress; the thirty-five-year time span required alterations of voice, posture, gait, and expression. At the end she moved the way a sixty-five-year-old woman with a heart condition would. The public might not have warmed to *Sister Kenny*, but the Academy of Motion Picture Arts and Sciences at least acknowledged Rosalind's dramatically rich performance with a best actress nomination, her second. Because *Sister Kenny* was such a tour de force for an actress known primarily for romantic comedy, there was always the possibility that the Academy would be impressed with her transformation. However, the transformation that impressed them was Olivia de Havilland's in *To Each His Own* (1946), in which the actress aged twenty years—not much of a stretch compared to Rosalind's thirty-five. Rosalind may have missed out on an Oscar, but she won a Golden Globe, a Blue Ribbon award from *Box Office* magazine, a New York Foreign Language Press award, the New York University Motion Picture Club's Citation of Merit, and the *Parents* magazine medal, which were at least a mark of recognition. But, as Rosalind reasoned, there was always next year, which also brought another nomination—but no statuette.

Sister Kenny provided Rosalind with a welcome vacation from comedy, which she had every intention of prolonging, until audiences were convinced that she could do more serious and, from her standpoint, more challenging roles. Rosalind's next film demanded even more from her public than did *Sister Kenny*: a three-hour version of Eugene O'Neill's Pulitzer prize–winning *Mourning Becomes Electra* (1931), with Rosalind as the sexually repressed, father-fixated, mother-loathing Lavinia Mannon.

Bringing *Mourning* to the screen virtually intact was the dream of Dudley Nichols, who had written the *Sister Kenny* screenplay, assisted by Rosalind's co-star, Alexander Knox, and Mary McCarthy, who, like Rosalind, also knew Elizabeth Kenny. *Electra* was another matter. In addition to being a theatrical monolith, *Electra* was a trilogy, modeled after the only extant one in Greek tragedy, Aeschylus's *Oresteia*.

The *Oresteia* traced the curse on the house of Atreus through a concatenation of actions involving adultery, infanticide, homicide, human sacrifice, matricide, and madness—enough material for a mini series, much less a trilogy. Aeschylus wrote for an audience familiar with its myths, thus enabling him to allude to events that occurred prior to the main action without having to explain them. The Greeks would have known, for example, that the house of Atreus was under an ancestral curse, resulting from Thyestes's seduction of the wife of his brother Atreus, who retaliated by murdering two of Thyestes's three sons and using their bodily parts for a stew that he served their unwitting father. Once Thyestes discovers what he has eaten, he curses Atreus and his descendants, Agamemnon and Menelaus. First, Agamemnon must come to the aid of his brother, Menelaus, whose wife, Helen, has been abducted (or seduced) by the Trojan prince Paris, thus precipitating the Trojan War. Next, Agamemnon, on his return from the war, is hacked to death in his bath by his wife, Clytemnestra, who has never forgiven him for sacrificing their daughter, Iphigenia, to obtain a fair wind to sail to Troy. Clytemnestra has also taken a lover, Aegisthus, whom she prefers to her husband. As fate would have it, Aegisthus is Thyestes's sole surviving son, making him an instrument in the execution of his father's curse. In keeping with the principle of retributive justice, Orestes and Electra, the children of Agamemnon and Clytemnestra, avenge their father's murder. Orestes, goaded on by Electra, has no other choice but to kill Clytemnestra, whose death still does not lift the curse. Since Orestes has committed matricide, he is hounded by the Furies, who are finally placated—not dramatically, but philosophically—as retribution yields to justice tempered by mercy.

O'Neill Americanized Aeschylus, substituting the Civil War for the Trojan War, switching the setting to New England, jettisoning the philosophical denouement, replacing matricide with suicide, and giving the characters names that are faintly evocative of their classical counterparts. Atreus and Thyestes become Abe and David Mannon; Agamemnon, Ezra Mannon; Clytemnestra, Christine Mannon; Electra and Orestes, Lavinia and Orin Mannon; Aegisthus, Adam Brant. No twentieth-century dramatist could have retained the infanticidal stew. Long before *Mourning Becomes Electra* opens, Abe Mannon, Ezra's father, and his brother, David, vied for the affections of Marie Brantôme, whom David seduced and then married after she became pregnant. Abe then disowned his brother, who took to drink and eventually hanged himself. When Marie begged Abe for financial assistance, assuming that he might have some feelings for his brother's son, whom she named Adam, Abe ignored her pleas, leaving her to die in poverty. Thus, filled with hatred for the Mannons, Adam changes his surname to Brant, a shortened form of his mother's. Like Aegisthus, Adam Brant becomes Christine's lover and accomplice, even supplying her with the poison that she administers to Ezra. Since Adam is Ezra's first cousin, as Aegisthus was Agamemnon's, the avengers in Aeschylus's and O'Neill's plays are an adulterous wife and a blood relative of her husband.

In both the *Oresteia* and *Electra,* the characters make choices and perform actions that forge their destiny, so that what seems to be fate is really free will: Christine takes Adam Brant as her lover and poisons her husband; Lavinia goads Orin into killing Adam Brant in retaliation for their father's murder; Christine chooses suicide to a life without Adam; Orin shoots himself like Christine when he realizes his sister is no substitute for the mother he worshiped; and Lavinia resolves to atone for the sins of the Mannons by spending the rest of her days with the family ghosts. Fate may have provided the background, but human beings occupy the foreground—acting freely, despite their allegations to the contrary, and living or dying by their choices. If anyone doubts that fate is character, the *Oresteia* and *Mourning* are proof that it is.

One of the most daring decisions any studio ever made was green lighting *Mourning Becomes Electra*. For one thing, O'Neill had not fared well on the screen; *The Emperor Jones* may have been a great stage vehicle for Charles S. Gilpin, but O'Neill's feverish language, which sounded as if had been written by someone with a body temperature of 104, translated poorly to celluloid, despite a towering performance by Paul Robeson in the 1933 film. *The Long Voyage Home* (1940) was atypical John Ford, although he caught the play's moody expressionism. *Strange Interlude*—an eleven-act drama with interior monologues and a cast of characters that included females in search of father surrogates, males in need of mothering, sons at odds with their birth fathers, and Apollonians clashing with Dionysians—required theatergoers to commit to an entire evening, spending five hours with a group of fascinatingly complex people whose lives span a twenty-five-year period. In 1932 MGM reduced *Strange Interlude* to a 110-minute movie, with the interior monologues delivered as voiceover, causing more laughter than shock in some quarters. O'Neill's diluted Freudianism lent itself to parody. Even before the film version of *Strange Interlude* was released, *Animal Crackers* (1930), the Marx Brothers' second film, parodied O'Neill's interior monologues in a scene in which Groucho starts speaking in asides, claiming that he is having a "strange interlude."

Unlike *Strange Interlude*, which resembled a chamber piece orchestrated by a disciple of Mahler, *Electra* plays like an opera libretto without music; in its place is language so emotionally raw that one can almost hear the turbulent orchestration. It was not surprising that composer Marvin David Levy turned *Electra* into a 1967 opera with a libretto that was uncommonly faithful to O'Neill; the trilogy was a disguised libretto from the outset.

Although Dudley Nichols functioned as both *Electra's* adapter and director, he claimed no screenplay credit, believing he was simply a stand-in for the playwright. Nichols excelled at turning complex literary and dramatic material into filmable scripts. He had adapted Maxwell Anderson's *Mary of Scotland* (1936) and O'Neill's *The Long Voyage Home* for John Ford. In his adaptation of Hemingway's novel of the Spanish Civil War, *For Whom the Bell Tolls* (1943), he neutralized the left-wing politics by making the Spanish Loyalists the equivalent of freedom fighters, who wanted a Spanish republic (albeit a Socialist one).

For Nichols, *Electra* was a labor of love. Since he really could not accept screenplay credit, he knew that *Electra* would never bring him the Oscar that kept eluding him, despite such exemplary scripts as *The Informer, Stagecoach,* and *For Whom the Bell Tolls* (for which he was not even nominated). Rosalind thought differently; *Electra* was prestigious enough to get her the statuette. Nichols and Rosalind convinced RKO production head Peter Rathvon, who was soon replaced by Dore Schary, that the studio would bask in the reflected glory of the screen version of a work by America's greatest playwright, who also happened to be a Nobel prize winner.

Mourning Becomes Electra—a co-production of RKO and the Theatre Guild, then the nation's premier producing organization, which presented the play in 1931—was the kind of property in which a studio is willing to invest because it knows it will reap critical accolades, but not great dividends. Yet neither RKO nor the Theatre Guild was prepared for the mixed reviews and the poor box office.

The Theatre Guild's name would have been known even to non-theatergoers because of the popular radio program, *The Theatre Guild on the Air*, which originated in 1943 as a showcase for radio adaptations of Broadway plays such as *Dead End, The Silver Cord,* and even *Strange Interlude*, which must have sounded like a soap opera with class.

Electra was too important a film to open in a movie theater; only a playhouse would do. And so, on Wednesday, 19 November 1947, at 8:30 PM, the world premiere of *Mourning Becomes Electra* took place at the Golden Theatre on West Forty-fifth Street. That evening, every theater on the block was occupied. On the same side of the street were the Royale, where Beatrice Straight was portraying Emily Dickinson in *Eastward in Eden*; the Plymouth, the home of the popular musical revue *Call Me Mister*; and the intimate Booth, where Thomas Mitchell was starring in J. B. Priestley's *An Inspector Calls*. Across the street at the Imperial, Ethel Merman was still belting out Irving Berlin's magnificent songs in *Annie Get Your Gun*; the hit comedy *John Loves Mary* was going strong at the Music Box and would reach the screen two years later; next door at the now defunct Morosco, John Van Druten's *The Druid Circle* was attracting the fans of Jane Cowl. To confer even greater respectability on a street that could boast of more playhouses than any other in New York, across Eighth Avenue at the Martin Beck, Maurice Evans was delighting Shaw lovers in a production of *Man and Superman*. George Bernard Shaw, Emily Dickinson, J. B. Priestley, Irving Berlin, John Van Druten, and now Eugene O'Neill, all had a presence here. *Mourning* opened in the right location—and at the right theater.

Throughout the war years, the Golden played host to one play, *Angel Street*, which enjoyed a run of 1,293 performances. With its ribbed ceiling, intricately paneled and embellished with random cameos, the Golden was the perfect venue for *Electra*, which was intended as a road-show engagement with two performances daily and three on Sunday. Ticket prices were more in line with Broadway shows than first-run movie theaters such as the Capital, Paramount, and Roxy: evenings, $2.40 (orchestra and mezzanine) and $1.80 (balcony); matinees, $1.80 (orchestra and mezzanine) and $1.20 (balcony). On the other hand, anyone wishing to see such Broadway luminaries as Ethel Merman in *Annie Get Your Gun*, Helen Hayes in *Happy Birthday*, or Bert Lahr in *Burlesque*—or long-running shows like *Oklahoma!* or *The Voice of the Turtle*—could get a mezzanine or balcony seat for around the same price. As for moviegoers who enjoyed live entertainment, as distinguished from live theater, there was *Forever Amber* at the Roxy, with a stage show headlined by Sid Caesar; and Lucille Ball in *Her Husband's Affairs* at the Capital, with Frank Sinatra in person. For a mere fifty-five cents, the Paramount on Times Square offered an early show featuring *Wild Harvest*, with Alan Ladd and Robert Preston battling over Dorothy Lamour, plus the King Cole Trio and Connie Haines.

There were no early shows for *Mourning*, which was advertised as more of a theater piece than a movie. The opening night audience was treated to a re-creation of O'Neill's trilogy, with each play identified by title, as O'Neill had intended—"Homecoming," "The Hunted," and "The Haunted"—and each beginning in front of the Mannon home with its Greek columns evoking a world both alien and familiar, at least to those who believed, as O'Neill did, that the past is never past.

On the stage, the curtain rose with Seth, the gardener, singing "Shenandoah." Nichols transferred the chantey to the main title, with the credits superimposed over an agitated sea, suggesting the emotional turmoil of the characters, eager to sail away to the blessed isles, where they hope to find the peace and freedom denied them in repressive New England. As if in counterpoint to the raging waters, a full-voiced chorus supplies the subtext with "Shenandoah": "Oh, Shenandoah, I long to hear you / A-way, my rolling river / Oh, Shenandoah, I can't get near you / Way-ay, I'm bound away / Across the wide Missouri." As the film proper begins, Seth sings a verse from the chantey, as he did in the play. Seth, too, yearns for some kind of Eden, which he associates with the Shenandoah Valley, far away from the ill-starred household that he serves. The Mannons, on the other hand, have their own Eden; it is somewhere in the South Seas, where they can be free of a past that continues to dog them.

Adam Brant, who lived for a time in some prelapsarian paradise, excites Lavinia with his description of a sinless world. When courting Christine, Adam conjures up the same image, filling her with the same longing as he did Lavinia. Ezra envisions an island where he can wash away memories of war and live peacefully with Christine. Every time the islands are mentioned, the characters respond knowingly, as if they have always been aware of their existence. Ezra and Christine never reach the islands; Lavinia and Orin do. Lavinia becomes so liberated that her behavior shocks Orin, who follows his mother in death—and in the same way. To Orin, the South

Sea Islands, where he planned to bring his mother, have become the islands of the blest, where he will be reunited with her.

To be able to bring such complex material to the screen without belaboring the symbols or the psychology is a tribute to Nichols. No one can deny that O'Neill can be pretentious in parading his classical erudition or that by contemporary standards his dialogue is the stuff of soaps and miniseries, best served by a British cast that could deliver the lines as if they were doing Ibsen, knocking out the kinks and making the language sound, if not natural, at least theatrical.

Although Nichols transferred the bulk of the trilogy to the screen, he knew he had to open it up to dramatize incidents that had to be narrated to eliminate the need for additional sets. As it was, *Mourning* required five sets, which, to the cost-conscious Theatre Guild, was enough of a concession to O'Neill's epic style, especially at the time of the Great Depression. Thus, instead of retaining O'Neill's expository prologue, in which Seth and the townspeople provide the necessary background about the Mannons, Nichols has Seth give curiosity seekers a tour of the mansion, identifying the Mannons by their portraits (and, in some cases, photos), thereby showing how similar in appearance they are—a fact that has to be considered when casting the parts.

When Nichols chose the Greek actress Katina Paxinou for Christine, he was not capitalizing on her international reputation or her Oscar-winning performance as Pilar in *For Whom the Bell Tolls*. In the play, Christine is described as "furrin lookin." Paxinou was the incarnation of Jung's Terrible Mother, who still retained a primordial appearance. Yet there was a physical resemblance between herself and Rosalind. With her dark beauty, coiled body, and banked-down emotions, Rosalind was the mirror image of Paxinou. But Lavinia also has her father's steeliness, which would sometimes splinter under the strain of regret, anger, and especially passion. Ezra cannot conceal his ambivalence about Christine, whom he desires and suspects—not of infidelity but of contempt for him. With as much subtlety as O'Neill's prose allows, Rosalind conveyed Lavinia's attraction to her father and her envy of her mother, who was willing to flaunt convention by taking a lover she knew was a Mannon. When Rosalind appeared alongside Paxinou and Raymond Massey (Ezra Mannon), it was obvious that this was not a family from Central Casting. If Michael Redgrave (Orin) had a fairer appearance, it seemed as if the love Christine lavished on him set him apart from the dark Mannons. Although Lavinia was the firstborn, she never received such attention from Christine, who associated her daughter with her traumatic wedding night. Apparently sex with Ezra had only become bearable after Orin was born, although even that was not enough to keep her faithful.

The chief criticism of the film was its stage-bound quality, which was intentional. Nichols's aim was to re-create the original, which *New York Times* drama critic Brooks Atkinson hailed as a masterpiece in 1931. The Theatre Guild concurred; a masterpiece is never altered, despite its transition from one medium to another. Whenever he could, Nichols dramatized what was only recounted on stage, such as Lavinia's trip to New York to spy on her mother, who had gone there for a tryst with Adam Brant. Nichols had Lavinia trail Christine in a carriage. In addition to providing a change of setting, the scene also had another function: it highlighted the similarity between mother and daughter. Each is not so much dressed in black as swathed in layers of it, as if their period attire with the requisite hoopskirts had become emotional holding cells. Each carries herself with the imperiousness of a matriarch. In later scenes, especially where they appear in profile or in shot–reverse shot compositions, Lavinia and Christine become doubles. To indicate that Lavinia is in love with Adam Brant herself, Nichols dissolved from a shot of Christine kissing Brant to a flashback of Lavinia kissing him also—but earlier. The dissolve has another function; it, too, is a visual one: Adam is a Mannon, and the sight of the dark-haired Leo Genn anticipates the later revelation, in addition to reinforcing the physical similarity between the Mannons.

Lavinia was an enormous challenge for Rosalind. There was nothing in the part that allowed her to draw on her repertory of sardonic expressions, sotto voce wisecracks, and stopwatch timing. Only the throb in the voice was familiar. Otherwise, she gave a scaled-down stage performance to convince audiences they were watching a play, but in the form of a movie—no easy feat. She had to suggest a woman so obsessively attached to her father, and so antagonistic toward her mother, that moviegoers without any knowledge of the Electra complex would at least understand, if not accept, her prodding Orin into killing their mother's lover.

There is also a sensuous side to Lavinia, first seen on the night of her father's return from the war; unable to sleep and knowing that her father and mother are alone in their bedroom, she walks out of the mansion into the moonlight—her hair shoulder length, and dressed in a columnar robe that seems to flow down her body in Grecian lines. She calls up to her father, seemingly to bid him good night, but hoping to interrupt their love-making. The scene is so subtle in its eroticism that one wonders if Lavinia unconsciously wants to change places with Christine.

Lavinia must deliver two lines that would challenge any actress. The first is the requiescat that she speaks over the body of Adam Brant after Orin has shot him in retaliation for their father's murder: "May God find forgiveness for your sins. May the soul of our cousin, Adam Mannon, rest in peace." A lesser actress would have spoken the lines portentously—like Puccini's Tosca, as she placed lighted candles on either side of Scarpia's body and intoned, "*Avanti lui tremava tutta Roma*" (Before him all Rome trembled). Perhaps it was a childhood of attending requiem masses that enabled Rosalind to speak the lines with such detached eloquence. Regardless, it was a theatrical moment, without "Theater" writ large.

The second line occurs at the end of the film. Fresh from a vacation in the South Seas that seemed to free her of her inhibitions (much to Orin's disgust), Lavinia is ready to marry the callow Peter Niles (Kirk Douglas in his second screen role). Clinging to him, she begs him to take her away from a home that has become a tomb; above all, Lavinia begs Peter to "want" her. Then she cries, "Take me, Adam!" Realizing what she has said (and the line is the most famous Freudian slip in all drama), Lavinia knows she is still obsessed with the memory of the man whose murder she engineered. Rosalind's "Take me, Adam!" is somewhere between a whisper and a command, delivered with genteel hunger and ladylike yearning, as if Lavinia was experiencing passion without lust because she had not yet achieved the final stage of liberation—the dissociation of shame from desire—that she hoped would occur on the islands but never did because she went there with Orin, not Adam.

Electra had a lukewarm reception from critics and public alike, although there was little carping about Rosalind's performance. The Academy of Motion Picture Arts and Sciences voted Oscar nominations for herself and Michael Redgrave, the latter in the best actor category, even though Orin is hardly a leading role.

By March 1948 the Hollywood wags had all but awarded Rosalind the Oscar for best actress. RKO also thought she was a shoe-in and planned a post-awards party. Rosalind's competition was not exactly formidable: Joan Crawford (*Possessed*), Susan Hayward (*Smash Up—The Story of a Woman*), Dorothy McGuire (*Gentleman's Agreement*), and Loretta Young (*The Farmer's Daughter*). Apart from Hayward, who played a frighteningly convincing alcoholic, there should have been no challengers. Crawford had never deprogrammed herself out of the high melodramatic mode after winning for *Mildred Pierce* (1945); Dorothy McGuire may have been the female lead in *Gentleman's Agreement*, but she was eclipsed by three other actresses in smaller but more significant roles: Celeste Holm, who won for best supporting actress, Anne Revere, and June Havoc; Loretta would have deserved the award if Oscars were given for mastering a Swedish accent.

On Oscar night, 28 March 1948, Frederic March was about to announce the name of the best actress of 1947. Rosalind, who was seated in the rear of the Shrine Auditorium, started to rise from her seat as March opened the envelope. It looked as if he were about to say "Rosalind Russell," but the card did not lie. It read, "Loretta Young for *The Farmer's Daughter*." As he was about to read the name, Rosalind had adjusted her gown and was about to start walking down the aisle when she heard "Loretta Young." Being the actress (and good sport) that she was, she stood in the middle of the aisle, leading the applause for her close friend (and fellow Catholic)—a gracious gesture from a decidedly disappointed woman. The party went on as scheduled; Rosalind and Frederick made their entrance to applause that would have been heartier if the predictions had come true. Since it was obviously not an evening that Rosalind cared to remember, she did not describe it in *Banquet*.

In retrospect, one can understand why Rosalind lost to Loretta for *The Farmer's Daughter*, also an RKO release but considerably more popular than *Electra*. If Academy members preferred Loretta's performance to Rosalind's, it may have been because they ranked popularity higher than prestige, or that more of them saw *The Farmer's Daughter*, which was intellectually less demanding, ran only 97 minutes compared to *Electra*'s 173, and, above all, made money. *Electra*, on the other hand, wound up losing more than $2 million; when it went on the RKO circuit, it was renamed *"This Strange Love"* to pull in the unsuspecting, with *"Mourning Becomes Electra"* in small print beneath the title. The stars were not Rosalind and Redgrave, but Rosalind and Kirk Douglas, who by 1948 was an icon in the making; and Redgrave, a transient Brit. Rosalind was still a "name" and would continue to be. Rosalind's performance in *Electra* did not go unacknowledged. She won another Golden Globe and a Laurel Award from the Motion Picture Exhibitors and Showmen's Trade Review; *Life* magazine voted her performer of the year, as did the students at UCLA. Close, but no Oscar. Rosalind's vindication came six years later when Eugene O'Neill, in deteriorating health, either dictated a letter to her or, more likely, wrote one that, because of his condition, had to be typed. It arrived a month after his death:

> My dear "Lavinia"
>
> Handwriting is hard for me now, but I want to express my deep gratitude for your splendid "Lavinia" and my thanks for your kindness in sending me that photograph and especially the inscription.
>
> The last time I saw the film, I was more moved by your performance than ever before. It grows each time you see it—and you *grow* with it.

Again, my deep gratitude for your splendid "Lavinia."

E. O'Neill.

Eugene O'Neill died on Friday afternoon, 27 November 1953. The typed letter was dated 31 December 1953. Recalling Rosalind's Lavinia may have been one of O'Neill's few happy memories at the end of his troubled life. Loretta Young won the Oscar, but Rosalind could claim recognition, however belated, from a Nobel laureate.

Becoming Rosalind Russell Brisson

When Frederick Brisson began the arduous process of applying for American citizenship, he filed a Declaration of Intent on 16 November 1934, giving his name at birth as Carl Frederick Ejner Pedersen, his place of birth as Copenhagen, Denmark, and his date of birth as 17 March 1913. At the time, he was 5 feet 11 inches and weighed 165 pounds. His weight rarely fluctuated. "Ejner," which was sometimes "Einer," eventually became the more familiar "Einar" (warrior chief). Frederick reserved his full name for official documents, but most of the time he was Frederick Brisson—the surname being the one his father adopted after switching from boxer to entertainer.

Occasionally, Frank Sinatra, one of Frederick's and Rosalind's closest friends, would address a letter to "Carl Frederick," but most of the time it was "Freddie." Sinatra was not being playful; Frederick could inspire either form of address: When Sinatra wrote, "Dear Carl Frederick," it was in a letter written on 23 December 1976, a month after Rosalind's death.

Frederick was named after his father, Carl Ejner Frederick Pedersen. When Carl turned to boxing, he shortened his name to Carl Pedersen. Once Carl made the transition from boxing to cabaret and musical theater,

"Pedersen" became "Brisson." By the time Frederick entered show business, but in a more circuitous way, Brisson—with an accent on the last syllable—had become the family name.

Frederick's mother, Marie Jorgensen (which Frederick spelled "Jorgenson" on his Declaration of Intent), had been an actress-singer who performed first as Cleo Jorgensen and later as Cleo Villard. As the latter, she scored a huge success in 1916 in Scandinavia, singing World War I songs. Although Cleo's stage career was brief, Carl's was not. Carl, in fact, had two careers, achieving fame in each. As "the Fighting Dane," Carl Pedersen became Europe's middleweight boxing champion in 1912. When a theater manager observed Carl coaching Cleo, he suggested that Carl also try show business, which was not entirely alien to him. Even as a boxer, Carl did a bit of performing. In fall 1913, Carl and Cleo, and perhaps Cleo's sister Tilde, also a singer, formed an act—possibly a trio, but at least a duo—known as "les Brissons."

"Brisson" was not an arbitrary choice; the name had been in Carl's family on his mother's side for a century, but went unused until Carl resurrected it for himself after realizing that a boxer's professional life is brief (in his case, five years, from around 1911 to 1916). And so Carl Pedersen, "the fighting Dane," became Carl Brisson, the international star, who capitalized on his seductive tenor voice which, combined with his personality—not to mention his reputation in the ring—provided him with a second act, along with a continental-sounding name. Carl was now an entertainer. The medium did not matter. He did not scorn movies and, in fact, made a few, beginning in his native Denmark with *De Mystike Fodspor* (1918). There would be others, twelve in all, first in England and later in Hollywood.

Although "ageism" had yet to be coined, Carl understood the consequences of revealing one's age in a youth-obsessed business. Carl, in fact, was so age-conscious that he passed Frederick off as his brother; according to Mitchell Leisen, who directed Carl in *Murder in the Vanities* (1934), Carl preferred to keep his wife at a safe distance in case she divulged his real age. Cleo no longer had an image to maintain, but Carl did. Although Carl was born in 1893, he preferred 1897. His future daughter-in-law would have understood. Both were well aware of "the enemy time," as Tennessee Williams stigmatized it in *Sweet Bird of Youth* (1958).

Frederick would also enter show business, but not immediately. Education came first. Until 1923, Frederick had been attending grade school in Copenhagen. That year, his father had the opportunity to appear as Count Danilo in a London production of Franz Léhar's operetta, *The Merry Widow*, with the extraordinary Evelyn Laye in the title role. Although most of the audience came to see (and hear) Laye, they were not disappointed with her co-star. Danilo became Carl's signature role, which he was still performing thirty years later until he contracted liver cancer and died on 26 September 1958. A London base for Carl and Cleo meant a British school for Frederick, who, at ten, spoke hardly any English. Thus Frederick was given a British education that would not only make him fluent in English, but also afford him opportunities he never would have had in Copenhagen. And once Frederick acquired the necessary language skills, London would provide the finishing touches.

Frederick was first sent to Emscote Lawn in Warwickshire; he completed his education at Rossall College, now the coeducational Rossall School, in Lancashire, which he attended from 1928 to 1929 as Carl Ejner F. Brisson. Rossall, which dates back to the mid-nineteenth century, has had its share of distinguished alumni, including the conductor Sir Thomas Beecham, who founded the London Philharmonic, and Leslie Charteris, one of the most literate practitioners of detective fiction, whose series detective was Simon Templar, "the Saint."

While Carl was appearing on the London stage, Frederick was learning how to manage in an English public school. Nothing in Denmark had prepared him for a class-conscious and regimented environment where privilege reigned and bullies thrived, and where the right combination of guts and brawn—intelligence was a given—was a prerequisite for survival. This was the world of William Golding's *Lord of the Flies* without the pig-sticking and blood-letting. Frederick survived and was all the better for it; Emscote and Rossall prepared him for the tough negotiating he would have to do as an agent and producer.

Carl's success on the stage did not elude Alfred Hitchcock, a regular theatergoer, who was working on a script for British International that became his sixth film, *The Ring* (1927). Since the setting was the boxing world, Hitchcock wanted an actor who looked like a boxer. Knowing that Carl had been one, and a champion, to boot, Hitchcock cast him as "One Round Jack" Saunders. Taken with his performance, Hitchcock offered him a more complex part in *The Manxman* (1929), the director's last silent film. *The Manxman* was a richly atmospheric work, set on the Isle of Man (hence the title, which refers to an inhabitant of Man), in which Carl played Peter Christian, whose attempt to make Kate (Anny Ondra) his wife nearly leads to tragedy. When Kate agrees to marry Peter, she is pregnant with the child of his best friend, Philip (Malcolm Keen). Kate's unsuccessful suicide attempt forces Philip to accept his responsibilities, even though it means both of them must leave Man. Since Hitchcock's sympathies lay with Peter, he reserved the final close-up for Carl, his face emblazoned with grief.

As soon as Frederick had completed his education, he landed a job as publicist for Moss Empires, Ltd., a vast theater chain dating back to the end of the nineteenth century and known for pampering the stars appearing in its venues that were scattered throughout Britain. Frederick learned not only how to publicize what were essentially variety acts but also how to accede to the performers' demands. One such performer was his father, who often played the Moss circuit. Since there could not be two Carl Brissons, Carl Einer F. Brisson became Frederick Brisson. During the early 1930s, Carl would tour when not making movies or appearing at the London Palladium and the Café de Paris. By occasionally accompanying Carl on his tours as a combination manager-publicist, Frederick discovered how extensive his father's reputation was. He then decided to become part of the entertainment world himself, but in a nonperforming capacity. Frederick's preference was the theater, although movies would do for the time being. And movies it was—at the beginning. Because of the tours, Carl started relying on

Frederick in the same way actors rely on agents: to provide them with work. Although Carl was essentially a stage performer, he was well aware of the ascendancy of film, a medium on which he also hoped to leave his mark. It was not coincidental that shortly after Frederick accepted a position at the Gaumont-British Picture Corporation, he became associate producer of *Prince of Arcadia* (1933) and *Two Hearts in Waltz Time* (1934), both of which starred none other than Carl Brisson. The former also featured an actress who later became a Hollywood star and one of the few women directors of the studio era: Ida Lupino.

Frederick, however, could not claim credit for his father's brief, gaudy hour in Hollywood. By 1933, Carl's reputation brought him to the attention of Paramount Pictures, which had developed a unique kind of movie—not exactly a conventional musical but rather a comedy (or drama) with musical numbers interspersed throughout without necessarily advancing the plot. The format, which admitted of variations, was simple: a bit of plot, a bit of music, more plot, more music, and so on until *The End*. In his Hollywood debut, Carl played opposite Kitty Carlisle in Mitchell Leisen's *Murder at the Vanities* (1934), which managed to get into the theaters by late spring 1934, before the newly enforced Production Code went into effect. Thus, Victor McLaglen could say "nuts," which later became a taboo word, replaced by the less offensive "nertz." And Gertrude Michael could sing "Sweet Marijuana," in which she extolled her drug of choice ("Sweet marijuana, help me in my distress"). Although the Production Code did not specifically forbid the use of the drug trade as a plot device, it did prohibit "scenes . . . which show the use of illegal drugs, or their effects in detail." Since marijuana was illegal, and "Sweet Marijuana" vividly described its effects, the number could never have been included if production began a year later.

The costumes were daring even by pre-Code standards. In one sequence, the ladies of the chorus wore flesh-colored body stockings with clusters of strategically placed mini sequins; in another, "Live and Love Tonight," with an idyllic setting that evoked the Garden of Eden, leaves served the same purpose. There was also a topless number in which the ladies demurely cupped their breasts, while blood dripped down from the flies (a murderer is loose in the theater) on a bare shoulder.

By contemporary standards, *Murder at the Vanities* may seem sexist and perhaps even racist. Leisen's ogling camera (in one number the chorines are lying on their backs with legs raised as a cowboy twirls a lariat over them) was in the Busby Berkeley tradition of geometrically arranged groupings where women are slowly panned, with the camera stopping just long enough to elicit a dirty thought, or photographed from on high so that the camera can look down at—or between—their legs elevated in V formation. LeRoy Printz and Larry Ceballos, who staged the dance numbers in *Vanities*, were more than familiar with the Busby Berkeley school of soft-core choreography. For the duration of the Production Code, "indecent or undue exposure is forbidden." In other words, no more breast-cupping, exposed navels, or nude-colored body stockings.

The musical numbers in *Vanities* ran the gamut from camp to kitsch. "The Rape of the Rhapsody" was the latter. The sequence was unusual; the cast was fully clothed, with only Gertrude Michael showing cleavage—and not much, at that. An elaborately staged version of Franz Lizst's "Second Hungarian Rhapsody" is interrupted by Duke Ellington's orchestra, which adds a welcome touch of lowdown to the stuffy proceedings. The conductor, however, thinks otherwise and proceeds to machine gun the intruders, most of whom are African Americans. Of course, blanks were used, except for the one that killed Gertrude Michael, who, as the cell block ladies in *Chicago* would have said, "had it coming."

Such was Carl Brisson's American film debut. *The Merry Widow, Vanities* was not. Although Carl headed the cast, followed by Victor McLaglen, Jack Oakie, and Kitty Carlisle, his name appeared after the title, not above it. Carl played "international star" Eric Linder making his first American appearance in an Earl Carroll's Vanities, a musical revue on the order of the Ziegfeld Follies but without the star power. When Rita Ross (Gertrude Michael) discovers that Eric, her former lover, and his leading lady Ann Ware (Kitty Carlisle) are planning to elope after opening night, she sets out to maim or, preferably, kill Ann before or during the performance. Instead, Rita ends up killing a female detective (Gail Patrick), whom Eric has hired to retrieve some items Rita has stolen. Rita herself is killed when someone fires a bullet from the wings that blends in with the gunfire at the end of "Rape of the Rhapsody." Revelations abound. The wardrobe mistress is really Carl's mother, whom he is trying to protect because she once killed a man (who also "had it coming"). Rita's killer is Norma, her maid (Dorothy Stickney), whom Rita has verbally and physically abused. But since Rita deserved to die, as everyone agrees, Eric promises to get Norma the best lawyer in New York. And with Stickney playing Norma with such disarming inno-cence, the audience can rest assured that Norma will not be doing much time, if any at all.

It is easy to see from *Vanities* why Carl was a matinee idol in Europe. Unlike, say, Maurice Chevalier, he did not rely on a twinkle in his eye or a mischievous grin; nor did he invest lyrics with Chevalier's worldliness. Although a Dane, Carl was the embodiment of old Vienna, not gay Paree. Understandably, *The Merry Widow* was the work with which he was most identified. *Vanities* was not the ideal vehicle for introducing Carl to American audiences. The title suggested a whodunit within the setting of a musical revue; the mix of song, dance, production numbers, murder, sleuthing, cover-ups, and red herrings resulted in a pastiche from which Carl emerged periodically to join the plot or sing a song (the most famous being "Cocktails for Two," with Kitty Carlisle). Paramount did not know how to market Carl any more than it did Metropolitan Opera star Gladys Swarthout or, for that matter, Kitty Carlisle. All of them were meant for the stage—or, in Carlisle's case, for the stage and television, where she was a regular panelist on the CBS show *To Tell the Truth* from 1957 to 1968. In the 1930s, American audi-ences expected European stars to exude an air of mystery heightened by a touch of the exotic: an emotionally veiled face like Greta Garbo's, which implied that she had seen it all but would not enumerate; and Charles Boyer's, which looked as if he were pondering some overwhelming question, whose answer kept eluding him.

Carl, on the other hand, never acquired a mystique. He communicated the joy of song without resorting to artifice. Carl's unfeigned sincerity, however, did not fit in with 1930s Hollywood. He was continental, but not a boulevardier; romantic but not a crooner; suave but not mannered. In short, he was a class act booked for a limited engagement. Carl made two more films for Paramount, *All the King's Horses* (1934) and *Ship Cafe* (1935), neither of which enhanced his reputation or the studio's. The former at least included "A Little White Gardenia" ("For I bring a little white gardenia / as refreshing as a day in May. / You may wear it if you care / or toss it away."), which furnished Carl with a hit record.

Since Carl mistakenly believed he was on the threshold of a Hollywood career in 1933, he urged Frederick to join Cleo and himself on the West Coast, hoping that they could revive the artist-manager relationship they had in London. In January 1934, Frederick was issued a temporary visa and booked passage on the SS *Aquitania*. He arrived in Los Angeles just as *Murder at the Vanities* started shooting on 5 February. If any year could be called Frederick's year of discovery, it was 1934. Once he experienced moviemaking, Hollywood style, he knew that Los Angeles would be his home. Frederick was determined to make a name for himself in the world of American entertainment, not knowing at the time that it would be primarily in the theater. In 1935, as Carl's film career was ending, Frederick's was beginning—but not in front of the camera.

Nineteen thirty-four brought Frederick in contact with two men who altered the course of his life: Cary Grant and Frank W. Vincent. By the time Frederick joined his parents in Los Angeles, Grant had become one of Paramount's stars, beginning with a bit part in *Merrily We Go to Hell*, followed by major roles in *Blonde Venus* opposite Marlene Dietrich; *Hot Saturday* with Nancy Carroll and a cast that featured Randolph Scott, who perhaps became his lover; *Madame Butterfly* with Sylvia Sidney in the title role; *Sinners in the Sun* with Carole Lombard; and *This Is the Night* with Lili Damita—all in 1932. Grant's persona—the urbane male personified, or, to use the new coinage, the ultimate metrosexual—had been forged. The real Grant was a brilliant actor of far greater depth than most of his films allowed him to reveal, except for a few such as *The Talk of the Town* (1942), *None but the Lonely Heart* (1944), and *Notorious* (1946).

Of the eight films Grant made in 1933, two confirmed his new image. Significantly, both starred Mae West: *She Done Him Wrong* and *I'm No Angel*. In the former, he held his own with Mae, who looked him over and sized up his character with four words: "You can be had." In the latter, Grant was striking but less memorable. How could he compete with Mae, who, in one scene, had to look into a lion's mouth? Grant, however, must have enjoyed *Angel's* not-so-subtle dialogue, especially in the scene in which Mae is trying to place a phone call but encounters an operator who has difficulty taking down the first letter of the person's surname. Exasperated, Mae shouts, "P as in 'pansy.'"

While Hollywood insiders speculated about Grant and Scott, to professionals like Frederick and his father, or even Rosalind, an actor's sexual orientation was unimportant as long as it did not interfere with his art. And Grant was an artist. Carl, however, was both an artist and a celebrity. Since Grant was aware of Carl's reputation, and Carl of Grant's ascendancy at Paramount, where Carl was now a contract player, however briefly, Grant must have been flattered to receive an invitation to the Brissons' dinner party in 1934. If Frederick knew what had occurred prior to the party, he would never reveal it. According to Grant's biographer, the actor arrived late, and alone; he had left his then wife, actress Virginia Cherrill (Chaplin's co-star in *City Lights*), at home. Virginia was in no condition to go anywhere that evening because a violent argument with her husband left her face in need of bandaging.

If Frederick witnessed Grant's dark side, he did not let it affect their friendship, which began with Frederick's arrival in Hollywood. Carl was looking for an opening at Paramount for his son, which led to Frederick's working briefly in the studio's publicity department. If Frederick did not meet Grant at his parents' home, it would have been at the studio. No stranger to film from his tenure at Gaumont, Frederick now saw the business from a different angle: it was a business that depended on agents to supply the talent the studios needed to function. Frederick may have even reached that conclusion earlier when he served as his father's manager during his tours. But it was never as evident to him as it was on his first trip to Hollywood.

In 1934, Frederick knew little about Frank W. Vincent, who would also play a major role in his career. But Grant knew a great deal about him. Frederick may have been a close friend of Grant's, but the Wisconsin-born, Wheaton College–educated Vincent was the actor's patron, benefactor, and business partner. In 1918, Grant—then Archie Leach, age fourteen—was a member of the Pender Troupe, a company of acrobats and stilt walkers. When the Penders were touring the Keith Circuit in 1922, Leach contracted rheumatic fever, bringing the tour to a standstill. After Leach recovered, the Keith Circuit was no longer interested in the Penders, but Frank W. Vincent was. Vincent, who then booked acts for the Orpheum Circuit, had seen the Penders before and was particularly impressed by Leach and the ease with which he walked on stilts. Vincent became the Penders' deus ex machina, and the Penders were now on the Orpheum Circuit. Grant never forgot Vincent's faith in him. But his relationship with Vincent did not end with an Orpheum booking.

By the time Archie Leach had morphed into Cary Grant, Vincent was part of H. E. Edington–F. W. Vincent, Inc., a talent agency that handled, among other stars, Greta Garbo, Ann Harding, Nelson Eddy, Basil Rathbone, Edward G. Robinson, Marlene Dietrich, and Douglas Fairbanks Jr. The agency was the creation of Harry E. Edington, a former MGM production executive, who would return to moviemaking in 1939. Meanwhile, he created a powerful agency, to which Vincent added his name when he joined it in 1932. Later, Grant also became part of Edington-Vincent, but in an unusual capacity: as a client and a silent partner, who invested in the same agency that represented him. Thus, while Edington-Vincent received 10 percent of Grant's salary, Grant got a percentage of that 10 percent. No other actor in Hollywood was in such a position.

By 1939, Edington was eager to return to production; the following year he was ensconced at RKO, where he produced such films as *Kitty Foyle* (1940), which won a best actress Oscar for Ginger Rogers, and Hitchcock's only attempt at screwball comedy, *Mr. and Mrs. Smith* (1941). Vincent, who was accustomed to working with a partner like Edington, did not have to wait long for a replacement.

Once Carl realized his Paramount days were over, he and Cleo headed back to London. Frederick did, too, planning to remain there only until he gained enough experience to return to Hollywood, where he sensed his future lay. In September 1935, the *Hollywood Reporter* announced it was planning to put out a London edition. Frederick was intrigued; in 1935, working for the *Hollywood Reporter* was the closest he could come to his goal. Within five years of leaving Rossall, Frederick had built up a resume that so impressed the *Reporter*'s editor and publisher, William R. Wilkerson, that he hired Frederick to cover the London theater and film scene. Although the *Reporter* was (and still is) a venerable trade publication in America, the British were indifferent to it. After slightly more than a year, the London edition ceased publication on 30 October 1936.

Frederick was by no means out of a job. In 1935, the same year he began writing for the *Reporter*, he joined the Ad Schulberg Agency. Schulberg, an American citizen, had set up an office in London specifically for the purpose of securing employment for British actors in America, and vice versa. Among the American actors for whom Frederick found work in Britain were Otto Krueger, Bruce Cabot, Victor Jory, and Phyllis Brooks, Cary Grant's great love, who almost became the actor's second wife.

Being a 10-percenter was not Frederick's idea of a career. Although he was successful as an agent, his heart was in producing, particularly for the theater. Film was his second choice. However, producing a play is riskier than making a movie. For one thing, movies had become an international mass medium. And even a film that was critically dismissed would have greater longevity and exposure than a poorly reviewed play that could close on opening night. Even so, Frederick engaged in a few theatrical ventures such as *Transatlantic Rhythm* (1936), a musical revue that he co-produced. *Transatlantic Rhythm*, which opened at London's elegant Adelphi Theatre in the Strand, featured British as well as American artists—the latter including the "Mexican Spitfire" Lupe Velez, who enjoyed a brief career in Hollywood before taking her life in 1944, and Ruth Etting, an impeccable vocalist whose renditions of "Ten Cents a Dance" and "Love Me or Leave Me" have become classics.

By 1938, Frederick was back in film. Theater may have been his first love, but it required the kind of financing which, at that point in his career, he could not obtain. Movies were easier. After making *Moonlight Sonata* (1938), Frederick worked out an arrangement with United Artists to distribute the film in Britain. The selling point was not the presence of the American actor Charles Farrell in the male lead (although that helped) but the screen debut of the greatest pianist of his generation, Ignace Jan Paderewski. An American release soon followed. But Frederick did not discount the appeal of Farrell, who had also appeared in other British films (including one of Carl's, *Song of Soho* [1930]). Recalling how British audiences responded to Velez and Etting in *Transatlantic Rhythm*, and to Farrell in *Moonlight Sonata*, Frederick realized that the Anglo-American rationale of the Ad Schulberg Agency was the show business version of an exchange program or a good neighbor policy. After leaving Schulberg in 1938, he opened his own agency the same year, which he called, appropriately, the Anglo-American Agency.

Once the Anglo-American Agency was established, Frederick started making contacts in Hollywood. On 19 January 1939, Frederick requested permission of the American consul in London to sail to the United States on the SS *Champlain*, scheduled for an 8 February departure. He did not specify the reason, which was to join the Frank W. Vincent Agency. Knowing that Edington would soon be leaving the agency and that Vincent would need a junior-level replacement, Grant may have recommended Frederick. On the other hand, Vincent may have already known about Frederick's track record of finding work in London for Hollywood actors, such as Brian Donlevy, who was one of Vincent's clients, or Phyllis Brooks. In 1939 Frederick became Vincent's junior partner; the agency was still Edington-Vincent at 9441 Wilshire Boulevard. It would never be the Vincent-Brisson Agency, as Vincent hoped, for several reasons, one of which was Frederick's not being an American citizen. And when he became one in April 1942, America was at war, and Frederick was about to enter the Army Air Force. But in 1939 Frederick was excited at the prospect of being Vincent's junior partner, returning to London to close his agency before relocating in Hollywood. He had picked a watershed year to change countries. With Hitler's invasion of Poland on 1 September 1939, Poland's allies, Britain and France, had no other choice but to declare war on Germany, which they did on 3 September. For France, it was the start of the Phony War; for Britain, the start of the Blitz. Although fall 1939 was not the most auspicious time to cross the Atlantic, Frederick left England on 20 September on the SS *George Washington*.

Some marriages are made in heaven, others on the high seas. Because of the war, the amenities were in short supply on the *George Washington*. By way of compensation, passengers were treated to MGM's latest release, *The Women*, which was shown three times a day. At first, Frederick avoided watching it, especially since he could hear the dialogue from his deck chair. On the last night of the voyage he succumbed. And when he did, he concluded, as did many of the critics, that the title was a misnomer. There was one woman, and her name was Rosalind Russell.

From New York, Frederick traveled to Los Angeles, staying briefly with Cary Grant. He arrived in Hollywood just as Grant was starting *His Girl Friday* at Columbia. When Frederick learned that his host's co-star was Rosalind Russell, he immediately asked to visit the set. Once Grant realized the extent of Frederick's attraction to Rosalind, he started playing matchmaker; Rosalind responded by playing hard to get. Frederick persisted, Rosalind weakened, and the proposal, which Rosalind insisted be in daylight, occurred at dawn, with Frederick on bended knee at Rosalind's door. Always the gentleman, Frederick asked Clara McKnight Russell in writing for permission to marry her daughter. Naturally, Mrs. Russell agreed. Although Carl Brisson was a

Lutheran, Cleo was Catholic, and Frederick was raised Catholic. That was all Clara needed to know.

Theirs was a long courtship. *His Girl Friday* wrapped up production on 20 November 1939, and the movie premiered in early January 1940. By spring of that year, Rosalind was at Universal making *Hired Wife* (1940), with star billing and a salary of $40,000—a far cry from the $750 a week she had been offered six years earlier. Next MGM loaned her out to Warner Bros. for *No Time for Comedy*, which hit the theaters in September 1940, the same month as *Hired Wife*. In 1941, there were four Rosalind Russell movies in release: *This Thing Called Love* (Columbia) and the trio that marked the end of her MGM contract, *They Met in Bombay* (1941), *The Feminine Touch* (1941), and *Design for Scandal* (1941). Filmmaking had become a roller-coaster ride, with Rosalind in the front car. And it was exhilarating.

Her stamina was extraordinary. The wedding was set for 25 October 1941. That gave the couple exactly one month before Rosalind had to report to Paramount for *Take a Letter, Darling* (1942), which was scheduled to start production on November 27.

Frederick wanted a Danish wedding, and Rosalind complied. It was not that she was playing the dutiful bride. She was quite emphatic about her new role as a married woman: "I shall adjust my career to my marriage, not the other way around," she told Gladys Hall in an interview for *Silver Screen* magazine. She also explained to Hall that freelancing would give her more time between pictures, noting that she would not make more than three a year, and maybe just two. "And if I have a child, I shall not, now, be breaking a contract during my absence from the screen." Any actress planning to make at least two films a year was hardly thinking in terms of a major adjustment. Rosalind never planned to retire from the screen to raise a family, nor did she ever believe that she would face the career-versus-marriage dilemma of some of her characters. She had accomplished too much as an actress to choose domesticity over professional recognition. Had she done so, she would have been miserable. Throughout her married life, Rosalind, a repertory veteran, never had a problem switching from Rosalind Russell to Rosalind

Russell Brisson. She had already mastered the art of playing two different roles a week in repertory.

The wedding was atypical by Hollywood standards. For one thing, it did not take place in Los Angeles. Once when Carl was lost, he came upon a Danish community in Solvang, California, about forty miles north of Santa Barbara. Carl was elated with his discovery, which evoked his native Denmark. So was Frederick, who, after visiting Solvang, knew he had found the perfect place for his wedding. The next step was to convince Rosalind. She, too, was taken with Solvang, particularly after she saw the church where the ceremony would take place: Santa Ynez, a Franciscan mission built in 1810 by Father Junipero Serra and never restored. To Rosalind, Santa Ynez represented the "till death do us part" kind of marriage that her parents had and that she wanted for herself and Frederick.

The priest who officiated was, naturally, a Franciscan—but Irish as well, Father Finnian Carroll. The wedding guests included Frank Sinatra; Barbara Hutton, whom Cary Grant would marry the following year; Claudette Colbert and her husband, Dr. Joel Pressman; the Herbert Marshalls; William and Diana Powell; Myrna Loy and her husband, Arthur; and Loretta Young and her husband, Tom Lewis. Cary Grant was the best man, and Charlotte Wynters was maid of honor. A stickler for authenticity, Rosalind commissioned Irene (Lentz), who succeeded Adrian as MGM's chief designer, to research Danish wedding gowns so that hers would be the genuine article, which it was—elegant but not ostentatious. It was not the kind a movie director would have requested; on the other hand, Rosalind's wedding was not taking place on a soundstage, but in a mission church 150 miles from Hollywood. Nor was there any resemblance between the gown Rosalind wore that day and the one that Adrian designed for her in *Reckless*; the latter was an ice-blue satin creation with a peplum that photographed as shimmering white, the trailing veil held in place by a pearl-studded coronet. And unlike her character in *Reckless*, Rosalind carried a bouquet of field flowers, not lilies of the valley. Rosalind knew the difference between a movie marriage and a real one.

Rosalind, class of 1929, the American Academy of Dramatic
Arts. American Academy of Dramatic Arts.

Rosalind in *China Seas* (1935) being cordial to Jean Harlow, who has eyes only for Clark Gable, as pipe-smoking C. Aubrey Smith notices. Private Collection.

Rosalind in Adrian's shimmering bridal gown from *Reckless* (1935). Springer/Photofest.

Rosalind as the neurotic Olivia drawn to the murderous Danny (Robert Montgomery) in *Night Must Fall* (1937). Academy of Motion Picture Arts and Sciences (AMPAS).

Rosalind as Sylvia Fowler in *The Women* (1939) with some of the title characters. Left to right, Hedda Hopper, Norma Shearer, and Joan Fontaine. Private Collection.

Rosalind as Hildy, the professional "newspaper man," and her managing editor (Cary Grant) in *His Girl Friday* (1940). Columbia Pictures/Sony Entertainment.

Rosalind on the set of *My Sister Eileen* (1942) with director Alexander Hall, her hairdresser, and her maid Hazel. Columbia Pictures/Sony Entertainment.

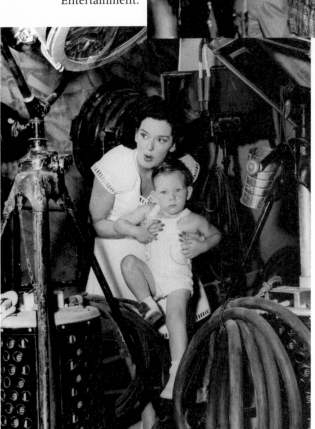

Rosalind introducing her two-year-old son Lance to moviemaking on the set of *She Wouldn't Say Yes* (1945). Columbia Pictures/Sony Entertainment.

Rosalind as the young Louise Randall Pierson in *Roughly Speaking* (1945). Private Collection.

Rosalind and the historical
Sister Kenny in the early
1940s. Private Collection.

Rosalind as the title
character in *Sister Kenny*
(1946). Private Collection.

Rosalind and Kirk Douglas as Lavinia Mannon and Peter Niles in *Mourning Becomes Electra* (1947). AMPAS.

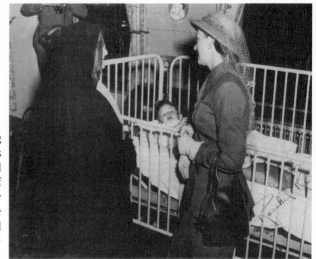

Rosalind visiting Waterbury's St. Mary's Hospital in 1949 and stopping by the bed of Bobby Keyser. Courtesy Hazel M. Keyser. (Note that Rosalind autographed the picture for Hazel.)

Rosalind as Mama Rose at the climax of *Gypsy* (1962). Private Collection.

Mother Superior (Rosalind) catching two of her "angels" (Hayley Mills and June Harding) smoking in the lavatory in *The Trouble with Angels* (1966). Columbia Pictures/Sony Entertainment.

Rosalind as Gillian, a contemporary witch, with her familiar from the 1952 tour of *Bell, Book and Candle*. Wisconsin Center for Film and Theater Research.

Rosalind and her co-star, George Gaynes, in the Broadway production of *Wonderful Town* (1953). Springer/Photofest.

Auntie Mame and her nephew (Jan Hanzlick) in the 1956 Broadway
production. Springer/Photofest.

Rosalind receiving the screenplay of *Auntie Mame* (1958) from Adolph Green and Betty Comden. Springer/Photofest.

Rosalind dining with Frank Sinatra and Ronald Reagan at the Los Angeles Biltmore in the mid-1950s. Springer/Photofest.

Rosalind and Frederick Brisson at their wedding reception on 25 October 1941. Springer/Photofest.

Rosalind and Frederick celebrating their twenty-fifth wedding anniversary in Las Vegas. Springer/Photofest.

Rosalind and Frederick at the London premiere of *Mrs. Pollifax—Spy* on 17 February 1971. Springer/Photofest.

Rosalind may not have wanted a Hollywood wedding, but she also did not want one in which the bridal procession came to a halt because the groom and best man had not appeared. Frederick and Grant were supposed to enter the church through a side door, which had been inadvertently locked. Unaware of their plight, Rosalind, escorted by her brother, James, proceeded down the aisle to the altar, where Frederick was supposed to be waiting with Grant. Fortunately, Grant spotted an open window and mimed their predicament to a guest, who immediately understood and unlocked the door. Rosalind's may not have been a movie wedding, but it was performed as if it were one uninterrupted long take with the same split-second timing that she and Grant displayed in *His Girl Friday*.

The reception was held in a field near the mission, where picnic tables had been set up. Candles provided the illumination; and the distant sound of a waterfall, the sound effects, as Rosalind and Frederick, standing between a Danish and an American flag, received the guests.

The couple returned from their honeymoon in Florida and Cuba in time for America's entrance into World War II. For Rosalind, the end of the honeymoon meant the start of a new movie; for Frederick, there were more pressing concerns: his citizenship application had not yet been approved. The process had become even more bureaucratic after the Japanese attack on Pearl Harbor. Furthermore, Frederick was still traveling under a Danish passport, but living at Rosalind's home on 631 North Elm Drive until they could sell it and move into their own. By early 1942, Frederick had enough friends to expedite the process, and on 10 April 1942, Carl Frederick Brisson, then twenty-nine, was sworn in as American citizen. A commission awaited him in the Army Air Force (AAF), where he rose to the rank of lieutenant colonel by the war's end. Because one of Frederick's responsibilities at the Vincent Agency was finding radio work for his clients, he was made producer of *The Fighting AAF* radio series. One such program was "Soldiers with Wings," on which Rosalind appeared occasionally. Both Rosalind and Frederick were honored for their contribution to AAF radio: Rosalind with a citation for her support and participation, and Frederick with the Legion of Merit.

By the time Frederick returned to civilian life (although remaining in the reserves), Rosalind had made six films—two each in 1942, 1943, and 1945. On 15 April 1943, *Flight for Freedom* opened at New York's Radio City Music Hall. Three weeks later, on May 7, Rosalind gave birth to a son at Good Samaritan Hospital in Los Angeles. He was christened Carl Lance Brisson, but "Carl" soon disappeared, just as "Catherine" had from Catherine Rosalind Russell.

In 1943, "Lance" was not as common a name as it is now. When Lance inquired about it, his parents replied that they came upon "Lance" in a book of children's names. Whether Rosalind and Frederick envisioned a film career for their son is uncertain. But if Lance decided to enter the business, he would never have had to change his name.

Rosalind made certain that Lance enjoyed the same kind of financially secure childhood that she had. That meant a home in a more fashionable section of Beverly Hills than Elm Drive: 706 North Beverly Drive. In 1945, *Modern Screen* magazine considered the Brissons' Beverly Drive home worthy of a color insert. The house was originally owned by the underrated comic actress, Mary Boland, whom Rosalind met during *The Women*. "Rosalind Russell's Modern Manor," as the piece was entitled, was a two-story, white stucco house with a circular courtyard. Downstairs was a dining room furnished in French provincial with the chairs upholstered in hydrangea blue to match the curtains; a living room that, except for the white marble fireplace, was a study in green; a spacious den that was partially glass-enclosed and opened onto a patio and garden; and a swimming pool with a greenhouse behind it. Upstairs was Rosalind's room, decorated in pink; Lance's nursery, which he would soon outgrow, also in pink, with a junior-size canopied four-poster and a fireplace; and Frederick's room, whose dominant color was yellow, from the drapes to the bed with its yellow headboard, footboard, and bedspread. The interior of 706 North Beverly Drive would be modified over the years, but in 1945, it was a reflection of Rosalind's taste.

Rosalind made certain that, initially, Lance would have a Catholic education. Thus, until the fifth grade, he attended Good Shepherd School in

Beverly Hills—the parish school of the Church of the Good Shepherd, where Rosalind worshipped and which she christened "Our Lady of the Cadillacs" because of its upscale congregation that, at the time, included the actresses Jane Wyman and Loretta Young. In 1952, when Rosalind began rehearsals for *Wonderful Town*, she was unable to find the equivalent of Good Shepherd School in New York. Since she believed Lance would not be in danger of losing his faith if he enrolled at a non-Catholic private school, particularly one near the Hotel Pierre on East Sixty-first Street, where she and Frederick would be staying, Lance finished grade school at Buckley, which was founded in 1912 and is still an all-boys elementary school. High school meant going out of state. While Rosalind was starring in *Auntie Mame* on Broadway, Lance was at the Hotchkiss School in Lakeville, Connecticut—an even more venerable institution than Buckley, dating back to 1891 and now coeducational. When Lance was ready for college, Rosalind was back in Los Angeles in the last decade of her film career. Lance attended both the University of Southern California and the University of California, Los Angeles, graduating from neither. He believed he had exhausted what higher education had to offer and embarked upon a career that took him from the *Los Angeles Times*, where he was a staff writer, to the consulting firm of Winner and Associates, where he is currently executive vice president.

Rosalind, who always wanted to write—or at least be an actress-writer—was proud of her son's pieces in the *Los Angeles Times*, as she had every reason to be. Lance knew how to paint a picture in words: "Towering surf diminished Monday after battering thousands of Southland swimmers for eight days, but the U.S. Weather Bureau predicted similar hazardous conditions may develop this week." (*Los Angeles Times*, 21 July 1964).

Lance was not the first Brisson to do a 180-degree career change. He was preceded by his grandfather and, in 1946, by his father. In July of that year, Frederick, Rosalind, and Frank Vincent decided to form their own production company. Vincent, then sixty-one, tried in vain to persuade Frederick to take over the agency, in which Rosalind was one of his many clients. Frederick was not interested; having been away from flesh-peddling for three years, he realized he was meant for something better. Although 1946 was a banner year in terms of box office, the picture was less rosy in 1947, when the winds of change began to blow. Americans were not the moviegoers they had been during the war, as other diversions such as miniature golf and especially drive-ins, which featured family nights at a dollar a car, offered alternatives to traditional moviegoing. By the early 1950s, a new mass medium emerged with a smaller (but ever widening) screen that did not require paid admission.

Long before "prioritizing" became a buzz word, Americans were doing exactly that. With many veterans, education under the GI Bill took precedence over entertainment; and a home, even a prefabricated one in the suburbs, became the goal of couples who had deferred starting families until, as the wartime song promised, the lights went on again all over the world.

When they did, some directors, producers, and stars—as if anticipating the eventual collapse of the studio system and knowing that the next decade would bring another generation eager for new, or at least different, kinds of films—began forming their own production companies. There had always been independent producers in Hollywood, the classic example being the founders of United Artists (D. W. Griffith, Mary Pickford, Charlie Chaplin, and Douglas Fairbanks). But that was in 1919, before the studio system came into being. By 1945, the system had been long established and, to the average moviegoer, seemed to be thriving. But there were actors and directors who wondered how the end of World War II would affect the industry, just as there were munitions plant workers who wondered about their job prospects in postwar America.

Early in 1946, Frank Capra, George Stevens, William Wyler, and Sam Briskin (whom Capra knew from his days at Columbia, where Briskin had been vice president and general manager in the mid-1930s) joined forces to form Liberty Productions, whose sole release was *It's a Wonderful Life* (1946). Rita Hayworth's Beckworth Corporation ("Beck" from her daughter, Rebecca, and "worth" from her surname) was also short-lived. Humphrey Bogart's Santana Productions and John Ford and Merian C. Cooper's Argosy Pictures lasted longer and delivered better films (e.g., Santana's *In a Lonely Place* [1950], Argosy's *She Wore a Yellow Ribbon* [1949]) than Beckworth's *The Loves of Carmen* (1948), *Affair in Trinidad* (1951), and *Salome* (1953).

Rather than become the Hollywood equivalent of Luddites, assuming that it would be business as usual in postwar Hollywood, Frederick, Rosalind, Dudley Nichols, and Frank Vincent agreed to form their own production company, Independent Artists, in July 1946, with offices at California Studios on North Bronson Avenue in Los Angeles. On 28 October, Vincent died suddenly of a heart attack, which meant the end not only of his involvement in Independent Artists but of his agency as well. Devastated by the death of his close friend, who had also been the best man at his wedding to Barbara Hutton, Grant scrambled to find representation for as many of Vincent's clients as he could. Vincent's death was also a blow to Frederick, who had hoped to interest the same clients in appearing in Independent Artists productions. Soon, Nichols bowed out, preferring to concentrate on what he did best: writing. The roster then consisted of Frederick as president-treasurer and executive producer, attorney Owen Ward as secretary, and Frederick and Rosalind as board members. The logo was an Olympic torch, and Independent Artists' first film was *The Velvet Touch*, released through RKO.

Rosalind had portrayed a stage actress before in *No Time for Comedy*, which required her to play second fiddle to James Stewart. In *The Velvet Touch* (1948), she was the star—Valerie Stanton, the queen of sophisticated comedy, who, like Rosalind, sought to venture into deeper waters and play Ibsen's Hedda Gabler. Here the resemblances end. Rosalind had already plunged into the depths in *Electra*, acquitting herself nobly but overwhelmed by a production that struck audiences and critics as stagy.

Rosalind's relationship with her producer-husband was quite different from Valerie's with her producer and ex-lover, Gordon Dunning (Leon Ames), who has become so proprietary that he threatens to reveal Valerie's past to her architect fiancé (Leo Genn, *Electra*'s Adam Brant) if she defects to another producer in order to play Hedda. *The Velvet Touch* opens in medias res with an argument between Valerie and Gordon that grows so ugly that

Valerie reaches for the only object at hand, a statuette that looks suspiciously like a Tony (but called a "Players Award") and brings it down on his head. In a typical noir composition, reminiscent of the opening shot of *Mildred Pierce* (1945), Gordon lunges into the frame, knocking down a lamp and falling to the floor. Although Valerie could have pleaded self-defense, she is so stunned that she leaves the scene of the crime, Gordon's apartment above the theater, and returns to her dressing room without being seen. When the stage manager drops by, it seems as if Valerie has never left. Valerie has an alibi. But will she use it? Or will she confess if her conscience gets the better of her if another is accused of Gordon's murder?

The film, which turned a profit, allowed Rosalind to do what she did best: play the bejeweled, impeccably coiffured, and elegantly gowned grande dame, tossing off bon mots like tennis balls, while at the same time yearning to be accepted as a serious actress. Lavinia seemed to have disappeared among the Mannon dead and returned as Valerie Stanton, the toast of Broadway, who, even when off stage, behaves as if she were on. At a cocktail party, she mistakes a publisher for a famous author, heaping praise on him, much to the amusement of Leo Genn, who politely informs her of her error. Rosalind is not even embarrassed until Genn asks what she does. Closing her eyes into slits, she purrs, "Did you say 'what do you do' or 'how do you do?'" And that is the beginning of a beautiful—but short-lived—relationship.

Although Rosalind was the star of the film, Leo Rosten's screenplay prevented her from usurping the spotlight, which she shared with Claire Trevor as her rival and Sydney Greenstreet as a wily police inspector. Trevor was on a roll in 1948: first as an alcoholic in *Key Largo*, winning a Best Supporting Actress Oscar for her performance; then as a self-destructive actress, in *The Velvet Touch*, who commits suicide after being suspected of Dunning's murder because she realizes no one will believe she is innocent. Another source of competition was Sydney Greenstreet, who nearly stole the film with the cat-and-mouse game he played with Valerie. Greenstreet is conflicted; although a seasoned theatergoer and fan of Valerie's, he still suspects her, but is stymied by the lack of a motive.

On opening night in the same theater in which she killed Dunning, Valerie can no longer bear her guilt. Although she is giving a spectacular performance, Valerie invites Greenstreet to her dressing room at intermission; before he arrives, she scrawls a confession on a page from the playbill ("I killed Gordon Dunning. Motive: Fear") and places it in one of the gloves she was wearing that fatal night. As a souvenir, she offers Greenstreet the glove, suggesting he might enjoy the rest of the performance from the wings. After the first triumphant curtain call, Valerie, purged and relieved, nods at Greenstreet, indicating her readiness to go with him. Greenstreet delivers the final line with great compassion: "Bring up the curtain once more for Miss Stanton." Rosalind gets the fade-out: a backward tracking shot as Valerie—gravely beautiful, her eyes glazed with a patina of tears—receives a standing ovation which, one hopes, will not be her last.

On 1 August 1948, two weeks before the *The Velvet Touch* opened at New York's Rivoli Theater, Rosalind appeared on Louella Parsons's radio show. Rosalind gave no indication that *The Velvet Touch* involved a murder, much less that she was the murderer. She knew how unsuccessful her last attempts at serious drama (*Sister Kenny, Mourning Becomes Electra*, and *The Guilt of Janet Ames*) had been. She told Parsons, "I enjoyed making [*The Velvet Touch*], but what made me particularly happy was it gave me a chance to play comedy again." Parsons, who claimed to have seen the film, went along with the ruse: "It's a swell picture and it convinced me more than ever you're one of our greatest comediennes, Roz." Rosalind replied humbly, "Thank you, ma'am."

Despite Rosalind's attempt to conceal the true nature of the film, *The Velvet Touch* was a hit because Rosalind, Sydney Greenstreet, and director John Gage took the title literally, imparting deftness and humanity to what otherwise would have been a clunky melodrama about neurotic theater folk. In fact, *The Velvet Touch* and the underrated *The Saxon Charm*, also a 1948 release, were more successful at re-creating a New York theater ambience than *All about Eve*, which was more of a reflection of Hollywood's image of the "theatah" than of the Broadway stage. *The Velvet Touch* aimed at authenticity; in fact, Dunning's theater, where Valerie enjoyed so many triumphs, was intended to evoke the Belasco on West Forty-fourth Street, where David Belasco had a duplex apartment above the second balcony. Dunning's was similar, but not as large (Belasco's had ten rooms) and without the stained-glass dome and the gothic decor.

Rosalind and Frederick realized they had to option properties for future Independent Artists films. When Rosalind read John Marshall's thirty-nine-page typescript, "You Can't Judge a Lady" (12 October 1948), she thought it could be developed as a vehicle for herself. The main character was a radio celebrity, "Mother Blake," who touts low-calorie Miracle Flour. Although Mother Blake's fans envision her as another "Ma Perkins" type because of her warm, maternal voice, Mother Blake is really the glamorous Jenny Blake. When a New England tea shop owner insists her biscuits made from a secret recipe are superior to anything made with Miracle Flour, Jenny is determined to get the recipe, even if it means disguising herself as her radio alter ego and taking a train to New England. At this point, the complications begin: Jenny is mistaken for a murder suspect who dabbles in disguises after she is seen without her Mother Blake padding.

By 15 March 1949, Rosalind became a pseudonymous screenwriter, using her mother's unmarried name, C. (Clara) A. McKnight. She took over the script, changing the medium from radio to television and making "Mother Blake" the aspiring actress Terry Mason. The plot points were the same: acquiring the recipe and being mistaken for a gangster's moll. Less than a month later, a third draft (5 April 1949) was ready, written by C. A. McKnight and Blake Edwards, who later became a major director but, at the time, had just switched from acting to writing, receiving his first screenplay credits for *Panhandle* (1948) and *Stampede* (1949). Thus Edwards was eager to work on the script with Rosalind. The two of them fashioned a denouement in which the tea shop owner admits she does not follow a recipe, and Terry leaves the business and marries a television announcer.

By 15 April, the script, now in its sixth draft, had become a satire on television commercials that ends with Terry, now married, returning to her old job for the last time to demonstrate a garbage disposal unit. "Lady" was never made; if it had been, the result would have been a minor comedy à la *Tell It to the Judge* and labeled a typical Rosalind Russell movie.

Rosalind eventually got story credit for Universal-International's *The Unguarded Moment* (1958), which starred Esther Williams in a nonswimming role and John Saxon. *Moment* originated as a screenplay by C. A. McKnight and Larry Marcus—then a television writer and later a screenwriter (e.g., *Petulia* [1968] and *The Stunt Man* [1980])—entitled "Teach Me to Love," the first draft of which was ready by 23 January 1951. The plot is similar to *The Accused* (1948), in which Loretta Young played a psychology professor stalked by a student, whom she kills in self-defense when he attempts to rape her. Rosalind's heroine, Lois Conway, is a high school math teacher who has been receiving threatening, unsigned notes. The writer is a disturbed athlete who manages to convince the entire school that Lois is pursuing him. Meanwhile, the student smashes her windshield and breaks into her apartment. Only a colleague, Harry Graham, believes Lois and comes to her assistance. The student is unmasked and later killed by the police, and Lois and Harry discover they have more in common than teaching in the same school.

Rosalind may have envisioned herself, at least in 1951, as Lois. However, *Wonderful Town* intervened, followed by *The Girl Rush* and *Picnic*, both 1955 releases, and it was not until that year that Rosalind returned to the script. By 1 December 1955, C. A. McKnight and Marcus had a temporary contract arrangement with Universal-International for their story that, in the interim, was known as both "The Lie" and "The Hidden Heart." When the film finally reached the screen as *The Unguarded Moment* (1956), Rosalind was credited with the story, on which Marcus and Herb Meadow based their screenplay. In the Marcus-Meadow version, the teacher, played by Esther Williams, actually tries to help the student, who victimizes women because he has become a misogynist like his father. Rosalind's lack of involvement with the script was partly due to rehearsals for *Auntie Mame*, which was scheduled to open in New York on 31 October 1956, just a few days before

The Unguarded Moment went into release. Another reason was that, in the gestation period between the time "Teach Me to Love" became *The Unguarded Moment*, Rosalind had found another project.

She and the Irish-born novelist Leonard Wibberley, best known for *The Mouse That Roared*, collaborated on "Little Mac," which by 7 September 1956 had taken the form of a fable in which Bud Simmons, the head of an American construction company, is proceeding with plans to build an airport somewhere in Ireland despite opposition from the locals, who claim it will uproot the leprechauns. To warn Simmons of the disasters awaiting him, McGillicuddy, the leprechaun "Little Mac," flies to New York, concealing himself in the plane's wing flap. Once in America, Little Mac drops in at the White House, where he convinces the president, a golfing enthusiast like Dwight D. Eisenhower, that he will never lose another golf ball if construction is abandoned. Naturally, the airport never materializes, and the fable ends with the St. Patrick's Day Parade.

The script was an adaptation of Wibberley's novel, *McGillicuddy McGotham* (1956), which may have appealed to Rosalind because, like Wibberley, she was Irish and enjoyed a bit of whimsy. The title page, "book by Rosalind Russell and Leonard Wibberley," indicates that "Little Mac" was conceived as a musical comedy. There are elements in the script that recall the Broadway musical *Finian's Rainbow* (1946) and the film *The Luck of the Irish* (1948), in which leprechauns prove to be wiser than humans. And since the plot was so evocative of *Finian's Rainbow*, Rosalind and Wibberley might have thought that, with the right composer, "Little Mac" would appeal to theatergoers of the mid-1950s, who had not seen a good musical fantasy since *Brigadoon* (1947). Apparently, "Little Mac" never moved beyond the draft stage, at least not with Rosalind; by 22 September 1956, she was in Wilmington, Delaware, for the first preview of *Auntie Mame*.

Although Rosalind continued to write for the rest of her career, she realized in 1948 that writing could not banish the restlessness that dogged her since *Electra* and *The Velvet Touch*, in which she projected such a natural stage presence that one almost wished she had joined the ranks of movie stars who periodically returned to the theater—or at least to summer stock, which, in the 1940s and 1950s, offered the over-forty contingent the chance to play considerably younger characters. Shortly after *The Velvet Touch*, Rosalind felt the urge to return to the theater, and within three years she was back on the boards. Perhaps without her realizing it, *Electra* and *The Velvet Touch* brought her closer to the stage, where, to be frank, she should have worked more often.

Part of the problem was Rosalind's unwillingness to become bicoastal—doing a film when a good part came around; if not, then committing to eight performances a week in a Broadway show to be reviewed by critics far more demanding than their Hollywood counterparts. And even if the reviews were favorable, there was still the question of whether theatergoers would pay more to see Rosalind Russell in person than they would on the screen. Some movie stars took the plunge and tried Broadway. Ingrid Bergman won the critics over in Maxwell Anderson's *Joan of Lorraine* (1945), as did Ruth Hussey in the Pulitzer prize–winning *State of the Union* (1945). Katharine Hepburn did Shaw's *The Millionairess*, first in London, then in New York (1951). Henry Fonda returned to the stage in *Mister Roberts* (1949), and for the rest of his career alternated between Broadway and Hollywood. Claudette Colbert followed suit—cautiously at first, replacing Margaret Sullavan in *Janus* (1956), and then co-starring with Charles Boyer in the highly success-ful *Marriage Go-Round* (1959). Bergman, Hepburn, Fonda, and Colbert—and later Greer Garson, Walter Pidgeon, Olivia de Havilland, Louis Calhern, and Shelley Winters, among others—found that while the stage is not as lucra-tive as the screen, it can revitalize careers that in Hollywood are considered moribund.

By the early 1950s, movie stars, both A and B list, had done theater with varying degrees of success. In August 1948, when *The Velvet Touch* was released, traversing the "straw-hat trail," as the *New York Times* dubbed summer stock, were such familiar names as Joan Caulfield, Marsha Hunt, Brian Aherne (Rosalind's co-star in *Hired Wife, My Sister Eileen*, and *What a Woman!*), Jackie Cooper, Lillian Gish, Janet Blair (her co-star in *Eileen*),

Sylvia Sidney, June Havoc, and Barry Sullivan (in *The Second Man*, the play that brought Rosalind to Hollywood). Until it was her turn, Rosalind brought the aura of theater to the millions who had never seen a star of her magnitude enter from the wings, gliding across the stage and taking command of it as if it were her home. The difference was that Rosalind was doing it on celluloid—and would continue to do so until 1951.

Nineteen fifty was a year of decision for Rosalind and Frederick. Although *The Velvet Touch* was successful, it was Independent Artists' only film. Unless it came up with another, Independent Artists would be a one-film company like Liberty. Although barely seven, Lance was unusually perceptive. That year, he sensed a feeling of uncertainty in both parents. Frederick headed a production company in need of product. Rosalind was stagnating in a profession that had once offered her a wide range of roles, of which only one seemed to resonate with the public: career woman/boss lady. The women she played in her last two films, *Tell It to the Judge* and *A Woman of Distinction*, were practically interchangeable. Only her wardrobe was different. She had not been on a stage since early 1934, except for Noël Coward's *Still Life* (filmed as *Brief Encounter* in 1945), a one-act play from *Tonight at Eight-thirty*, in which she and Herbert Marshall appeared in 1940 at the palatial El Capitan on Hollywood Boulevard (soon to become the Paramount Theater) as part of a benefit for the British Red Cross. Otherwise, radio drama, of which she did a great deal between 1937 and 1950, was the closest she came to performing before a live audience. Although Rosalind had made twelve appearances on *Lux Radio Theatre*, she must have wondered how long the program would last after *Lux Video Theatre* debuted on CBS TV in October 1950. *Lux Radio Theatre* had five more years, but Rosalind could not wait that long. If she were to return to the stage, it must be soon. And if Frederick wanted to reclaim his theatrical heritage, he should follow her lead.

Financially, 1950 was not a good year for the Brissons, as Lance realized when he overheard his parents discussing the purchase of a second car. The Brissons had been accustomed to Cadillacs. But there would be no

Cadillac in 1950. The second car would be a black Pontiac. But at least there was a second car.

Frederick and Rosalind understood they were in a business where reinvention was the only alternative to oblivion. Neither was ready for an oubliette or a gap-filled resume. Rosalind was ready for the theater, where a woman in her early forties could play a woman in her early thirties, or even late twenties, and be given better dialogue than the kind she was saddled with in her last two movies.

As 1950 came to an end, Rosalind was determined more than ever to return to the theater, if for no other reason than to play someone other than a career woman in tailored suits with shoulder pads—a contemporary witch, for example. If Lilli Palmer could play one in *Bell, Book and Candle* on Broadway, why not herself on tour? The question was whether she could do live theater. Despite her long absence from the stage, Rosalind had been doing live theater in a different medium—radio—as early as 1937. That summer, she co-starred as Beatrice with Leslie Howard as Benedick in a one-hour version of Shakespeare's *Much Ado about Nothing* on CBS's *Shakespeare Cycle*. Two years later, her co-star was James Stewart in "First Love" on CBS radio's *Silver Theatre;* "First Love" was a stream-of-consciousness radio play, for which Rosalind and Stewart had been asked to memorize their lines rather than read them. In 1944, Rosalind re-created her memorable Hildy Johnson opposite a new Walter Burns, Walter Pidgeon, in *His Girl Friday* for the CBS series *The Star and the Story.* In 1949, she became one of the four stars in NBC's *Four-Star Playhouse*, which was aired during that summer. The other three were Fred MacMurray, her former co-star from *Take a Letter, Darling* and *Flight for Freedom;* Robert Cummings, with whom she had just finished making *Tell It to the Judge;* and her good friend Loretta Young. Clearly, this was not a randomly chosen quartet. Although Rosalind could usually hold her own with any actor, even a scene-stealer like Cary Grant, nothing prepared her for CBS radio's broadcast of *The Man Who Came to Dinner* on Christmas Day 1949. It was a stellar cast: Dorothy McGuire, Gregory Peck, Gene Kelly, and Rosalind as the flamboyant stage star Lorraine Sheldon. Monty Woolley was not repeating his famous characterization of the acerbic Sheridan Whiteside. The Whiteside on this occasion was Jack Benny, who fumed where Woolley bellowed. One could even imagine Benny delivering his lines, cupping his cheek with his right hand and an "Oh, my!" look on his face. Since Benny had turned *The Man Who Came to Dinner* into the "Jack Benny Show," everyone, including Rosalind, played to the star. After all, it was the equivalent of his own CBS show, *The Jack Benny Program,* with Rosalind, Peck, McGuire, and Kelly as guests.

Rosalind's best known radio work was for Lux Radio Theatre, where she reprised some of her movie roles and occasionally played parts originated by others. Her Lux debut was as Terry Randall in *Stage Door* (20 February 1939). For those who knew the 1936 film, in which Katharine Hepburn appeared as Terry, it was like hearing Hepburn's patrician voice running in counterpoint to Rosalind's. Rosalind *played* Terry; Hepburn *was* Terry, just as Joan Crawford *was* Mildred Pierce in the 1945 film that won the actress her only Oscar. Rosalind was a believable Mildred on radio (6 June 1949), but could not compete with Crawford's tough-as-nails characterization of a woman who rose from selling the pies she baked to founding a restaurant chain.

Although Irene Dunne had played the female lead in *My Favorite Wife* (1940) on the screen opposite Cary Grant, Rosalind was very much at home in the Lux adaptation (9 December 1940). *Wife* was the kind of quasi-screwball comedy at which Rosalind excelled: a comic riff on Tennyson's *Enoch Arden* with a change of gender and a happy ending. Enoch Arden was now Ellen Arden, who disappeared during an archaeological expedition and, after seven years, was declared deceased, only to return to civilization and find that her husband has remarried. Rosalind played the part as if it had always been hers; her co-star, Laurence Olivier in the Grant role, kept up with comic pace and, apart from an occasional "bean" for "been," sounded authentically American.

Except for *Wife*, Rosalind was at her best on Lux Radio Theatre when she re-created her own film roles: *Craig's Wife* (12 May 1941), with Herbert

Marshall as Walter Craig; *My Sister Eileen* (5 July 1943), with Rosalind reunited with Brian Aherne and Janet Blair; *Flight for Freedom* (20 September 1943), with George Brent and Chester Morris in the parts originally played by Fred MacMurray and Herbert Marshall, respectively; *Roughly Speaking* (8 October 1945), again with Jack Carson; *The Velvet Touch* (10 January 1949), with her co-star Sidney Greenstreet; *What a Woman!* (14 March 1949), with Robert Cummings standing in for Brian Aherne; *A Woman of Distinction* (23 October 1950), with Cary Grant in the Ray Milland role.

The year before Lux Radio Theatre left the air, Rosalind played Agatha Reed in *Goodbye, My Fancy* (28 June 1954), opposite Robert Young, who had co-starred with Joan Crawford in the 1951 film. Although a tape of the show is unavailable, one suspects that Rosalind came much closer to the character—a congresswoman invited to deliver the commencement address at the college from which she had been expelled—than Crawford. One could imagine Crawford getting expelled from a women's college, but not getting elected to Congress.

Live radio was not the equivalent of live theater, only a substitute. A closer approximation was live television, where the dialogue had to be memorized. By fall 1951, there were several television programs devoted to live drama, such as *Studio One, Starlight Theatre, Academy Theatre,* and *Robert Montgomery Presents*. The *Schlitz Playhouse of Stars* joined the lineup on 5 October 1951. Frederick was considering a property, *Never Wave at a WAC*, originally called "The Private Wore Skirts," as his next Independent Artists release. With Rosalind on the eve of a seven-city tour in John Van Druten's *Bell, Book and Candle*, starting in Philadelphia on 25 December 1951, he thought a shortened version of *WAC*, done live on *Schlitz Playhouse of Stars*, which then had a one-hour format, would serve two purposes: it would introduce Rosalind to a new medium, on which Helen Hayes, David Niven, Claudette Colbert, Jane Wyatt, Marsha Hunt, and Zachary Scott, among others, had already appeared. It would also enable him to test the audience's reaction to a potential film about a Washington hostess who enlists in the WACs for reasons having nothing to do with patriotism. *Never Wave at a WAC* was telecast at 9:00 PM on Friday, 19 October 1951. After carefully studying a kinescope of the live performance, Frederick believed *WAC* had the makings of a hit movie and commissioned Frederick Kohner and Fred Brady to write the script; later, Ken Englund joined the team, with all three sharing screenplay credit.

Rosalind had barely returned from the *Bell, Book and Candle* tour at the end of March 1952 when *WAC* went into production, and Rosalind was back playing another moon goddess/snob/madcap, knocked off her pedestal by a man who knows what is best for her—namely, himself. Rosalind is now a senator's daughter—irresponsible and self-absorbed—who joins the WACS so she can be stationed in Paris with her fiancé. Her father cooperates because he feels the experience will humanize her; however, he never informs his daughter that he will not use his contacts to get her preferential treatment. Rosalind, who arrives for basic training with a car full of luggage and a makeup kit, quickly learns the truth but decides to stick it out.

WAC was another comedy of remarriage. Rosalind's ex-husband (Paul Douglas), a chemist, is given permission to use some WACs, including Rosalind, for experiments in determining the effect of the elements on specially treated clothing. It is humiliation time again for Rosalind, who, trouper that she is, groans and grimaces, but comes through beautifully. She even succeeds in finishing basic training, after which she decides to leave the service, despite having formed some close friendships. But no senator's daughter leaves the WACs—at least not in a movie—while the Korean War (also known as Police Action) is on. Rosalind's love of country is revived, along with her affection for her ex, who is off to Korea. If the only way she can join him is by becoming an officer, then it's officer's candidate school for her. That the Korean War would be over by the time she got there is irrelevant. What mattered was the reconciliation of two people who should never have married in the first place, much less remarry after they divorced. Rosalind had strange bedfellows before (for example, Paul Lukas and Don Ameche), but no one stranger than Paul Douglas, a fine character actor who could be bearish, blustery, and touchingly sincere when courting a woman, as he was in

A Letter to Three Wives (1949). In that film, his diamond-in-the-rough persona worked because he was pursuing a woman (Linda Darnell) from the same class as himself, except that he was a millionaire and she was from the wrong side of the tracks. Rosalind Russell, however, was not Linda Darnell, and Paul Douglas was not in the Cary Grant–Robert Montgomery–Brian Aherne mold. How someone like Douglas could ever have met, much less married, a socialite requires not just a suspension of disbelief but a leap of faith, which the writers must have anticipated, since the divorce has occurred before the film begins, thus sparing the audience the sight of a marriage made in the writers' collective imagination.

If anyone hoped for a sequel with Rosalind gadding about the Far East, she and Frederick had other plans. *WAC* marked the end of Independent Artists, although Rosalind, who seemed to pick up an award wherever she went, received a citation for making a film that aided the Women's Army Corps in its recruiting efforts. Whatever success the film had was largely attributable to the timing of its release with Rosalind's opening in *Wonderful Town* at the end of February 1953. Once *WAC* was completed, Rosalind was Broadway bound. So was Frederick, who was about to play a role that he had been coveting for two decades: the producer of a hit Broadway musical.

CHAPTER 7

A Return to the Roots

As the 1950s began, Rosalind wanted desperately to be on Broadway but knew she was not ready. Since she had been away from the theater for sixteen years, there was much she would have to relearn—particularly, the art of reacting not just to a co-star in a conversation or an intimate scene, but to a stage full of actors, if necessary. Unlike a film, in which a group scene would begin with an establishing shot, followed by close-ups, shot–reverse shots, and perhaps a two- or a three-shot, the same scene on stage was continuous, requiring reactions that were sometimes verbal, but often facial or even gestural. Rosalind had been accustomed to a director's calling "Cut!" for a close-up or reaction shot that would be edited seamlessly into the film to maintain continuity. But perhaps the most daunting prospect was mastering the entire text of a two-and-one-half-hour play performed eight times a week, as opposed to memorizing several pages of a script at a time over a couple of months.

Knowing she had to reactivate her stage technique before trying Broadway, Rosalind embarked upon a seven-city tour of John Van Druten's *Bell, Book and Candle*, a hit of the 1950–51 Broadway season that starred Rex

Harrison as a publisher and his wife at the time, Lilli Palmer, as a witch who falls in love with him. This was not the typical single-set drawing-room comedy with a soigné leading lady and her co-star, in tailored suits and perfectly knotted ties, sprinkling charm like fairy dust and seducing the audience into believing that they, too, could reach the same level of sophistication if they dressed well and drank martinis.

Frederick was determined to generate as much publicity as he could from the tour. He hired Shirley Herz as Rosalind's publicist, thus launching her fifty-year career as a theatrical press agent. As recently as 2004, Herz recalled her experience with Rosalind on the *Bell, Book and Candle* tour and told her interviewer, "I learned more from [Rosalind] than anyone I've worked for since." What Herz learned was to feed *Variety* and *The Hollywood Reporter* information about advance sales, weekly grosses, reviews, and audience response.

The tour began in Philadelphia on Christmas Day 1951 for a three-week run. The date may have been intentional, since the play begins on Christmas Eve. After Philadelphia, there were one-week engagements in Pittsburgh and Cleveland, followed by three days each in Dayton and Columbus, a week in St. Louis, and four weeks in Chicago, where the company had to face one of the toughest drama critics in America, Claudia Cassidy. When *Bell, Book and Candle* arrived at Chicago's Great Northern Theatre on 25 February 1952, the production, which Van Druten himself had directed, was ready for Cassidy's scrutiny. Surprisingly, Cassidy implied in her *Chicago Tribune* review (26 February 1952) that she preferred the touring version to the original, in which Harrison and Palmer "were rather like the Lunts of older days on a sofa." Although Cassidy was the kind of critic who concentrated on the overall production rather than individual performances, she had nothing but praise for the five-person cast. Rosalind was "quite a girl, amused and amusing, striking to look at, and altogether beautiful when the lighting [did] her justice." Her co-star, Dennis Price in the Rex Harrison role of Shep, was "expert at his trade." The entire company was "carefully chosen . . . [and] adroitly directed." None of the cast could have wished for a better blurb: "I see a better play than I remembered."

There was little in Rosalind's film career to prepare her for Gillian Holroyd. For one thing, Gillian is on stage when the curtain goes up; not only does she deliver the opening lines, but she delivers them to a cat, speaking to it as if it were her confidant: "Oh, Pye—Pye—Pye—Pyewacket—what's the matter with me? Why do I feel this way? It's all such a *rut*." Actually, the cat is a sort of confidant: Gillian is a witch, and Pyewacket is her familiar.

Animals, no matter how well trained, have always posed problems for stage actors; they have been known to relieve themselves in full view of the audience, upstaging the cast and getting laughs for doing what comes naturally. Although Pyewacket was the equivalent of a character, there was no guarantee that the cat would cooperate whenever Gillian had to cast a spell, or when Shep had to be scratched on cue. As if Pyewacket were not enough, there was a paper-burning ritual requiring a match that can't ignite, indicating that Gillian's powers are waning. On a movie set, if Pyewacket leapt off Gillian's lap before she could enchant Shep, or the match caught fire by mistake, the director could call, "Cut!" But not in the theater.

Rosalind could have picked a play that did not involve talking to a cat or striking nonflammable matches, but she would not have found one that gave her the chance to play a woman who mastered the dark arts at the expense of her humanity, which she now wants to reclaim. Rosalind may not have dabbled in witchcraft, depicted as a parlor game in the play; but, like Gillian, she, too, was in a rut. Gillian found herself at the crossroads of witchcraft and womanhood, enjoying the power to enchant but yearning to experience basic human emotions—the kind that bring on tears, which witches are unable to shed.

Rosalind understood Gillian. Although Rosalind had no problem crying on cue, and did so in a number of films, she had also arrived at her own crossroads, where her desire for more challenging roles clashed with the ones she was offered, which were so similar it hardly mattered whether she was an advertising executive, a psychiatrist, a judge, or a dean.

Gillian was a challenge. As she grows to love Shep, she becomes less of a witch and more of a woman. The end of act 3, scene 1, is a challenge for any actress. When Gillian tells her aunt, also a witch, that she is in love with Shep, the aunt innocently asks, "What is love like?" Gillian does not answer but weeps uncontrollably. The aunt is both awed and moved: "Oh, darling. Tears. Real tears." This is not a case of "tears, idle tears." Gillian's are tears of emotional release. Although she is still drawn to sorcery, a field in which she has few rivals, she has progressed too far in her humanization to return to her former life. Gillian is torn between a secure past and an uncertain present; she laments the loss of her powers, while realizing, at the same time, that love is not dependent on spells, incantations, and familiars. Van Druten is suggesting that love is the ultimate form of disenchantment, in which enchanter and enchanted divest themselves of their roles, becoming just woman and man about to embark on the magical journey of mutual discovery.

The satisfaction that Rosalind must have experienced from playing the most complex role she had in any comedy since *His Girl Friday* dissipated when the tour ended in late March 1952; by early April she was on location in Fort Lee, Virginia, for *Never Wave at a WAC*.

Meanwhile, in New York, a musical version of *My Sister Eileen* was in the final planning stages, which began several years earlier when producer Robert Fryer purchased the rights to the 1940 stage play and hired the original authors, Joseph Fields and Jerome Chodorov, to write the book. In 1952 Fryer was a relative newcomer to producing. The year before, the musical version of *A Tree Grows in Brooklyn* opened on Broadway with Shirley Booth as Aunt Cissy for a disappointing run of 267 performances. It was a George Abbott production in every sense; in addition to coauthoring the book, the legendary "Mr. Abbott," as he was usually addressed, directed as well. According to the playbill and the liner notes for the original cast recording, Mr. Abbott also produced the musical, but not alone: "George Abbott *with* (italics mine) Robert Fryer Presents Shirley Booth and Johnny Johnston in *A Tree Grows in Brooklyn*." But there would be no "with" in the playbill for the as yet untitled musical that became *Wonderful Town*. That playbill read: "Robert Fryer presents Rosalind Russell in the Musical Comedy *Wonderful Town*."

Since *Wonderful Town* was Fryer's first solo production—followed by a string of others that included *The Desk Set* (1955), again with Shirley Booth, and Rosalind's second and last Broadway show, *Auntie Mame* (1956)—every effort was made to ensure a hit. Mr. Abbott, who had few peers when it came to staging musicals, would direct. There was never any question about the Fields-Chodorov book. There was, however, a question about the star.

Although Fryer, Mr. Abbott, and the writers wanted Rosalind to re-create her film role, there were two matters that had to be resolved; first, a score had to be commissioned that a non-singer like Rosalind could handle; second, and more problematic, was whether Rosalind was willing to undertake a Broadway musical when she had never even appeared in a movie musical. Comedy, yes. Drama, yes. But musical comedy? Although Rosalind frequently broke into song at parties, the guests were not paying the then record price of $7.20 for an orchestra seat.

Bell, Book and Candle had been a revelation to Rosalind in terms of the critical accolades, audience reaction, and box office grosses, which amounted to $600,000 at the end of the tour. Although Fryer was impressed by the figures, which proved Rosalind was a bankable stage actress, he also knew she was a film star with other commitments. If he were to acquire her services, it would have to be soon.

At first Rosalind was noncommittal. She had not been on Broadway since 1931 in *Company's Coming!* which Brooks Atkinson reviewed without mentioning her name, noting only that her character was tiresome. On the other hand, *My Sister Eileen* was especially meaningful to Rosalind because it brought her her first Oscar nomination. If *Eileen* were to become a musical, the book had to reach an even higher level of sophistication than the play, much less the movie, which sanitized the original.

If critics hailed *Wonderful Town* as the best musical since *Guys and Dolls*, it was because of the book, the music, and the lyrics. That would not have been the case if the original team of composer Leroy Anderson and lyricist Arnold B. Horwitt had been retained. Horwitt was a Broadway veteran who wrote the book for the classic revue *Pins and Needles* (1937); the lyrics for the musical *Are You with It?* (1945), which had a modest run of 267 performances; and both book and lyrics for another revue, *Make Mine Manhattan* (1948), which ran almost a year. Horwitt also contributed sketches to two revues: one a hit, *Call Me Mister* (1946) with Betty Garrett, and the other a failure, *Two's Company* (1952) with Bette Davis, which was supposed to capitalize on her movie star image, except that the actress was ill suited to the musical stage. Horwitt, however, had no trouble writing material for Beatrice Lillie in another long-running revue, *Inside U.S.A.* (1948), which co-starred the Tin Man from *The Wizard of Oz* (1939), Jack Haley.

Writing Broadway-style lyrics was second nature to Horwitt. Writing them for the composer of *Fiddle-Faddle* and *The Syncopated Clock* was another matter. Although classically trained, Leroy Anderson was essentially a composer of popular music. One reason Fryer had originally commissioned Anderson to write the score was precisely his popularity, which was evident after his Decca recording of *Blue Tango* remained on the charts throughout 1952, sold a million copies, and became a gold record.

But composing popular music is not the same as composing for Broadway. There is a huge difference between the Great American Song Book, in which show music is heavily represented, and American popular song, in which it is far less prominent. Although many songs from Broadway shows became hit singles during the American musical's golden age, the recording artists were rarely from the original cast. When Jo Stafford, an artist in her own right, recorded "Use Your Imagination" from Cole Porter's *Out of This World* (1951), it was transposed to accommodate her voice, which was not a clarion soprano's like Priscilla Gillette's in the original. On stage, Gillette sang the number as if it were an aria; Stafford, as a warm exhortation to enter a world where "every day will be a dream."

Stage songs for mass audiences require interpretations less theatrical, even less expressive, than a stage performer's. Often, the songs are reorchestrated, the classic example being Bobby Darin's "Mack the Knife," where the beat, delivery, and lyrics are radically different from the "Ballad of Mack the Knife" that opens Brecht and Weill's *Three Penny Opera*. The composer of the musical version of *Eileen* had to understand the difference between writing music for Broadway and writing for the charts. If some of the songs scored with the public, all the better. But Broadway came first.

When Rosalind, Fryer, and Abbott heard Anderson's score, they knew they had to look elsewhere. Anderson was a musical populist, not a Broadway composer. He had, however, not given up on Broadway. A few years later, Anderson composed the score for a musical that at least was produced: *Goldilocks* (1958), with Elaine Stritch and Don Ameche, and a book by Walter and Jean Kerr. The show's failure cured Anderson of his urge to compose for Broadway.

Horwitt did not even have to wait until 1958. In 1955, *Plain and Fancy* opened to moderately favorable reviews; Albert Hague was the composer; and Horwitt, the lyricist. Morton Da Costa, who a year later directed Rosalind in *Auntie Mame*, staged the production, which featured the relatively unknown Barbara Cook. Horwitt's lyrics complemented both the book and the score, neither of which was the last word in sophistication. But then a show about Amish life, with a barn-raising first-act finale, did not require any. If *Plain and Fancy* is remembered at all, it is for "Young and Foolish," originally sung by David Daniels and reprised in a duet with Daniels and Gloria Marlowe. However, it was Frank Sinatra's and Dean Martin's recordings that popularized the song and gave it an afterlife. Horwitt's lyrics suited *Plain and Fancy*. Whether they would have suited the kind of musical that Abbott and Fryer envisioned for Rosalind is doubtful.

Rosalind may have felt relieved by the departure of Anderson and Horwitt, perhaps even hoping that it spelled the end of her Broadway musical debut. But George Abbott had no intention of giving up. He immediately phoned Betty Comden, who, with Adolph Green, had written the book and lyrics for Leonard Bernstein's first Broadway show, *On the Town* (1944), which enjoyed a run of 436 performances; five years later, *On the Town* (1949) became an MGM musical with Gene Kelly, Frank Sinatra, and Jules Munshin as three sailors on a twenty-four-hour pass and Betty Garrett, Ann Miller, and Vera-Ellen as the women they encounter on their day in New York. On the stage, *On the Town* opened as the sailors envisioned their day in the big city: "New York, New York's / a helluva town / the Bronx is up / and the Battery's / down." Since the Production Code forbade "hell," "helluva town" became "wonderful town" in the film. "Hellava Town" would have been too vulgar, if not off-putting, for *Eileen*, the musical; but "Wonderful Town" caught the spirit of the original play, which was an affectionate tribute to a bygone New York.

And *"Wonderful Town"* is what the title became. But first Abbott asked Comden to cajole Leonard Bernstein into writing the score, which had to be completed in three weeks, along with the lyrics, to keep Rosalind from defecting to Hollywood. Bernstein had just returned from Mexico when Comden contacted him. When she and Green were deep in discussion with Bernstein at his apartment, the phone rang. It was Abbott. "Have you made up your mind yet?" he asked impatiently.

They had. Miraculously, they finished in three weeks. But Rosalind was ambivalent. It was fall 1952. *Wonderful Town* was scheduled for a late February 1953 opening at the Winter Garden, preceded by tryouts in New Haven and Boston. Rosalind had about three months to prepare for the greatest challenge of her career.

It was one of the few times that Rosalind panicked. She phoned Frederick, who essentially told her to make up her own mind. Rosalind did. "I am not going to do the musical," she informed Fields and Fryer. Disconsolate, she started walking back to her hotel, only to realize that Fields and Fryer were accompanying her. Rosalind was so conflicted that afternoon that she had to pause for a few tears—Gillian's kind, that arise from complex emotions ranging from trepidation to self-punishment for disappointing Bernstein, Abbott, Comden, and Green because of her fear of failure. When the trio arrived at her hotel suite, Rosalind's maid Hazel reminded her of a dinner party. Even while Hazel was styling Rosalind's hair, the men continued to offer alternatives to a long run, such as a three-month engagement, which, if successful, could be extended with another star. Rosalind knew Fryer could never recoup his investment in three months. Eager to dress for the party and impressed by the men's low-key powers of persuasion, she consented.

Although Rosalind swore she was petrified of doing a musical, Comden insists Rosalind was naturally musical and could sing better than she claimed. Bernstein realized she had a limited range with four good notes that he used brilliantly in Ruth's duet with Eileen, in which the sisters lament leaving Ohio: "Why, oh why, oh why-oh / Why did I ever leave Ohio?" The number was deceptively simple; although it seemed that Eileen (Edith, later Edie, Adams) and Rosalind were performing a duet, Rosalind was actually harmonizing with Adams. At first, it was not easy; Adams, who attended Juilliard and studied voice with former Metropolitan opera soprano Helen Jepson, had to hum it for Rosalind, who, in return, taught Adams how to apply stage makeup.

The middle section of "Ohio" was much easier for Rosalind since it required what Comden correctly called "speech song," in which the lyrics had to be musically inflected rather than sung full voice: "Now, listen, Eileen / Ohio was stifling / We just couldn't wait / To get out of the place." Ruth's solo in act 1, "One Hundred Easy Ways to Lose a Man," was also speech song. All Rosalind had to do was accentuate the lyrics, neither speaking nor singing them, but just giving them a musical cast. The lyrics are not the most feminist ever written, although they reflect Ruth's self-deprecating sense of humor as she recalls all the men she has alienated by correcting their grammar, flaunting her knowledge of automotive mechanics, and predicting the outcome of a baseball game.

In *Banquet*, Rosalind wrote that she requested such a number from Comden and Green; naturally, Bernstein had to be involved, even for a melody that ran under the lyrics, not in tandem with them. Comden recalls the creation of "One Hundred Easy Ways" differently. Rosalind had come down with the flu, and Comden placed a chair outside her room and sang the number that she and Green had just written. They devised a song that made few vocal demands and was essentially a monologue showing how the disillusioned resort to self-criticism to maintain a sense of humor. For the number to work, the audience, especially women, must realize that Ruth is joking about her inability to play the dating game, while at the same time wishing she could—but not by batting her eyelashes or acting helpless.

In the finale, Ruth and Eileen must perform a wittily dissonant duet, the "Wrong Note Rag," which has to be sung slightly off key without sacrificing the melodic line. Bernstein was composing for Broadway, not the avant-garde. Since Rosalind had not studied voice, she had no problem with the music; at least, she didn't have to be on key. The operatically trained Adams looked upon "Wrong Note Rag" as just another song in the show. Just as Abbott enlisted the uncredited help of Jerome Robbins to fine tune *A Tree Grows in Brooklyn*, he asked Robbins to do the same for *Wonderful Town*. What particularly bothered Abbott was the finale, which he felt was too static. After deciding against choreographing "Wrong Note Rag," Robbins instructed Rosalind to respond to the music with her entire body, including hands and feet. This was something Rosalind could manage; after working in Hollywood for almost twenty years, Rosalind knew how to make her body as much of a performing instrument as her voice. Once Robbins saw Rosalind perform the number, which grows into an ensemble piece, he realized what was lacking in the rest of the company: spontaneity. He then told the cast to take their cue from Rosalind, absorbing the rhythm in the same way as she had.

Although Rosalind's vocal resources were limited, her dancing ability was not. Rosalind rarely danced on the screen; yet when she did in *What a Woman!*, *Tell It to the Judge*, and *A Woman of Distinction*, she proved she was no stranger to the dance floor. The dancing in those films was genteel compared to the sequence in *My Sister Eileen*, in which Ruth and Eileen form a conga line to lead the Brazilian cadets out of their basement apartment into the street.

The conga sequence in *Wonderful Town* is better motivated. Ruth strikes a deal with the cadets, offering to teach them the conga if they agree to an interview, unaware that they do not speak English. Musically, "Conga!" the first-act finale, was easy enough for Rosalind, who just had to inflect the lyrics rhythmically. The number is orchestrated in such a way that it begins with Ruth asking the cadets a few simple questions; gradually, the beat intensifies, as Ruth becomes increasingly frustrated by their lack of response. Soon the interview turns into a Dionysian revel, with Rosalind getting tossed around like a duffle bag. At one point, she crawls between the cadets' legs; at another, she ends up perched on their backs, as two of them take her by the legs and turn her around clockwise before returning her to an upright position. By the time Rosalind left the show, she had incurred 1,004 bruises.

The closest approximation of Rosalind's opening night performance is the kinescope of the two-hour (9:00 PM–11:00 PM) live telecast of *Wonderful Town* aired on CBS TV on 30 November 1958. To view that kinescope, now part of the collection of the Museum of Television and Radio in both New York and Beverly Hills, is to see a fifty-year-old woman, looking half her age and dancing as if she had been taking lessons since she was a child. Rosalind's performance is even more impressive when one realizes that between the time she left *Wonderful Town* and the telecast, she had starred in *Auntie Mame,* which she left in January 1958. After a brief vacation, Rosalind arrived at Warner Bros. in April 1958 for the movie version of *Mame,* returning to New York in early November for the television production of *Wonderful Town.*

Rosalind admitted that she could never top the performance she gave on opening night, 25 February 1953. Subsequent performances were never less than professional but never equaled the evening of the premiere. For the telecast, Rosalind had to re-create that evening in a medium that magnifies awkward stage business, strained expressions, and mannered acting. Doing the movie version of *Wonderful Town* would have been simpler. Actually, Columbia, which released *My Sister Eileen* in 1942, was interested, but decided that acquiring the rights to the score was too costly. However, the studio was determined to remake *Eileen* as a musical with the same title, but with an original score by Jule Styne, which was tuneful but undistinguished. The movie's outstanding features were Bob Fosse's choreography and the Broadway-worthy performances by Betty Garrett (who would have been the ideal replacement for Rosalind when she left the show in early 1954, instead of Carol Channing, who took it over) as Ruth, and Janet Leigh as Eileen, who revealed a previously untapped flair for musical comedy that became even more evident in the movie version of *Bye, Bye Birdie* (1963).

Rosalind's co-stars from the original company, George Gaynes and Edith (Edie) Adams, did not appear in the telecast. Gaynes was a former opera singer with a richly expressive baritone, whose Broadway experience was then limited to Gian Carlo Menotti's *The Consul* (1950) and Cole Porter's *Out of This World* (1951), which opened with Gaynes's lusty rendition of one of Porter's most wickedly risqué songs: "I Jupiter, I Rex" ("am positively teeming with sex").

In 2003, Gaynes recalled what a fine colleague Rosalind was:

> She was a lady in the best sense of the word, very straightforward and decent. We never had a squabble, or dispute. At the time WT was cast some of the managing group were keen on another leading man, and I remember a revolving door sort of thing when, having finished early rehearsals, the other guy could come waltzing in for another audition. Roz always supported keeping me—I am a slow worker and it has often dismayed some producers. George Abbott was also on my side. Finally they won out, and so did I after the first tryout in New Haven.

Gaynes did not appear in the telecast, perhaps because his dark baritone was not what television viewers were accustomed to hearing. Instead, Sydney Chaplin, who had played opposite Judy Holliday in *Bells Are Ringing* (1956) and had a more generic but less interesting voice, was cast as Bob Baker. Adams expected to reprise her Eileen and even went for fittings. But when it came time for the final fitting, Adams was told her services were no longer required. It could not have been that she had lost the winsomeness that Eileen needs to be convincing. The previous season, she was a thoroughly believable Daisy Mae in the musical *Li'l Abner*. According to Adams, Rosalind implied that, in the five-year interim, Adams's taste had deteriorated. Unable to explain her reasons for not wanting her, Rosalind gave an example that cut to the quick: "It's something like . . . well, who else could go to Mark Cross and buy an alligator bag in bad taste?"

Adams did not speak to Rosalind until years later, after Rosalind had become arthritic. If Adams is reporting the incident accurately, it was one of the few times Rosalind was deliberately cruel. Perhaps to make amends,

Rosalind asked Frederick to cast Adams in the movie version of *Under the Yum Yum Tree* (1963), which he had produced on Broadway and was doing the same for Columbia Pictures. Adams got the part.

In March 1953, *Wonderful Town* had become Broadway's newest hit; crowds gathered nightly at the Winter Garden's stage door on Seventh Avenue to watch Rosalind exit into a waiting car, waving to the fans who wanted an autograph but were grateful just to get a look at her. Frederick, meanwhile, wanted a hit of his own.

Rosalind understood Frederick's desire to return to his roots, as she had to hers. Who could blame him for being envious of Rosalind's success in *Wonderful Town*, particularly after he saw her mobbed at the stage door every evening? Rosalind knew producing was his goal; as the toast of Broadway, she was now in a position to help him achieve it. The production manager of *Wonderful Town* was Robert E. Griffith, a Broadway veteran who began as an actor in 1929, appearing in such shows as *Brother Rat* (1936) and *Best Foot Forward* (1941), both directed by George Abbott, with whom he enjoyed a long association. When Griffith decided to stop performing, he stage managed Abbott's productions of *Barefoot Boy with Cheek* (1947), *Billion Dollar Baby* (1949), *Call Me Madam* (1950), *A Tree Grows in Brooklyn* (1951), and *Wonderful Town* (1953). Griffith's assistant in *Call Me Madam* and *Wonderful Town* was a young man, then known as Hal Prince, who, early in the run of *Wonderful Town*, also understudied the role of the drug store manager, Frank Lippencott; a few years later he became Harold Prince, one of the foremost producer-directors in the history of the American theater. *Wonderful Town* brought Griffith and Prince in contact with Frederick, who sympathized with their frustration at stage managing a show when they would rather be producing one.

Griffith had been around George Abbott long enough to learn the rudiments of producing a musical. *A Tree Grows in Brooklyn* began with Abbott's acquiring the rights to Betty Smith's best-seller and then bringing Robert Fryer on board; *Wonderful Town*, with Fryer's acquiring the rights to *My Sister Eileen*. Since so many musical hits of the late 1940s and early 1950s were adapted from other sources (for example, *South Pacific*, *Where's Charley?*, *Kiss Me, Kate*, *Gentlemen Prefer Blondes*, and *Guys and Dolls*), Griffith ruled out an original musical for his first production. He discovered a novel, Richard Bissell's *7½ Cents*, about labor-management problems in a pajama factory, that he thought would work as a musical. He approached Abbott, who at first questioned the idea of converting a novel involving a strike into a Broadway show. Yet the more Abbott thought about the project, the more he believed in it, even coming up with a sexier title, *The Pajama Game*. Since Griffith and Prince were part of the *Wonderful Town* company, they approached Rosalind, hoping she would be a backer. Realizing this was the ideal opportunity for Frederick, she informed them that Frederick would raise half of the cost in return for his being part of the production team. The result was a show that ran longer than *Wonderful Town*'s 559 performances, not all of which starred Rosalind, whom Carol Channing had already replaced when *The Pajama Game* opened on 13 May 1954 at the St. James Theatre, where *Oklahoma!'s* premiered a decade earlier. *The Pajama Game* never matched *Oklahoma!*'s 2,248 performances. But for a show that lacked star power, a recognizable composer and lyricist, and a known production team, *The Pajama Game* racked up 1,063 performances and became a hit movie four years later.

The Pajama Game's success came as a surprise to everyone. The three producers—Robert E. Griffith, Frederick, and Harold Prince—ranged in age from forty-six (Griffith) to twenty-six (Prince). In between was Frederick, then forty-one. Except for Frederick, none of them had ever produced a play or a movie. And Frederick's production experience was limited to a few British films, *The Velvet Touch*, and a musical revue in London. George Abbott and Bissell did the adaptation, making certain it would offend neither unionists nor managers. Abbott also shared the direction with Jerome Robbins. As for the 7½-cent raise the workers are demanding, the lyrics make it clear that "seven and a half cents / doesn't mean a hell of a lot" except in terms of hours, days, and months, in which case it means much more—a philosophy with which even anti-unionists would have to agree. The provocative title and the playbill cover—a Peter Arno sketch of a woman wearing only a pajama top pulled down over her shoulders, as five male faces scrutinize her with expressions ranging from gleeful curiosity to disapproval—discouraged deconstructionists from looking for a political subtext.

The Pajama Game's producers were not the only Broadway neophytes; so were the composer and lyricist, Richard Adler and Jerry Ross. In fact, they were so inexperienced that Richard Rodgers decided against investing in the show after hearing the score, which he called mediocre. Rodgers may have been judging the music by other standards—his own, perhaps. The Adler-Ross idiom was not that of Rodgers and Hammerstein; nonetheless, it was pure Broadway, 1950s style. *The Pajama Game* also generated a hit song heard by millions who had never seen the show, in which Sid (John Raitt), the new superintendent at the Sleep-Tite Pajama Factory, sings the ballad "Hey, There," wondering if he has alienated Babe (Janis Paige), the grievance officer to whom he is attracted. Since the song is virtually a soliloquy, with Sid talking to himself, the script calls for him to sing the first part into a Dictaphone as if he were composing a memo to himself. "Hey, There" achieved a life of its own, independently of *The Pajama Game*. A song of great warmth and introspection, "Hey, There" needed no gimmickry to reach the non-theatergoing public; what it needed was a sensitive singer, which it received in Rosemary Clooney, whose recording made the song a standard.

Within a year, Frederick, Griffith, and Prince came up with another winner, *Damn Yankees*, by repeating the same formula: a novel, Douglas Wallop's *The Year the Yankees Lost the Pennant*; book by the author and George Abbott; direction by Abbott, this time without Robbins; a score by Adler and Ross; and choreography by Bob Fosse. The female lead was Fosse's future wife, Gwen Verdon. For a musical with a title that spelled baseball in capital letters, *Damn Yankees* was even riskier than *The Pajama Game*. Baseball may be the great American pastime, but not the basis for the great American musical. Yet *Damn Yankees* ran almost as long as *The Pajama Game*: 1,019 performances. The reason had little to do with baseball, but with a Faustian plot about rejuvenation, treachery, and an attempted seduction in a locker room. At first, the *Damn Yankees* ads showed Verdon in a ball player's uniform, which she never wore in the show; when the baseball motif turned off ticket buyers, the ad and playbill cover featured Verdon in a sexy hands-on-hips pose, wearing the same tights from the locker-room striptease. The advance sale improved enormously.

Although Verdon was billed above the title, hers was not a starring role. Yet after she did her famous locker-room strip near the end of act 1, *Damn Yankees* became her show. Verdon, who caused a sensation two seasons earlier in Cole Porter's *Can-Can*, played Lola, who does the bidding of Mr. Applegate, the Mephistopheles figure, whom Ray Walston played as if the devil were a song-and-dance man. Applegate materializes when Joe Boyd, a middle-aged fan of the Washington Senators, exclaims that he would sell his soul if his home team could wrest the pennant from the New York Yankees. After turning Boyd into the much younger Joe Hardy, Applegate summons Lola to keep Boyd's mind off the wife he left behind. Lola sings to Joe, "Whatever Lola Wants, Lola Gets," as she does a striptease that is alternately comic and sensuous. Purists, whose Faust is Goethe's or Gounod's, had no cause for alarm. *Damn Yankees* was musical comedy, "the two most beautiful words in the English language," as the director in *42nd Street* rhapsodized. Lola helps Joe break the Faustian pact, so there can be a happy ending, with the Senators winning the pennant and Joe reunited with his wife.

In 1957, Frederick, Griffith, and Prince applied their formula of adaptation and direction by George Abbott to a far more literary source: Eugene O'Neill's Pulitzer prize–winning play, *Anna Christie*, renamed *New Girl in Town*, with music and lyrics by newcomer Bob Merrill. Despite a revelatory performance by Gwen Verdon as Anna and a brothel ballet, choreographed by Bob Fosse, that left little to the imagination, *New Girl in Town* failed to generate the same excitement as did *The Pajama Game* and *Damn Yankees*. Still, it ran a year, from 14 May 1957 to 24 May 1958. Although Abbott softened the tone of the original and brightened O'Neill's fogbound world, he was still dealing with subject matter—a former prostitute's regeneration and her lover's acceptance of her past—that would have made a better opera than a Broadway musical.

New Girl in Town was the trio's last production. Griffith and Prince teamed up to produce the revolutionary *West Side Story* (1957); the Pulitzer prize–winning musical *Fiorello* (1959), and the less successful *Tenderloin* (1960), with Maurice Evans showing a surprising flair for musical comedy. Their partnership ended with Griffith's death in 1961. Prince went on to a career of his own, directing such classics as *She Loves Me* (1964); Stephen Sondheim's *Company* (1970), *Follies* (1971), *A Little Night Music* (1973), *Pacific Overtures* (1976), and *Sweeney Todd* (1979); Andrew Lloyd Weber's *Evita* (1979) and *The Phantom of the Opera* (1988); and an extraordinary revival of *Show Boat* (1994), in which Prince subtly brought out the racism implicit in Oscar Hammerstein's adaptation of Edna Ferber's novel by depicting a segregated showboat where African Americans were seated apart from whites.

Frederick did not have the same kind of career as Prince, who is better known as a director than a producer. Of the fifteen plays Frederick produced between 1959 and 1983, seven were hits: *The Pleasure of His Company, The Gazebo, Five Finger Exercise, Under the Yum-Yum Tree, Generation, Coco,* and *Twigs.* Perhaps because of his experience with *New Girl in Town,* he avoided musicals until he decided to produce *Coco* (1969), which had been conceived as a vehicle for Rosalind and instead became one for Katharine Hepburn. Meanwhile, he concentrated on straight plays, two of which ran for more than a year: Samuel Taylor's *The Pleasure of His Company,* the best comedy of manners since the playwright's *Sabrina Fair,* and Peter Shaffer's *Five Finger Exercise,* which proved there was an audience for a British psychological drama about oedipalism and repressed homosexuality. That Broadway became aware of Harold Pinter was due to Frederick's production of *The Caretaker* (1961), which ran for nearly five months. Although *The Caretaker* could not qualify as a hit, it was an opportunity for New Yorkers to sample the work of a future Nobel Prize winner. Another gamble was Tom Stoppard's *Jumpers,* the author's most demanding—and often irritatingly obscure—play. Despite its brief run, *Jumpers,* along with *The Caretaker,* established Frederick as a producer of taste as well as daring.

Once Frederick's producing career had been launched, Rosalind began looking for another stage vehicle for herself. Meanwhile, she was off to Las Vegas and Kansas for two films, one that she would rather forget (and conveniently did in her autobiography) and the other that established her as a character actress and might have brought her an Oscar nomination if she had agreed to be billed as a member of the supporting cast. But as Norma Desmond (Gloria Swanson) observed in *Sunset Boulevard*, "Great stars have great pride."

CHAPTER 8

The Last of Boss Lady

If, for some reason, Robert Griffith and Harold Prince had been able to produce *The Pajama Game* without Frederick, he still would have become a producer—not of a smash Broadway show but of a mediocre movie musical. Frederick realized it would be several years before Rosalind could return to Broadway in a tailor-made vehicle like *Wonderful Town*, especially since she had agreed to appear in Joshua Logan's film version of *Picnic*. Another stage musical was out of the question in 1954, but a movie musical was not. Since Rosalind was not the female lead in *Picnic*, she could fit in another film for a 1955 release. Frederick envisioned a movie that would showcase Rosalind's musical comedy skills for the millions who had not seen *Wonderful Town*. Those who did, however, were struck by the disparity between Rosalind's Broadway musical debut and her first—and only—movie musical, *The Girl Rush* (1955). It need not have been the case. The creative team that Frederick assembled for *The Girl Rush* may not have been of the caliber of Bernstein, Abbott, Fields and Chodorov, and Comden and Green; on the other hand, no one involved in the film was a novice.

On paper, the project looked promising: a musical set in Las Vegas, which, in the early 1950s, was on its way to becoming a tourist mecca known for its casinos and entertainers, such as Mae West, Jimmy Durante, Noël Coward, and Marlene Dietrich, who were among the first to appear there. In August 1953, while *Wonderful Town* was attracting capacity audiences at the Winter Garden, Frederick was planning an Independent Artists production with Rosalind as star and RKO as distributor. By 15 August 1953, Ken Englund, who had worked on the script of *Never Wave at a WAC*, had completed a treatment of *The Girl Rush*, whose main characters were a lawyer and his wife (Rosalind), living in a New York apartment with a Joshua tree on their terrace. One can only conjecture about the significance of the Joshua tree, a species of yucca indigenous to the American Southwest and supposedly given that name by nineteenth-century Mormons, who first saw one when they were trying to convert the Paiute Indians in what is now Las Vegas; the Mormons associated the tree's beckoning appearance with Joshua, who led the Israelites into the promised land. In a nonbiblical way, Las Vegas had become another promised land for mobsters, hoteliers, high rollers, slot-machine players, and performers whose careers were headed in either direction. *The Girl Rush* would have seemed a natural for RKO, then owned by Howard Hughes, which released *The Las Vegas Story* in 1952. Other films with a Vegas setting would follow, but Frederick intended to cash in on the current fascination with America's Xanadu.

As the script evolved, Rosalind's character ended up in Vegas either because she inherited her grandfather's (Leonard Gershe's revised first-draft screenplay, 10 May 1954) or her father's (final screenplay, 17 November 1954) hotel. By the time *The Girl Rush* opened in September 1955, RKO was two years away from closing, Independent Artists had been dissolved, and the film was now a Paramount release. Englund and Gershe were no longer involved in the screenplay, which was credited to Robert Pirosh, who also directed, and Jerome Davis. Davis seemed the right kind of collaborator, having worked on several MGM films, including the Esther Williams musicals, *The Duchess of Idaho* and *Pagan Love Song* (both 1950). Henry and Phoebe

Ephron received story credit for what eventually became the final screenplay, which made no reference to a Joshua tree. For a movie that Rosalind later dismissed as "ghastly," declining even to mention it in *Banquet*, *The Girl Rush* involved a number of talented people—not A list perhaps, but well credentialed.

Although the Ephrons were primarily known for comedy, they had written the screenplays for a few musicals, including *On the Riviera* (1951) and *There's No Business Like Show Business* (1954). Pirosh was the odd man out. An odder one would have been George Cukor, whom both Rosalind and Frederick wanted. For Rosalind, it would have meant a reunion with the director who gave her one of her most famous roles, Sylvia in *The Women*. Although Cukor later directed a few musicals, such as *A Star Is Born* (1954) and *Les Girls* (1957), he was unimpressed with the script. Unwilling to offend Rosalind, Cukor asked his agent, Bert Allenberg, to "manage a few tears in his voice with a suppressed sob or two" when he conveyed Cukor's regrets.

Pirosh, who had seen action in World War II and won an Oscar for the story and screenplay of MGM's *Battleground* (1949), received his first directing credit for another World War II film, *Go for Broke* (1951), which he also wrote. *The Girl Rush* was his fourth film as director; it was also atypical of his output. Perhaps Frederick thought Pirosh could inject some realism—or at least authenticity—into the film, although whatever authenticity *The Girl Rush* had came from location shooting. As for realism, all that can be said in the film's favor is that it lacked the soundstage look of the typical movie musical. That *The Girl Rush* looked realistic is unimportant; any movie shot on location will "look" realistic. But in terms of plot, *The Girl Rush* was not realistic, although with Pirosh and Davis coauthoring the screenplay from a story by the Ephrons, it should at least have made narrative sense.

It did, at the beginning. Kim Halliday (Rosalind) and her aunt Clara (one wonders about the name, given its significance to Rosalind), played by scene-stealer Marion Lorne, operate the Providence Historical Museum, where Kim answers queries with the ease of a quiz kid, even though she is obviously bored by the routine. Like her father, Kim has the instincts of a gambler, which explains her willingness to "take a chance," the film's theme as well as the title of one of the songs. When Kim learns from her late father's partner, Ether Ferguson (James Gleason), that she has inherited a half interest in a Las Vegas hotel, she and Clara immediately hop on a plane. Pirosh and Davis fashioned the character of Kim to conform to Rosalind's screen persona; Rosalind is boss lady with a takeover mentality, even though she has no idea what she is taking over. Because her father's dilapidated hotel is next to the elegant Flamingo, Kim assumes that her half interest is in the latter and proceeds to order everyone around, including the entertainers. Vic Monte (Fernando Lamas), the Flamingo's owner, brings her down a few pegs, and, as invariably happens in this kind of movie, finds himself more attracted to her than to the much younger Taffy (Gloria De Haven). After Ether gambles away the money that had been set aside for renovating the hotel, a deus ex machina arrives in the person of millionaire Elliot Atterbury (Eddie Albert), so that the renovation can proceed, and the couples pair off.

Of the three potential couples, only Clara and Ether were a sure thing because of Gleason's and Lorne's age. Age, however, was not a factor with the others. If it were, it would have been Vic and Taffy, and Elliot and Kim. Since Lamas, the Argentinian heart throb, had been cast in the male lead, it was inevitable that he would end up with Rosalind. That left Albert and DeHaven, who, in real life at least, had a musical comedy background in common.

More implausible than the denouement was the miscasting. Rosalind and Lamas seemed to be in two different pictures: Rosalind was playing boss lady humbled and turned amorous; and Lamas, the Latin lover who had to romance her because the script required it, although he acted as if he would rather be back on the set of *The Merry Widow* (1952) and *Sangaree* (1953), making love to his co-stars, Lana Turner and Arlene Dahl, respectively, whose notion of sex appeal was more to his taste. Apart from being eight years younger than Rosalind; Lamas was also not in her league. He was just one more in a long list of actors (for example, George Raft, Robert Young,

Don Ameche, Robert Cummings, Ray Milland, and Paul Douglas) for whom Rosalind had to feign affection, hoping the audience would not realize that her character had nothing in common with theirs. Kim and Elliot would have made a more believable couple; they sang "Birmingham" with the kind of ease that suggested they were meant for more than harmonizing. At least Rosalind looked closer in age to Albert, who was one year younger than she. That would have brought Monte and Taffy back together, along with some semblance of verismilitude. Gloria DeHaven, however, was not the star. The leading lady gets the leading man; and the supporting actress gets the supporting actor.

Then there were the dance numbers, only one of which, the mildly risqué "An Occasional Man," performed by DeHaven, had any style. If the credits had not identified the co-producer as Robert Emmett Dolan and the associate producer and choreographer as Robert Alton, one would have thought that Frederick had hired a couple of amateurs. That, however, was far from the truth. Throughout the 1940s, Dolan had been the musical director of a number of Paramount films (e.g., *Holiday Inn* [1942], *Lady in the Dark* [1944], *Going My Way* [1944], *Blue Skies* [1946]) in addition to composing the background music for such Paramount releases as *Sorrowful Jones* (1949), *Let's Dance* (1950), and *My Son John* (1952). Alton had choreographed both Broadway and Hollywood musicals: for Broadway, the original production of Rodgers and Hart's *Pal Joey* (1940) and the acclaimed 1952 revival, *Hazel Flagg* (1953), and Rodgers and Hammerstein's *Me and Juliet* (1953); for Hollywood, the Judy Garland musicals, *The Harvey Girls* (1946); *Easter Parade* and *The Pirate* (both 1948); as well as Paramount's *Annie Get Your Gun* (1950), MGM's *Show Boat* (1951), and Fox's *There's No Business like Show Business* (1954). If *The Girl Rush* ended up as a Paramount release, Dolan's connection with the studio must have played a part, particularly since, in 1955, RKO was moribund.

As talented as Alton was, there was little he could do with Hugh Martin and Ralph Blane's score; only "An Occasional Man" lent itself to Broadway-style choreography. One expected more of the team responsible for *Best Foot Forward* (1941), filmed in 1943, and for most of the songs in one of America's best loved movie musicals, *Meet Me in St. Louis* (1944), which included "The Trolley Song" and "Have Yourself a Merry Little Christmas." As bland as the production numbers were, Alton's choreography at least allowed Rosalind to show those who never saw *Wonderful Town* what an extraordinary dancer she was. The numbers were photographed in long shot, then standard in musicals, so that there was no doubt that Rosalind was doing her own dancing. One only wished she had better music for dancing. The nadir was "Hill Billy Heart," in which she stomped around like Mammy Yokum in *Li'l Abner*.

Frederick had great hopes for *The Girl Rush*: "Frederick Brisson Presents" came on the screen in glittering letters after the Paramount logo, setting the tone for a film that would show audiences Vegas's fabled "Strip," in addition to the interior of its first casino hotel, "Bugsy" Siegel's Flamingo, which opened in 1946. Naturally, no reference was made to Siegel, much less to his reputation as a mobster and member of Meyer Lansky's circle, although Lamas's character could easily have passed for a mafioso.

Frederick also sought out the powerful columnist Hedda Hopper, whom producers and stars cultivated to get a favorable mention in her syndicated column. Rosalind always expressed her gratitude to Hopper on personalized gray note stationery. Two months before Rosalind opened in *Wonderful Town*, Robert Fryer wrote to Hopper, introducing himself as the show's producer and thanking Hopper "for sending [Rosalind] to us," as if she had issued Rosalind a green card to perform on Broadway. Fryer asked Hopper not to publish the letter, stating that its purpose was "to inform you what a wonderful impression one of your stars is making in New York." Ironically, the show had not even opened. Fryer just wanted Hopper's blessing and was taking no chances. Frederick behaved similarly, sending Hopper a special-delivery letter inviting her to Vegas during the filming of *The Girl Rush* and offering her and a guest free transportation and "the very best the Flamingo affords." Hopper begged off, claiming she had to finish her Christmas shopping, although Christmas was more than a month away.

Determined to generate as much publicity for the film as he could, Frederick scheduled the world premiere for Thursday, 18 August 1955, at the State Theatre in Rosalind's hometown of Waterbury. Arriving the day before with Gloria DeHaven, Rosalind spent that Wednesday being feted and visiting with her brothers, James and John, and her mother, who was living at 72 Country Club Road. Clara McKnight Russell, then seventy-nine, was not in good health and would die three years later. After her mother's death, Rosalind knew she would not be returning as regularly to Waterbury as she had in the past and, in 1959, asked her brother James, a Waterbury attorney, to negotiate the sale of the property to St. Margaret's School for Girls for faculty housing. Fifteen years later, the Russell family's last home in Waterbury became St. Margaret's–McTernan School, the name that St. Margaret's acquired after merging with the McTernan School in 1972. With the Russells' Willow Street home now the site of the Snyder Funeral Home, and the Country Club property that of a nondenominational school, the Russell presence is still felt in Waterbury.

The Russell name was even more prominent that Wednesday in 1955 when Rosalind arrived on a special train along with reporters from Hollywood, Chicago, and Baltimore. Little did anyone realize that the next day Connecticut would experience the worst flood in its history. The rain, the after effects of Hurricane Diane, started falling in the early morning, becoming heavier as the day wore on. By evening, it was torrential. Still, the Mattatuck Drum Band and the U.S. Marine Color Guard escorted Rosalind, who was wearing a white satin beaded dress, to the theater, where some ten thousand people with umbrellas lined the streets to get a glimpse of "Waterbury's own." Immediately after the premiere, Rosalind left Waterbury. Since train service between Waterbury and New York had been temporarily suspended, Rosalind rented a car, and Hazel did the driving. After reaching New Haven, they made their way to New York.

The 20 August 1955 headline of the *New York Times*'s front page read, "Floods Batter The Northeast; 73 Killed, Damage In Billions; Four States Declare Emergencies." One of the states was Connecticut. Below the headline was a picture of the Waterbury flood scene, which resembled a shot from a disaster film. Rosalind was fortunate to have left when she did; the bridge over the Naugatuck River collapsed, and power lines fell victim to the flood.

Gloria DeHaven had to wait until train service was resumed to return to New York, but Rosalind was determined to get there well before Sunday, 21 August at 8:00 PM, when she, DeHaven, Eddie Albert, and Marion Lorne were scheduled to appear live on the hour-long *Ed Sullivan Show*, performing scenes from *The Girl Rush*. Unfortunately, no amount of publicity could make the film a hit; it was not so much "ghastly" as ill conceived, but less of a disaster than the flood that coincided with the premiere, although believers in portents might argue otherwise. Rosalind had survived worse—*The Feminine Touch* and *The Guilt of Janet Ames*, for starters.

Rosalind's other 1955 film, on the other hand, gave her enormous satisfaction: the movie version of William Inge's Pulitzer prize–winning play, *Picnic*, in which she played Rosemary Sydney, the same role that won Eileen Heckart a 1953 Theatre World award. Although there is sometimes a hairbreadth difference between a lead and a supporting part, there was no doubt, even in Rosalind's mind, that Rosemary was not the female lead. The stars of the play were Ralph Meeker and Janice Rule; and of the film, William Holden and Kim Novak. Rosemary is a high school teacher, living in a rented room in a small Kansas town. If played too broadly, Rosemary could become tiresome and unsympathetic. Although she refers to herself as an "old maid schoolteacher," as if it were a badge of honor, sex is constantly on her mind. She conceals her frustration behind a façade of self-deprecation and faux puritanism that breaks down at the sight of a shirtless male or a young couple caught up in the erotic rhythms of a dance. After a few drinks, Rosemary becomes raucous, broadcasting—and probably exaggerating—her love life, behaving with an abandon that, for an "old maid schoolteacher," is unseemly. She revels in having started a petition to unsex the statue of a male nude with exposed genitalia, using inoffensive but suggestive language that underscores her obsession with male anatomy. Had she used the vernacular, it would have at least indicated that she was human.

Along with practically everyone in the play, Rosemary is leading a life of quiet desperation until Hal Carter (William Holden), a young drifter, appears seemingly out of nowhere on a Labor Day morning and, within twenty-four hours, alters everyone's life. After drinking too much, Rosemary loses her inhibitions and demands that Hal dance with her. Hal is reluctant, but Rosemary is insistent, grabbing onto his shirt and accidentally ripping it as he pulls away. When Howard (Arthur O'Connell), Rosemary's last chance for marriage, delicately explains to her that Hal would rather dance with the younger Madge (Kim Novak), Rosemary publicly humiliates Hal.

It is an ugly moment and can seem uglier if the audience does not understand that Rosemary cannot conceal the panic she feels at impending spinsterhood, which she hopes will end with a proposal from Howard. And when Howard calls attention to the couple's youth, Rosemary, who has watched her own slip away, unleashes the anger that has been building up from years of living in furnished rooms and waiting for a man to rescue her from a dead-end job. A simple reference to "young people" triggers an attack on Hal, whom Rosemary accuses of being a stud and a fraud, mocking his dreams of self-improvement and predicting that he will "end [his] life in the gutter . . . 'cause the gutter's where you came from and the gutter's where you belong."

Since Logan wanted a screenplay that was scrupulously faithful to the original, Oscar-winning screenwriter Daniel Taradash (*From Here to Eternity*) provided him with one that made no attempt to soften Rosemary's character. Although Rosalind had participated in a murder in *Mourning Becomes Electra* and committed one in *The Velvet Touch*, she had never played so unsympathetic a part. But if Eileen Heckart, who created the role, left such an indelible impression on theatergoers in addition to winning their sympathy, Rosalind would have to work even harder to win over moviegoers, who are more inclined to judge a character by what they see on the screen than by analyzing motivation and background.

Since Rosemary was just a high school teacher, there would be no classy wardrobe. She is first seen in a bathrobe, framed in a window as she slathers cold cream on her face, speaking in a kind of lazy drawl and stretching out the syllables as if she were trying to extend the Labor Day morning indefinitely because the next day marks her return to the hated classroom and another year of spinsterhood. When Rosemary sees the bare-chested Hal for the first time, she registers both disapproval and interest. She sneaks a peek, and when he nods at her, she turns away in a huff. Her ambivalence immediately defines Rosemary as a woman so trapped in her role of maiden lady that she feels guilty about enjoying the sight of a well-built male.

Logan moved Rosemary's attack on Hal from the backyard, where the entire action of the play took place, to the picnic grounds, which could never be shown on the stage. The Labor Day picnic in the film is a glorious piece of Americana that profited from location shooting. Thus Rosemary's outburst is even more jarring in a setting where neighbors renew old friendships amid strains of traditional American folk songs that provide a nostalgic coda as twilight descends and the work week, shortened by one day, beckons.

In the film, Rosemary excoriates Hal so loudly that someone turns a spotlight on her, causing her to shield her face with her arms. Rosalind played the scene as if she had come out of a trance, unaware of what she had done. The question lingering in the audience's mind is how her outburst will affect her relationship with Howard.

The most difficult scene in *Picnic* is the one in which Rosemary begs Howard to marry her. Radical feminists may be appalled, but Rosemary has reached such a state of desperation that she has no other choice. As Rosalind played the scene, Rosemary is at first belligerent, demanding that Howard marry her. As in the play, there is a cryptic reference to what they did after the picnic ("You were awfully nice to me tonight, Rosemary"). Rosemary believes that whatever niceties she provided merit a proposal. Howard is reluctant, countering with arguments that Rosemary will not accept. Finally, in the most poignant moment of both the play and the film, Rosemary pleads with Howard, who insists that she at least say "please." Sinking to her knees, she asks contritely, "*Please* marry me, Howard."

For the scene to work, the audience must be on Rosemary's side. They must understand that she lashed out at Hal because he could have any woman he wanted, while she can only attract a middle-aged bachelor with a fear of commitment. *Picnic* could have ended with Rosemary as an embittered spinster, venting her frustration at her students. It seems to be moving in that direction after Howard refuses to give Rosemary an answer, saying only that he will be back in the morning.

That morning, some of Rosemary's colleagues stop by on their way to school as Howard arrives. Hearing that Howard is waiting for her and assuming the answer is "yes," Rosemary is elated. We never know what he has planned to tell her, since the other teachers, all women, conclude from Rosemary's euphoria that marriage is in the air. If Howard were planning to renege, he is too embarrassed to do so in the presence of the women. This may not literally be a shotgun marriage, but it comes close.

In the main title, Rosalind is not listed in the supporting cast. The first credit reads, "William Holden in *Picnic*"; the next, "Costarring Rosalind Russell as Rosemary, the school teacher." The billing doomed Rosalind's chance of being nominated for best supporting actress of 1955. Because she considered herself a star, a perception that was even more justified after her Tony award–winning performance in *Wonderful Town*, she declined to be nominated in the supporting actress category. It was a mistake. That year, five women were nominated for supporting actress: Betsy Blair in *Marty*, Peggy Lee in *Pete Kelly's Blues*, Marisa Pavan in *The Rose Tattoo*, Natalie Wood in *Rebel without a Cause*, and Jo Van Fleet, who won for *East of Eden*. Interestingly, Arthur O'Connell was nominated for his portrayal of Howard in *Picnic*, but lost to Jack Lemmon in *Mister Roberts*. O'Connell knew where Howard belonged in the cast of characters—and it was not as a co-star.

Rosalind probably would have received a supporting actress nomination if she had agreed to be billed either at the head of the supporting cast or in a special credit at the end ("And Rosalind Russell as Rosemary," for example). And if nominated, she might have won, if for no other reason than for being gracious enough to take on a supporting role in a movie after conquering Broadway and making the cover of *Time* magazine. Her performance did not go unrecognized: The Motion Pictures Exhibitors and Showman's Trade Review honored her with a Laurel Award for *Picnic* without designating the category. To them, she was a star, regardless of the size of the role. But in 1955, Rosalind had more on her mind than an Oscar nomination. Early that year, she discovered a novel that she thought could be turned into a play with herself in the lead. The novel was Patrick Dennis's *Auntie Mame: An Irreverent Escapade*.

CHAPTER 9

Auntie Roz and Mama Rose

In 1973, Frederick told a journalist that Patrick Dennis had sent Rosalind the manuscript of his novel, *Auntie Mame*, accompanied by a note in which he declared, "You are my one and only Auntie Mame."

In *Banquet*, Rosalind first wrote that Dennis had sent her the typescript of his novel; seventy-five pages later, she claimed to have read the novel in galleys. In whatever form Rosalind read *Auntie Mame*, she was first struck by the resemblance between the free-spirited Mame and her sister, Clara, "the Duchess"; then, she suddenly realized that Mame was more like herself than her sister, and, if properly adapted, *Auntie Mame* could become her next Broadway triumph.

This much is clear: Rosalind read the novel in either December 1954 or early January 1955. She was looking for a vehicle over which she could exercise some control, so that her second Broadway venture would not be an anticlimax after *Wonderful Town*. Control was not an issue with *Wonderful Town*, which was far from a maiden voyage. Joseph Fields and Edward Chodorov coauthored the hit play, *My Sister Eileen*; the screen adaptation; and the book for *Wonderful Town*. Since Rosalind had already played Ruth

Sherwood in the film, the character was familiar to her. And with music that lay within her range, and lyrics that could almost be treated as dialogue, Rosalind only had to go on stage and give the audience its money's worth.

Auntie Mame was another matter. Unlike *My Sister Eileen*, which premiered on Broadway in 1940, became a movie in 1942, and a stage musical in 1953, *Auntie Mame* was just a novel that became an instant best-seller after its publication in January 1955. However, the novel underwent even more incarnations than *My Sister Eileen*: a 1956 stage play starring Rosalind, the 1958 film version again starring Rosalind, Jerry Herman's 1966 musical, *Mame*, starring Angela Lansbury, and a 1974 film version of the musical starring Lucille Ball.

Although *Auntie Mame* (1956) proved to be a bigger hit than *Wonderful Town*, it was inferior to it in other respects. Herman's musical, which ran even longer than *Auntie Mame* (1,508 performances versus 639), revealed what was missing in the dramatization by Jerome Lawrence and Robert E. Lee: music. Everything about Lawrence and Lee's *Auntie Mame*, from its cast of thirty to its multi-set production, suggested not so much a straight play as a book for a musical without a score. There is no way of knowing whether Rosalind ever considered doing *Auntie Mame* as a musical in 1955. More likely, she was anxious to be back on Broadway, and a musical would have meant waiting for a composer to deliver a score that she could negotiate. Martin and Blane tried to do as much in *The Girl Rush*, but only succeeded in providing her with numbers that were manageable but mediocre. On the stage, *Auntie Mame* was more of a series of blackout sketches than a fully integrated play. It was almost as if Lawrence and Lee took the novel's subtitle, "An Irreverent Escapade," literally and created a series of escapades for Mame/Rosalind, with a costume change for each.

The play had a promising beginning and an exquisite ending. The problem was the middle. Like the novel, it opens with the arrival of the recently orphaned Patrick Dennis and his late father's housekeeper, Nora Muldoon, at 3 Beekman Place, where Patrick's aunt, Mame Dennis, now his legal guardian, resides. One of Mame's fabled soirées is in progress, the first of many to which Patrick will be exposed, and from which, Mame assumes, he will grow up to be as broad-minded as she is. In the novel, Mame makes her first appearance in the foyer. But if the apartment has a staircase, what better way for Rosalind to make her entrance than by sweeping down the stairs, as she greets her guests, identifying them by name so that the audience becomes familiar with her circle? Mame's first appearance, then, serves a dual purpose: it is the kind of an entrance expected of a star, as well as a way of introducing characters who appear in later scenes. After some confusion, Mame finally figures out who the ten-year-old awestruck boy with Nora is: "But darling, I'm your Auntie Mame." From that point on, the play becomes a series of skit-like scenes, alternately farcical, cartoonish, and occasionally touching, until the coda, which is straight out of the novel and the play's finest moment: Mame, nearly twenty years older, slowly ascends the same staircase with her nephew's young son, Michael, ready to introduce him to a world beyond his imagination, as she had done for his father.

Lawrence and Lee, whose *Inherit the Wind* (1955) was a far better play, tried to maintain the episodic nature of Dennis's novel, which, if one did not know otherwise, seems to have been written in installments. Brooks Atkinson, who began his *Wonderful Town* review with a suggestion that Rosalind run for president, did not retract his endorsement after *Auntie Mame*. In his opening night assessment (1 November 1956) Atkinson muted his disappointment with the play, noting that Lawrence and Lee were fortunate to have Rosalind, since *Auntie Mame* would have been "a major crisis without her."

On the other hand, Jerry Herman's musical, *Mame* (1966), never even approached the crisis stage. Although Lawrence and Lee also wrote the book for *Mame*, it was not appreciably different from their play. The revelation was Herman's score, which moved the plot along, revealing a Mame who was less frivolous, less eccentric, and more human. Mame makes her entrance at the top of the staircase with a bugle, calling her guests to attention and then expounding her philosophy in her first number, "It's Today." In the play, Mame does not deliver her famous "Life is a banquet, and most poor sons of bitches are starving to death" line until the second act. "It's Today," on the other hand, immediately establishes Mame's character; the song is not a hedonist's credo, but Mame's belief that each day is a celebration of, if nothing else, just being alive. That philosophy carries over into the next number, "Open a New Window," in which she describes what she has in store for Patrick—not prescriptively, as Mame did in the play, but pedagogically, with a curriculum that will have him opening doors and windows and traveling highways that he never knew existed. In the musical, Mame takes charge of Patrick's education without sounding like a flighty liberal determined to create a mirror image of herself. "Music hath charm," but it can also deepen a characterization that, without it, would merely be a composite of plot points and dialogue. And Jerry Herman's music filled in the hollows of the book.

In the play, Mame never questions her decision to expose Patrick to only one world, hers. Any other is an anti-world, inhabited by closed-minded bigots. In Herman's musical, Mame is not so certain. Midway in the second act, Mame sings the best-known number in the show, "If He Walked into My Life," in which she wonders whether she has raised Patrick properly. The song is a soliloquy, with Mame posing a series of questions to herself, as she tries to come to grips with the possibility that she may have failed Patrick by turning him into an adult before he had a chance to be a child: "Was there too much of a crowd / All too lush and loud / And not enough of me?" If Mame had been given a similar moment of self-reflection in the play, she would have revealed a maturity that came not from age, but from introspection. But Lawrence and Lee (and, no doubt, Rosalind) had already decided on the characterization: Mame as free thinker whose bohemian lifestyle is the right one and whose liberal philosophy is the only kind worth espousing. Even after Patrick has sampled conventional society, becoming critical of his aunt's circle, Mame retaliates by calling him a snob. Mame can do no wrong, nor can there be any suggestion that her theory of child rearing is not as inclusive as she thinks, since it leaves out anyone with a traditional upbringing.

If Lawrence and Lee had an easier time with *Mame* than they did with the 1956 dramatization, it is because they had done most of the work a decade earlier: selecting what they would use from the novel, developing episodes that were stageable, and dropping those that were not. Mame's encounter with the British refugee children from hell was wisely abandoned, along with several others, including Patrick's affair with "Bubbles," a Newark waitress, and Mame's attempt to prove she is still desirable by flirting with her nephew's college-age friends. And why two fox hunts, when one would suffice? Lawrence and Lee pared Dennis's novel down to a two-and-a-half-hour play flexible enough for Rosalind to add material of her own.

Rosalind had been in enough comedies, classic and otherwise, to know that a bit of stage business or a line of snappy dialogue could add sparkle to an otherwise lackluster scene. She took an unusual interest in Lawrence Roman's comedy, *Under the Yum-Yum Tree* (1960), which Frederick was producing on Broadway with Roger L. Stevens. The premise—Robin, a Berkeley student, proposes that she and her fiancé, Dave, live together platonically to see if they are compatible—must have brought back memories of *This Thing Called Love*, in which Rosalind's character argued for sexual abstinence during the first three months of marriage. Both *Love* and *Yum-Yum Tree* were rife with double entendre, although some critics found *Yum-Yum Tree*'s suggestiveness excessive.

Suggestiveness never mattered to Rosalind, who, years earlier, had mastered the art of double entendre. She knew the term was a misnomer; only one meaning was ever intended—the one she made certain the audience got. In *Auntie Mame*, both play and film, Claude Upson takes Mame into his confidence and whispers the name of the ingredient that makes his daiquiris unique: honey. "I beg your pardon!" Mame replies icily, taking "honey" as an unwelcome display of familiarity. It is only after she realizes that Upson was speaking literally, that her expression changes.

What mattered to Rosalind was the waste of comic potential. When she referred to a scene in *Yum-Yum Tree* as "shit," she immediately sensed that she had offended Roman and apologized. Roman later agreed with Rosalind. The scene—in which Hogan, Robin's voyeuristic landlord, is conversing with Dave in Robin's apartment as he waters her plants—was both needlessly expository and humorless. Rosalind had an idea: the traditional setup-payoff formula. Suppose the plants were artificial. Setup: Dave (to Hogan), "Look, I hate to tell you this, but those plants aren't real." Payoff: Hogan (to Dave), "Doesn't matter, the can was empty." Rosalind's contribution brought one of the biggest laughs in the play. *Under the Yum-Yum Tree,* which ran for 173 performances in New York and enjoyed a long afterlife in summer stock because of its small cast and single set, became a 1964 film with Jack Lemmon as Hogan, grossing $10 million.

As an actress-writer, Rosalind had no qualms about offering suggestions to playwrights, nor did it matter whether or not she was appearing in their play. There is no doubt that she contributed to the *Auntie Mame* dramatization, although her additions were not as numerous as she led others to believe. Lance Brisson recalls his mother working away at her desk, changing and inserting lines, some of which would be used, and others discarded. In *Banquet,* Rosalind alluded to a few of her contributions—stage business, mostly—which were then incorporated into the script. Rosalind's brother-in-law, Clara's husband, Chet La Roche, once told Rosalind about the way martinis were made at the Yale Club. The standard martini consists of two ounces of gin and one and one-half ounces of dry vermouth. At the Yale Club, the vermouth was only used to rinse the glass, into which straight gin was then poured from an ice-filled cocktail shaker. Early in the first act, Mr. Babcock, the trustee appointed to oversee Patrick's education, pays Mame a visit. While Mame is upstairs, frantically trying to affect a matronly appearance, Patrick offers Babcock a martini, which he proceeds to make in exactly the same way. A ten-year-old offering a cocktail to a middle-aged man guarantees at least mild laughter. But when the cocktail is prepared unconventionally, and the man is a conservative banker staring in astonishment at the young but experienced bartender, the laughter intensifies. However, the martini bit is merely the setup for another down-the-staircase entrance from Mame in a tailored brown suit and ready to deliver the pay-off: She proceeds to chide Babcock for drinking during business hours but promises not to tell anyone.

There is another, more significant addition that Rosalind does not mention in *Banquet* but may well have been her own. In the novel, Mame's husband, Beauregard Jackson Pickett Burnside, affectionately known as "Beau," dies after being kicked in the head by a horse. Since the novel has declared itself to be "irreverent," Beau's death seems like the punch line of a cruel joke. But then, nothing is sacred in the novel except race; everything else, including pregnancy, is treated so lightly, and at times flippantly, that Beau's death seems no less bizarre than the experimental school where Patrick and the other children romp around in the nude playing "fish families," or the fox hunt in which Mame, unable to ride because of a sprained ankle, participates by car, injuring horses and running over the fox.

Beau must also die in the stage version, so Mame can play the merry widow, but not one whose husband perished from a lethal kick in the head by a horse. Apart from being more ludicrous than comic, the incident would have to be recounted, causing either a guffaw or shocked silence, depending on the audience. In *Roughly Speaking*, Louise Randall Pierson warmly recalls her mountain-climbing grandfather, who fell to his death from Mont Blanc but at least died doing what he loved best. Whether Rosalind's memory of the film prompted the change, which she then suggested to Lawrence and Lee, is unknown. Regardless, in the play Beau dies taking a picture from atop an alp. There is no other way that the scene can be played, except for laughs. But better a fall from a mountaintop than a kick in the head by a horse. And yet the audience knows something is bound to happen after Mame warns Beau not to climb any higher. Determined to take a picture, Beau starts yodeling; then the yodel becomes an echo as he falls—not to his death, because "death" implies tragedy, but into the abyss of discarded characters.

A few more scenes were added in the film version to prepare the audience for Beau's exit. Beau is obsessed with taking pictures. Before the fox hunt, he insists on photographing Mame. On their honeymoon, Beau and Mame visit Egypt, where Beau climbs onto a rock to take a picture of a pyramid. "No higher, dear," Mame cautions. When they return for Patrick's graduation from St. Boniface, Beau insists on getting a shot of Mame and Patrick from a third-story window. Heights pose no problem for Beau, who is not even afraid of climbing to the top of the Eiffel Tower to get a picture. By the time Mame and Beau are mountain climbing, Beau's departure from the world as well as from the plot is inevitable. In a serious play, Beau's death would have been tragic; but in an amalgam of high and low comedy, the bottom line is, "Anything for a laugh." A dead fox, a dead husband—what's the difference, when neither was taken seriously to begin with? The incongruous—the disparity between what is and what should be—has always been at the heart of comedy. In Billy Wilder's *A Foreign Affair* (1948), an Iowa congresswoman (Jean Arthur) explains to an army captain (John Lund) how uneventful life is in her home town, where the last time anything unusual happened was when a boy took a blow torch to his grandmother. Out of context, the line is shocking; in context, it is not. The audience laughs, not at the act but at the disparity between the act and the circumstances under which it is recounted—as someone's idea of a major event, told in a matter-of-fact voice.

Despite Rosalind's additions and suggestions, the *Auntie Mame* dramatization was primarily the work of Lawrence and Lee, even though at the time of the premiere rumors were circulating that Rosalind not only had written the script but also had purchased the rights to the novel, rumors that Richard Tyler Jordan has discounted. In his definitive study of *Auntie Mame*'s various transformations, Jordan makes it clear that the producer, Robert Fryer, bought the rights and Rosalind bought shares, like any backer. Financially, she did extraordinarily well. It might not have been the case if the script had been more drawing-room comedy than crowd pleaser.

If Rosalind had become so obsessed with the adaptation, it was partly because she did not have a team on the order of Bernstein, Abbott, Comden and Green, and Fields and Chodorov. The *Auntie Mame* quintet were professionals, but not of the same caliber as the creators of *Wonderful Town*. Robert

Fryer, who produced *Wonderful Town*, was again on board, this time with Lawrence Carr, with whom he had produced the Shirley Booth vehicles, *By the Beautiful Sea* (1954) and *The Desk Set* (1955). Although Fryer had a string of hits to his name when he died in 2000 (e.g., Kander and Ebb's *Chicago* [1975]; Neil Simon's *California Suite* [1977], *Chapter Two* [1977], *Brighton Beach Memoirs* [1983], and *Biloxi Blues* [1985]; Stephen Sondheim's *Sweeney Todd* [1979]; and Michael Frayn's *Noises Off* [1983]), in 1956 he had only five shows to his credit, including the disastrous *Shangri-La* (1956). Lawrence and Lee had written the book for *Look Ma, I'm Dancin'* (1948) and one of the finest plays of the mid-1950s, *Inherit the Wind* (1955), which still remains their best work. *Auntie Mame*'s director was Morton DaCosta, who started in the theater as an actor but had just turned to directing with *Plain and Fancy* (1954) and *No Time for Sergeants* (1956); the latter was as episodic as *Auntie Mame*, which DaCosta directed in the same style as *Sergeants*, assuming that theatergoers understood the difference between a play that was a series of loosely connected but fast-moving scenes and a meticulously crafted comedy of manners. If it is true that Rosalind originally wanted Noël Coward to adapt Dennis's novel, *Auntie Mame* might have been a better play. For one thing, the dialogue would have been wittier; and the characterizations, sharper. It is hard to imagine Coward writing a line with a pun like "Hounds! Sons of bitches!"—Mame's reaction on the morning of the fox hunt, when she is expected to "ride with the hounds." Plays on words are not the highest form of humor, even though Shakespeare reveled in them, and the ancients endorsed such figures of speech as antanaclasis (using the same word twice in a sentence but with different meanings) and paronomasia (using words similar in sound but not in sense). She would also have been working with a playwright with considerably more experience in the theater than Lawrence and Lee; as a playwright, composer, director, and actor, Coward would have been loath to take suggestions from Rosalind, nor would such a collaboration have given her the kind of control she was seeking.

Rosalind realized if *Auntie Mame* was to be *her* vehicle, the play would have to be structured quite differently from the novel, in which Patrick was not only the narrator but also a character as central to the story as Mame. The novel-as-reminiscence was scrapped, and Patrick was demoted from co-star to supporting cast. Even the playbill made that evident. The names of the actors playing the young and the older Patrick, Jan Handzlik and Robert Higgins, respectively, were listed in tenth and twelfth place.

The show was all about Mame and little about Patrick, whose primary function was to set the plot in motion with his arrival and appear whenever necessary, which was not all that often. Vera Charles, the flamboyant, Tallulah Bankhead–like actress, had a much larger role in the play (and film) than she did in the novel. With Patrick relegated to the background, Vera moved to the foreground, never usurping the spotlight but becoming the equivalent of Mame's sidekick.

Auntie Mame was a challenge to both the adapters and the production designer, Oliver Smith. In the novel, Mame had three addresses: first, a duplex on Beekman Place; then, a more modest apartment in Murray Hill; and, finally, a house on Washington Square. Lawrence and Lee restricted Mame to Beekman Place so that the play could end where it began. Once the playwrights determined the number of scenes, Smith had an easier time. Lawrence and Lee, however, still had to confront a major problem: Mame herself, who had to be transformed from a name-dropping and often petulant narcissist into a woman whose maternal instincts were strong enough to compensate for her eccentricities. Dennis's Mame was no more an orphan's dream than Patrick was a surrogate son. Patrick may have been docile as a boy; but as he grows older in the novel, he becomes openly critical of his aunt and her self-absorption. Both go through periods where they virtually disown each other. Patrick also knows Mame's vulnerable spot, her age, and thinks nothing of taunting her about it. When Mame insists she is not much older than Patrick, he replies, "Only about twenty or thirty *years*. Just what the hell kind of a trick you think you're playing, Grandma Moses?"

The sparring scenes between Mame and Patrick, in which they behave like Bette Davis and Miriam Hopkins in *Old Acquaintance* (1943), would have defeated the playwrights' purpose, which was to depict Mame as a woman of strong motherly instincts and liberal convictions, determined to raise her nephew in an environment free of the kind of racial and religious prejudice to which he would have been exposed if he had been brought up as his father intended.

Dennis's Mame posed another problem: she could become tiresome. Even Patrick occasionally found her a drag. And if he did, so would the audience, who did not have the luxury of skimming the text. In the play, Mame is blameless, even when she sabotages her nephew's engagement to the vapid Gloria Upson, whose anti-Semitic parents live in a restricted Connecticut community appropriately named Mountebank.

In the novel, Mame and Patrick visit the Upsons' home, "Upson Downs," which indicates their level of wit. Mame can put up with Claude Upson's honey-sweetened daiquiris, but when he launches into a tirade against Jews, she rebuts each of his charges calmly and rationally.

> I have known dozens of Jews in my life and it has also been my sorry experience to have heard quite a few gentiles who have talked about Jews the way you do. I know the adjectives—all of them. Jews, you will tell me, are Mean, Pushy, Avaricious, Possessive, Loud, Vulgar, Garish, Bossy people. But I've yet to meet one, from the poorest pushcart vendor on First Avenue to the richest philanthropist on Fifth Avenue, who would ever hold a candle to you when it comes to having all of those qualities. (216–17)

This is Mame's finest hour, which Lawrence and Lee have omitted; had the speech been included, liberal theatergoers might have applauded, but it would have meant a detour into social consciousness that would only have darkened the mood. On the other hand, those who paid $7.90 for an orchestra seat to see Rosalind in person would not be interested in hearing her stand up to anti-Semites.

Furious, Upson tells Mame to leave, which she gladly does, along with Patrick, spelling the end of his engagement to Gloria, the Aryan. The novel, however, was only the play's point of departure. Once Mame's centrality has been established, with the other characters orbiting around her, no one throws Mame out of the house, particularly someone who uses ethnic slurs that, if delivered on stage, would have cast a pall over the play and diminished its audience appeal.

In the stage version, Upson does not voice his anti-Semitism so blatantly, although he is obviously opposed to having Jews as neighbors. Thus there is no occasion for Mame to berate Upson or be evicted from Upson Downs. Instead, she feels the Upsons should be taught a lesson: She invites them to a party at her apartment, celebrating Patrick's engagement to Gloria.

There is no such party in the novel, which is little more than a string of vignettes. A play, on the other hand, needs a climax, a point at which the action peaks, followed by a denouement; or in the adaptation, by an epilogue-like coda. The playwrights refashioned three episodes from the novel, arranging them sequentially so that they culminate in the party: Beau's death, Mame's memoirs, and her visit to the Upsons. In the novel, Mame's attempt at writing her memoirs is such a fiasco that she has to be given an editor, a third-rate Irish poet, Brian O'Bannion. In the play, Mame's autobiography is a triumph; Lawrence and Lee—and perhaps Rosalind—determined at the outset that Mame does not fail, except at jobs for which she is unsuited, such as selling roller skates at Macy's. In the play, her publisher friend and former suitor, Lindsay Woolsey, believing that writing would be therapeutic for Mame after Beau's death, arranges for a collaborator, O'Bannion, and a secretary, Agnes Gooch, whom Peggy Cass played magnificently in both the play and the movie, dominating the second act and doing the same in the latter part of the film.

After meeting Brian, Mame stops playing the bereaved widow: "Do you think you and I can get anywhere? I mean, with the book?" she asks suggestively. At that point, it is obvious that Beau has become a memory, and a dim one at that. Mame now does for (or to) Agnes what she had done to/for Patrick. Before Mame sends Agnes off to a party she was supposed to attend with O'Bannion, she delivers the play's most famous line (which is not in the novel): "Live! Live! Live! Life is a banquet and most poor sons of bitches (changed to "most poor suckers" in the film) are starving to death." When Agnes returns from the party in a daze, all she can say is that she has "lived," her euphemism for having had sex with O'Bannion, who promptly deserts her. Their one-night stand, however, has left Agnes pregnant.

Agnes's pregnancy was less of a running joke in the novel than it was in the play. In the novel, Mame brings Agnes to the fictitious town of Apathy, Massachusetts, where Patrick is attending St. Boniface, expecting him to run errands for them until Agnes is ready to give birth. The sixth chapter, "Auntie Mame on a Mission of Mercy," might have worked on the screen, but not on the stage. In the novel, Mr. Pugh, an English teacher at St. Boniface, comes upon Patrick and Agnes in the woods while he is searching for a night-blooming plant. The scene is a true "meet cute"; Pugh becomes so attracted to Agnes that he marries her, thus saving her from being an unwed mother.

Instead, Lawrence and Lee ignored the sixth chapter, dropped Pugh, and placed Agnes in Mame's care. With a noticeably pregnant Agnes as part of Mame's household, Peggy Cass raised the laugh quotient in the party sequence by stretching out on the staircase or waddling into the parlor, to the amazement of the Upsons. A pregnant Agnes is not the only surprise Mame has in store for her never-to-be in-laws. Instead of an intimate gathering, Mame has invited her old friends, including her former enemy, Mr. Babcock. Unlike the gulling of Malvolio in *Twelfth Night* or the tormenting of Falstaff in *The Merry Wives of Windsor*, the party is not so much an occasion to "get the guests" as it is to expose the Upsons to Mame's world, which, to some extent, is also Patrick's. Still, Mame cannot resist serving the Upsons pickled rattlesnake and "Flaming Mame" cocktails that have to be ignited. Meanwhile, Mame becomes the center of attention as the galleys of her memoir arrive.

Trying to be sociable, Mrs. Upson inquires about "Mr. Gooch," whom Agnes interprets to mean her father. When Agnes remarks that he is dead, Mrs. Upson's response, "No, I mean your husband," brings Agnes to tears. Then Vera describes a dreadful party she attended where the daiquiris were made with honey. While everyone is gushing over Mame, Gloria Upson tries to take over the conversation by recalling the time she stepped on a ping-pong ball. When no one reacts, Gloria tries again, but in vain. Vera then proposes a toast to the young couple, meaning not Patrick and Gloria, but Patrick and Mame's private secretary, Pegeen Ryan, who is adjusting a mobile while Patrick holds the ladder for her. (In the novel, Pegeen was a high school French teacher whom Patrick met during a summer vacation.) Vera is just being perverse, knowing full well that Patrick is engaged to Gloria. When corrected, Vera replies sardonically, "Pity!" Having had their fill, the Upsons leave in a huff. But since this is "Mame knows best" night, Patrick realizes that his aunt has his interests at heart, which she does because they coincide with her own: giving bigots their comeuppance and saving Patrick from marrying "an Aryan from Darien with braces on her brain." By interconnecting the three episodes, Lawrence and Lee made the party the natural climax. If Beau had not died, there would have been no memoir, no O'Bannion, and no Gooch. There might have been a party, but it could never have been as wickedly amusing if Agnes was not weaving about, looking as if she were about to give birth any moment, and the guests were not reading the galleys, in which Agnes discovers, to her delight, that she has been singled out for "fighting the stigma of the unwed mother."

There is no doubt that Lawrence and Lee came up with a stageworthy adaptation, if not a comic masterpiece. To prevent Mame from becoming a caricature, Rosalind had to soften what otherwise would have been a brittle characterization in order to reveal the woman beneath the haut couture wardrobe. That she succeeded is evident from the myriads who think of Rosalind as "Auntie Mame"—not from the play, but from the 1958 film version.

On 18 January 1958, Rosalind played Mame for the last time on stage, never suspecting that it was also the last time she would be appearing on Broadway. Two days later Greer Garson assumed the role, despite Rosalind's insistence that her final performance should mark the end of the run. Rosalind not only invested in the production, but also invested in the role, which she declared her own. Producers, however, think differently. If a show has proved to be such a hit that it can continue to attract audiences with another performer, no producer would close it simply because the original star had left—unless the star was truly irreplaceable, as was the case when Hugh Jackman left *The Boy From Oz* on 12 September 2004. That the show had been critically panned did not matter; what mattered was that a replacement could not be found to lure audiences to a mediocre musical, as Jackman had been able to do. *Auntie Mame*, however, was not a mediocre play; it was a jerry-built comedy that needed an actress who could invest a larger-than-life character with human feelings on those few occasions when they were allowed to surface—not by programming herself suddenly into a warm and loving mode, but by suggesting that she was always capable of tenderness even when behaving outlandishly.

Rosalind was overruled; as of 18 January 1958, she was only a backer. *Auntie Mame* continued for five more months, first with Garson, and finally with Beatrice Lillie. But in a way, Rosalind was right in claiming ownership of the role; Rosalind Russell will always be Auntie Mame. If *Auntie Mame* is ever revived on Broadway (and there has been no New York revival since the play closed in June 1958), her Mame will be the standard by which any other is judged. But it will be the Mame of the 1958 movie, not the 1956 play. Like Katharine Hepburn's Tracy Lord in *The Philadelphia Story*, Marlon Brando's Stanley Kowalski in *A Streetcar Named Desire*, Julie Harris's Frankie Addams in *The Member of the Wedding*, and Shirley Booth's Lola Delaney in *Come Back, Little Sheba*, Rosalind's Mame Dennis has been preserved on film, giving those who never saw her on the stage the opportunity to experience what it must have been like. Actually, she was better in the movie.

Ordinarily, the movie version of a play or a novel falls short of the original. *Auntie Mame* is an exception. The film, a Warner Bros. release, was the result of a three-picture deal, with Rosalind as star, that Frederick struck with Warner Bros.; Rosalind fulfilled her commitment to the studio by following *Auntie Mame* (1958) with two other adaptations of Broadway hits, *A Majority of One* (1961) and *Gypsy* (1962). Since Rosalind had played Mame from the 22 September 1956 tryout in Wilmington, Delaware, to 18 January 1958 in New York, the characterization had crystallized by the time filming began in April 1958. There are two scenes that are far more poignant on the screen than they were on the stage. The first is the disastrous opening night of Vera's play, in which Mame, in the inconsequential part of Lady Iris, catches her bell-festooned bracelet on Vera's gown and, unable to disengage it, clings to Vera for the duration of the scene and into the curtain call as well, as if she were the co-star. After Vera publicly humiliates her back stage, Mame is desolate; only young Patrick, who came down from the Massachusetts boarding school where Babcock had placed him, is there to comfort her, reminding his aunt that at least she was noticed. Knowing that Lady Iris was supposed to exit with Lord Dudley, Patrick plays the gallant and says, "Lady Iris," offering her his arm. Mame, visibly touched, replies, "Charmed, Lord Dudley." The same lines are repeated at the end of the party as Mame awaits Patrick's reaction. Realizing that Mame has saved him from a family that would have made him an honorary Aryan, Patrick gazes tenderly at his aunt and says, "Lady Iris," as the lights begin to dim. And Mame, deeply moved, replies, "Charmed, Lord Dudley."

The serious moments in the film—Babock removing Patrick from Mame's care, Mame losing her job at Christmastime, and, of course, Patrick appearing after the opening-night fiasco—reveal an actress who is not emoting, as she might on stage, burying her face in her hands if the tears fail to well up on cue. Close-ups did not allow Rosalind to simulate despondency. In the movie, Mame achieved a dimension that she never did on the stage, even for those sitting in the first five rows of the orchestra. There is nothing like a reaction shot in a movie to capture a mood or an emotion; the actor is enclosed not within the set, but within the frame, where there is just a face and perhaps a bit of background. The camera can lie, of course, but when an actor feels an emotion and expresses it truthfully, that emotion is reflected in the face alone. It is different in the theater, where mood lighting, line readings, bearing, and gesture combine to produce the reaction. If any play benefited from the technology of film, it was *Auntie Mame,* in which Mame was allowed to drop her persona, however briefly, to register a human emotion. But once she does, the audience realizes that they are watching not a mannequin, but a woman who can be outrageous and cunning, but always loveable. And the last quality is the most important. If Brooks Atkinson warmed more to Rosalind than he did to *Auntie Mame*, it was that, on stage, Mame was an unfinished woman. As a stage production, *Auntie Mame* was a triumph of style over script and bravura over acting. When it came time for filming, Rosalind had thought out the role so carefully that, although the movie was shot out of sequence, she knew exactly how much she should give to each scene, how far Mame had developed previously, and where she was heading. Mame was more credible on the screen than she was on the stage, where character development consisted of changing costumes and wigs, so that by the end of the play Mame had gone through an entire wardrobe but not much of a trajectory. The unsung heroes of the stage play were Rosalind's dressers.

Rosalind's Mame in the film was more nuanced because she had to build a character, not just change costumes. She used a range of vocal inflections, from attenuated whispers and feminine purrs to baritonal patter and throaty suggestiveness. "Are we all *lit?*" she asks, making "lit" sound suspiciously risqué as she ignites the Upsons' "Flaming Mames." When she pulls off Agnes's clothes to get her ready for her date with O'Bannion, she exclaims, "Agnes, you do have a bust! Where have you been keeping it?" At times she would speak Patrick's name, softening each syllable, so that it took longer to pronounce because she was investing it with such tenderness.

Because Rosalind was pleased with the lyrics Comden and Green had written for *Wonderful Town*, she requested them as the screenwriters, knowing that they had written the scripts for such successful films as *Good News* (1947), *On the Town* (1949), and arguably the greatest of movie musicals, *Singin' in the Rain* (1952). Their *Auntie Mame* script was not that different from Lawrence and Lee's. What Comden and Green did was provide cohesiveness to what otherwise would have been a montage of scenes. DaCosta again directed, ending each scene with a blackout, as he had on the stage, to preserve an air of theatricality. The screen gradually darkens, leaving the actors momentarily spotlighted until the next scene fades in and ends exactly the same way. The blackouts were so much like fades, with which movie-goers were familiar, that only those who saw the play would have made the connection.

Since the Production Code was still in effect, Comden and Green had to excise the profanity and either discard or modify the considerable amount of double entendre. Surprisingly, they retained Mame's line about a sculptor: "Such talented fingers! Oh, what he did with my bust!" Since she now speaks the line to young Patrick, Mame has to explain "bust": "That's a head, you know." In the play, she did not have to explain; the audience knew she did not mean "head." In the play, as in the novel, Mame asks Patrick if his father had ever told him anything about her. Patrick hesitates before answering: "He only said that you were a very peculiar woman and to be left in your hands was a fate he wouldn't wish a dog, but beggars can't be choosers and you're my only living relative." Mame replies pithily, "That bastard." Since the word is unfamiliar to Patrick, Mame writes it out for him, explaining that it is a seven-letter word for his father. In the film, Mame naturally does not speak the *b* word but writes each letter out so carefully that she does not have to, saying only that it is a seven-letter word, beginning with *b*, ending with *d*, and meaning Patrick's late father.

When Mame objects to the amount of time being spent on her mem-oir, O'Bannion remarks, "Flaubert spent thirteen years on *Madame Bovary*." Mame's rejoinder in the play, "How did she stand it?" obviously did not reach the screen, where Rosalind just threw him a look that made it obvious that she took "on" literally. The most problematic aspect of the plot, at least in 1958, was Agnes's seduction by O'Bannion that left her pregnant but unmarried. To circumvent objections by the Legion of Decency and make *Auntie Mame* as much of a family film as the material allowed, Comden and Green took their cue from Preston Sturges's *The Miracle of Morgan's Creek* (1943), in which Betty Hutton faced a similar situation (just as Sturges did with the Legion). Originally, Betty Hutton's character, Trudy Kockenlocker of the telltale name, goes out with some soldiers on leave, becomes inebriated, and later discovers that she is pregnant but unable to recall by whom. Sturges finally had to add a few lines implying that there was a marriage ceremony, which Trudy cannot remember. Hoping that a comic finale will divert the audience's attention from the transparent and implausible explanation, Sturges has Trudy gives birth not to one child but to sextuplets. Likewise, Agnes has a eureka moment in which she remembers a ceremony before a justice of the peace, which mollified the Legion.

Comden and Green knew they could not change the ending, in which the sari-clad Mame returns to the Beekman Place duplex, now occupied by Patrick, Pegeen, and their young son, Michael. Mame persuades Patrick and Pegeen to let her take Michael to India, promising to return before the beginning of the school year. Placing her arm around Michael, Mame leads him up the staircase, enumerating the wonders India has in store for him. As they near the top, golden light floods the stairs, transfiguring them. That sublimely cinematic touch validates Mame's mission, which, in retrospect, seems less idiosyncratic than it was in the play. Although Mame would have balked at the phrase "spiritual development," the enlarging of Patrick's soul—in the humanistic, rather than the religious, sense—was her goal. In the film it is apparent that Patrick is all the better for the way he has been raised, while in the play he seems to have escaped from bohemia into marriage and fatherhood; and Mame, into another adventure, this time in India. The luminous touch at the end provided Mame with a nimbus, as if she had just been canonized; and Auntie Mame is now Saint Mame, patron of multiculturalists.

While the play is a footnote in Broadway history, the movie is a perennial, available on VHS and DVD and frequently aired on cable television. Mame was an aunt for all seasons. She became a gay icon for her convention-flaunting and flamboyance. But she also appealed to the myriads, gay and straight, who longed to thumb their noses at convention but could not risk the consequences. To Mame, living life on one's own terms without harming others was all that mattered. If bigots like the Upsons needed a lesson in tolerance, Mame's apartment was the classroom.

Although Rosalind admitted that she wished she could be like Mame, she was the Catholic equivalent. Unlike Mame, Rosalind did not hobnob with surrealists and progressive educators. Hers was a more international circle, consisting of celebrities such as Aristotle Onassis, Maria Callas, Coco Chanel, and Frank Sinatra, along with five American presidents: Franklin D. Roosevelt, Harry S. Truman, Dwight D. Eisenhower, Lyndon B. Johnson, and Richard M. Nixon.

What *Auntie Mame* allowed Rosalind to reveal—and at the same time revel in—was the *joie de vivre* that was part of her and Mame's credo. However, Rosalind also subscribed to another creed, the one that every Catholic schoolchild had to memorize: the Apostles' Creed, a summary of the main tenets of Catholicism, where the only mention of life is "life everlasting," which follows logically from a belief in the "resurrection of the body." What Rosalind exhibited on the screen was a free spirit who did not subscribe to any religion but was nonetheless an admirable human being. There is no doubt that Mame raised Patrick to be as much like herself as she could, even though it meant exposing him to a lifestyle that most 1950s Catholics would have considered unwholesome. Certainly *Sign* magazine, a publication of the Passionist Fathers, thought that about that play, which it classified as "Completely Objectionable." The film version encountered less opposition because it was less bawdy. However, Rosalind played the role as if Mame's belief that life was meant to be lived to the hilt was an article of faith; it may not have been part of the Apostles' Creed, but it was part of Rosalind's—and Mame's. Long before diversity became a politically correct buzzword, Mame was practicing it under the rubric of tolerance. Even at her wackiest, Mame was so devoted to Patrick that she could hardly be faulted for her unortho-dox approach to his education.

Other actresses played Mame differently on the stage: Greer Garson as a sophisticate, whose swearing was always ladylike; Beatrice Lillie as an inaudible eccentric; Sylvia Sidney as a tough dame in designer clothes and a Beekman Place address. Rosalind understood the contradictions within the character and resolved them, which she could not do on the stage when she was changing costumes and wigs in practically every scene. Although Rosalind's stage Mame resides in the memories of an ever-diminishing number of theatergoers, the film, minus the dialogue cuts required by the Production Code, is the next best thing.

Auntie Mame brought Rosalind her fourth and last Oscar nomination. She won Golden Globe and Laurel awards for her Mame, but that was the extent of it. The competition was not as formidable in 1958 as it was in 1942, when Rosalind was up against Greer Garson, Bette Davis, and Katharine Hepburn. This time it was Deborah Kerr (*Separate Tables*), Shirley MacLaine (*Some Came Running*), Elizabeth Taylor (*Cat on a Hot Tin Roof*), and Susan Hayward (*I Want to Live!*). But on Oscar night, 6 April 1959, when Kim Novak and James Cagney walked onto the stage of the Pantages Theatre to announce the name of the best actress of 1958, the winner was Hayward for her performance as the real-life Barbara Graham, who died in the gas chamber at San Quentin for a crime, the film implies, she may not have committed. If sentiment played a role in the voting, as it often does, Hayward was the favorite, having received five nominations to Rosalind's four: *Smash-Up: The Story of a Woman* (1947), *My Foolish Heart* (1949), *With a Song in My Heart* (1953), *I'll Cry Tomorrow* (1955), and *I Want to Live!* (1958). And just as Rosalind was expected to win for *Electra*, so was Hayward for her realistic portrayal of Lillian Roth in *I'll Cry Tomorrow*. Hayward lost that year to Anna Magnani (*The Rose Tattoo*), just as three years later Rosalind would lose to Hayward. In Hollywood, the scales of justice are regulated by measurement standards known only to Academy members, who, like all voters, cast their ballots for various reasons, ranging from the desire to reward excellence to the determination to right a wrong. If any Academy member felt that Rosalind had been overlooked in the past, there were no further opportunities to make amends. However, there would be Golden Globes for *A Majority of One* (1961) and *Gypsy* (1962), the latter being Oscar material, if any film was.

On 21 May 1959, *Gypsy* opened in New York and redefined the nature of musical theater. In *Gypsy*, book and score were so interconnected that they seemed inseparable. And yet, a close study of Arthur Laurents's book reveals that, despite the greatness of Jule Styne's score and Stephen Sondheim's lyrics, *Gypsy* might have worked as a straight play if Laurents had written dialogue equal to Sondheim's lyrics, which, in turn, were meant to serve Styne's music: in other words, dialogue that would have accomplished through language what Styne and Sondheim did through music and lyrics.

Although Laurents is an accomplished playwright and screenwriter, it is hard to imagine a nonmusical version of *Gypsy* that would have rivaled the original; at the very least, it would have required vaudeville skits and burlesque routines. However, once Laurents's book was given musical life, *Gypsy* became not just another musical but musical theater, which, at the time, consisted of a handful of shows such as *Show Boat, Pal Joey, Oklahoma!, Carousel, South Pacific, Guys and Dolls,* and *The King and I.* In fact, Laurents's book for *Gypsy* surpassed the one he wrote for *West Side Story,* in which characterization derived, to a great extent, from Jerome Robbins's choreography, particularly the way he gave the Sharks and the Jets their own identity through dance, so that the audience understood the psychological makeup of each gang. In *Gypsy,* Robbins's choreography was not so much geared to character as setting, specifically, the vaudeville and burlesque houses mandated by Laurents's book. Thus, unlike *West Side Story, Gypsy* was never perceived as a dance musical; in fact, "choreography" is not even a term associated with *Gypsy,* where the only numbers that had to be choreographed were the vaudeville and burlesque acts and a solo dance routine, which were all intrinsic to the plot.

Laurents adapted *Gypsy* from Gypsy Rose Lee's memoir of the same name about her career as America's most famous ecdysiast (or "stripper," in the vernacular) and the circumstances under which she entered a form of show business where the performers were not exactly known as artists or even artistes. Laurents was faced with a difficult task: Gypsy's story could not be told without including her mother, Rose, and her sister, June. Either Rose or Gypsy had to become the central character—or, in box-office terms, the star. And since *Gypsy* would be a musical, the star would have to come from the musical stage. Despite the title of the memoir, Laurents decided against making Gypsy the main character, since neither her story nor June's could be told apart from their mother's. It was Rose who built a vaudeville act around June, whom she considered the more talented daughter. When June could no longer bear being billed as "Dainty June," even though it was an improvement over "Baby June," she eloped with a dancer. Rose then concentrated on making a star of Louise, who became one by default when the act was booked into a burlesque house, and Louise realized all a stripper needed was a gimmick. And hers was to add a touch of playful mockery to her striptease, with an emphasis on "tease," by removing less than the average ecdysiast but doing it tastefully, as if there were such a thing as the art of disrobing. If anyone popularized that art, it was Gypsy Rose Lee. And if any Broadway star could play Rose Hovick, it was Ethel Merman of the mega-phonic voice and larger-than-life persona, for whom Styne composed a score that was so demanding that Merman ended up missing several performances for the first time in her career. Even so, Merman's Rose answered the ques-tion that critics and audiences never had to pose until she took on a role that required a singing actress: Could Ethel Merman act?

If Merman had acting skills, she never had to draw on them until *Gypsy*. Her best-known musicals—*Anything Goes; Red, Hot, and Blue; Something for the Boys; Annie Get Your Gun; Call Me Madam*—called for her to deliver the lines and belt out the songs without a body mike and amplification. Yes, Merman acted Mama Rose, whose drive coincided with her own. Merman did not have to go the Method route, resorting to emotional memory to con-vey the frustration of a woman who stood by while her daughters achieved the fame that always eluded her. In Merman's case, it was watching Holly-wood stars play the roles that she had created on Broadway: Ann Sothern in *Panama Hattie*, Lucille Ball in *DuBarry Was a Lady*, Betty Hutton in *Annie Get Your Gun*, and her greatest disappointment, Rosalind in *Gypsy*, in the role that was as much hers as Mame was Rosalind's. If Merman regarded *Gypsy* as her personal property, so much so that she toured with it after the Broadway run (something Rosalind did not do with either *Wonderful Town* or *Auntie Mame*), it was because she finally had a role that allowed her to break the mold of the brassy belter in which she had been encased throughout her career. In *Gypsy*, Merman succeeded in reaching the heart of the character as well as the back of the rear mezzanine. Just as Rosalind's Mame set the standard for subsequent interpreters, so did Merman's Rose. There were other Roses—Angela Lansbury, Tyne Daley, and Linda Lavin—but it was not until 2001, when Bernadette Peters took on the part, that one could feel compassion for a woman who lived vicariously through her children and who could only find her moment of glory on a stage in an empty theater, with an audience of one—Gypsy, who finally realizes that she owes her career to her mother.

Once Laurents made *Gypsy* Rose's story, he had to determine the importance of each daughter to the plot. June's life would have constituted a play—or better, a movie—in itself. As June Havoc, she became a successful stage and screen actress as well as an author and playwright. Louise, who achieved greater celebrity as Gypsy Rose Lee, also tried her hand at writing, although she never produced anything as memorable as her sister's memoirs, *Early Havoc* (1959) and *More Havoc* (1980), and her play, *Marathon '33* (1969), for which June drew on her experiences competing in the dance marathons of the 1930s, in which couples danced for prize money, often for days at a time, with fifteen-minute rest periods every hour.

Gypsy was also a writer, although not as highly regarded as June. Gypsy provided the story that became the basis of the Fox musical *Doll Face* (1945), which ended up being more about vaudeville than burlesque. Simon and Schuster published *The G-String Murders* (1941), purportedly by Gypsy Rose Lee, despite rumors that the novel was ghost written by her friend, Craig Rice (pseudonym of Georgiana Ann Randolph). Rice may have helped Gypsy revise the novel, which was made into a film, *Lady of Burlesque* (1943). However, Rice could never have had the firsthand knowledge of burlesque that Gypsy had, leading one to suspect that, except for the editing, the novel was Gypsy's.

June's memoirs were favorably reviewed; as an actress, June Havoc was as much at home on the musical stage (Rodgers and Hart's *Pal Joey* [1940], Cole Porter's *Mexican Hayride* [1944]) as she was in classic theater, where her roles included Jocasta in Jean Cocteau's *The Infernal Machine* and Titania in

Shakespeare's *A Midsummer Night's Dream*. When June was in *Pal Joey*, she must have taken great delight in "Zip," sung by a female journalist who recounts her interview with Gypsy, describing her as an intellectual stripper who thinks about Schopenhauer, Picasso, and Confucius while shedding her clothes. Similarly, in *Gypsy*, Rose accuses her daughter of lapsing into French and reading book reviews instead of books. Although the historical Gypsy Rose Lee could be pretentious, she had no reservations about the way she or her mother were portrayed in the musical. June was more critical. However, June only appears in the first act, in which she has several numbers, including some vaudeville routines and a duet with Louise. While vaudeville dominates the first act, the second, in which Louise Hovick becomes Gypsy Rose Lee, is devoted to burlesque, as one form of entertainment gives way to another.

Like June, Gypsy was self-educated. In the mid-1960s, Gypsy had an afternoon talk show in which she was perfectly comfortable discussing playwrights and novelists. When Ethel Merman was a guest on the show and remarked that her son was stage-managing a production of *Six Characters in Search of an Author*, it was obvious Merman had no idea who the playwright was, or even what the play was about. Gypsy was impressed; she knew the playwright was Luigi Pirandello.

In 1959, when *Gypsy* opened at New York's Broadway Theatre, Rosalind had her first bout with mortality. She discovered a lump in her breast, which led to a mastectomy in 1960, according to Frederick, although Lance insists it was 1961. Frederick knew that she would not be returning to Broadway immediately, if at all. Meanwhile, Rosalind owed Jack Warner two more movies.

Around the same time as Rosalind's first mastectomy, Frederick acquired the sobriquet "the lizard of Roz" because of his determination to find starring roles for Rosalind, preferably in film versions of plays, all of which, except for *Gypsy*, she might have done on the stage. As recently as 2001, a few theatergoers reacted to Elaine Stritch's reference to "the lizard of Roz" in her one-person show, *Elaine Stritch at Liberty*, as if they understood the meaning. On the other hand, they might have been laughing at the word play. No one seems to know who coined the phrase; it suggests Schadenfreude, from which performers are not exempt, despite Irving Berlin's claim to the contrary. "The lizard of Roz" probably originated among the slighted and the spiteful, who felt that Rosalind was playing leads in respectable films with Broadway pedigrees, while Bette Davis and Joan Crawford were appearing in gothic melodramas, Myrna Loy in touring companies, and Barbara Stanwyck in a television series. If Frederick allegedly campaigned for suitable properties for Rosalind, it was not because he wanted producer's credit. Except for *Five Finger Exercise*, which he produced for Columbia Pictures, and her last film, *Mrs. Pollifax—Spy*, which was adapted from a novel, Frederick received no screen credit for Rosalind's other 1961–1972 films. However, he knew that any studio that bought the rights to *A Majority of One, Gypsy, Five Finger Exercise, A Very Rich Woman* (renamed *Rosie!* for the movie), and *Oh, Dad, Poor Dad* would never hire Gertrude Berg, Merman, Jessica Tandy, Ruth Gordon, and Jo van Fleet, respectively, to reprise their stage roles. In the 1960s, even Jessica Tandy's name would have meant little at the box office; Tandy did not re-create any of her Broadway roles on the screen—Blanche in *A Streetcar Named Desire*, the title character in *Hilda Crane*, Agnes in *The Four Poster*. In short, Rosalind was still "bankable"; the others were not.

Lawrence Roman called Frederick a great producer because "he could get things done." If he was a hard bargainer, it was something he learned to do as an agent in the 1930s. The difference was that now he was a producer, acting like an agent with one client: Rosalind. It is not hard to imagine Frederick convincing Jack Warner to make *Gypsy* with Rosalind. Warner was obviously impressed with the success of *Auntie Mame*. Warner also knew that movie audiences never responded to Merman, whose only real success in Hollywood at the time was *Call Me Madam* (1953), in which she had starred on Broadway. Her latest, *There's No Business like Show Business* (1954), was less successful, despite the presence of Dan Dailey, Mitzi Gaynor, Marilyn Monroe, and Donald O'Connor in the cast.

Yet one wonders how much convincing Frederick had to do. Even before *Auntie Mame* opened on Broadway, Jack Warner knew his studio would be making the movie version. Unable to attend the New York premiere, Warner sent Rosalind a basket of chrysanthemums. Thanking him for the "beautiful symbol of [his] good wishes and devotion," Rosalind added, "You are very special to so many." Rosalind liked Jack Warner, even though his biographer dubbed him "the clown prince of Hollywood." But then Rosalind also liked "white fang," Harry Cohn. Warner and Cohn respected Rosalind as much for her talent as for her integrity. Warner even made a point to remember her birthday; and she, to convey the good wishes of his friends abroad after returning from a European trip ("It seems that each and everyone loves you just as much as we do"). Flattery, perhaps, but there was a kernel of sincerity. Frederick may have acted as his wife's unofficial agent; after all, she was responsible for his becoming one of the producers of *The Pajama Game*. But one also suspects Rosalind could have gotten parts on her own—and perhaps better ones than the terrible mothers in *Oh, Dad* and *Five Finger Exercise*. She could probably have even gotten *Gypsy* on her own.

Gypsy was a huge gamble. By agreeing to play Rose, Rosalind was inviting comparison with Merman. There are stage musicals identified with a particular star whose interpretation becomes a touchstone, the standard against which others are measured. Mitzi Gaynor's Nellie Forbush in the movie version of *South Pacific* was a poor relation of Mary Martin's; Barbara Streisand's nasal Dolly Gallagher Levi in *Hello, Dolly* suggested that her inspiration was Mae West, not Carol Channing. Since *Gypsy* required a Rose who could both sing and act, Rosalind may have thought that her acting could carry the film. She knew that Merman, who was never a favorite with moviegoers, was incapable of scaling down her persona, not to mention her voice, to fit the dimensions of the screen. Rosalind also must have been aware of the show's genesis. From the outset, *Gypsy* was conceived as a book musical, in which the musical numbers advanced the plot, so that they could not be rearranged without affecting it.

Anyone who saw Merman as Mama Rose—or at least heard the original cast recording, still a popular CD—could sense the complementarity
between Merman's voice and Styne's music. Of the show's sixteen numbers,
seven—the most demanding—are Rose's. Rose does not so much sing the
first number, "Some People," as tear into it; "Some People" is not a scene-set-
ter, but an expression of Rose's contempt for people who "have the dream,
yeah, but not the guts" to pursue it. Rose has both. En route from Seattle to
Los Angeles, she manages to throw an act together, with June as star. With
June's elopement, Rose turns to the faithful Louise, the "no talent" daughter,
little knowing that Louise will become a headliner—not in vaudeville, which
is moribund, but in burlesque, where the former Louise Hovick metamorphoses into Gypsy Rose Lee.

The first act closes with the triumphant "Everything's Coming up
Roses," in which Rose, determined to make a star out of Louise, envisions a
glorious future for her daughter—a future that Rose has every intention of
sharing. The finale is even more powerful; it is the ultimate eleven o'clock
song, "Rose's Turn," an aria, as Merman herself realized, that strings together
musical motifs and snatches of previously heard lyrics. Rose lashes out at the
world and her daughters, implying that, without her, "Baby June" would
not have evolved into June Havoc, the successful memoirist, playwright,
and stage and screen star; or Louise, into the class-act stripper, Gypsy Rose
Lee. Rose is even convinced that she could have been better than either
of them; and if "Rose's Turn" is performed properly, the audience believes
it, too.

For the first time in her career, Rosalind was competing with a legend. In the other adaptations of stage plays in which she appeared (*Craig's
Wife, Night Must Fall, The Women, My Sister Eileen,* etc.), Rosalind was not
measured by the original stars. Although *A Majority of One* might seem an
exception, it was the presence of Gertrude Berg in the lead that kept
Leonard Spiegelgass's slight comedy-drama running for 577 performances.
Gypsy was something else. Merman was a Broadway icon; Berg, a familiar
name from radio and television, was not.

In *Gypsy*, Rosalind would be following in the footsteps of a star to whom John Gielgud once wrote, "I certainly compare your art to that of Edith Evans in our country." And Gielgud was referring to Merman's acting! There was no question that Rosalind could act the role and, in fact, succeeded so well that she received her fifth Golden Globe award. But the songs were, and always will be, Merman's.

Although *Gypsy* came to the screen virtually intact, producer-director Mervyn LeRoy initially had trouble finding a screenwriter. When Delmer Daves, LeRoy's first choice, bowed out because he thoroughly disliked the subject matter, Leonard Spiegelgass took over. Realizing he could not improve upon Laurents's book, Spiegelgass simply rearranged some of the scenes (Rose meets Herbie before she leaves Seattle, resulting in "Small World" coming before "Some People") and removed whatever would have run afoul of the Production Code, which was still in effect—but not for much longer. Thus Tessie Tura did not say "tough tittie," as she had in the original; and her snide remark about the Vatican was replaced with one about the Louvre.

The script changes were minor; more problematic was Rosalind's voice. Although Rosalind insists that she did her own singing, the production files tell another story. Since it was common knowledge in Hollywood that Rosalind could not handle the entire score, agents bombarded LeRoy with suggestions. Leonard Hirsham from the William Morris Agency encouraged him to test pop singer Gogi Grant. Another 1950s vocalist, Eileen Wilson, was briefly considered. When Rosalind learned that LeRoy was leaning toward a singer with an operatic voice, she objected vehemently: "Everyone knows I don't sing operatically." If Rosalind knew the singer's identity, she never revealed it. Karl Malden, who played Herbie in the film, thought it might have been Patricia Morison, the original Lili Vanessi in *Kiss Me, Kate*, who could pass for an opera singer.

Malden was not far off. The artist, whose voice was heard in almost all of Rose's numbers, was Lisa Kirk, also from *Kiss Me Kate*, in which she stopped the show with "Always True to You in My Fashion," as she enumerated the ways her various lovers improved her quality of life, while at the same time swearing fidelity—in her fashion—to her latest. Although Rosalind had already recorded Rose's songs, Kirk was hired at twenty-five thousand dollars as her "voice double" but without screen credit. A memo from the head of Warner's music department, Victor Blau, specified that there was "no limit to the number of songs that Miss Kirk will be required to do." The same memo confirmed that "Mr. Goldstone, I Love You" and "Together, Wherever We Go" were sung entirely by Rosalind, who also half spoke and half sang a brief reprise of "Small World." Rosalind also sang the beginning of "Everything's Coming up Roses," with Kirk taking over with "Starting now." In short, most of "Roses" is Kirk's, and most of "Rose's Turn" is Rosalind's. At the end of "Rose's Turn," Rose wills the same "rosy" future for herself that she once predicted for Louise: "And everything's coming up Rose / Everything's coming up roses / Everything's coming up roses this time for me." "Rose's Turn" is a brilliant example of word play, Sondheim's passion. Rose takes "roses" personally, first changing the plural to a singular with a capital *R*, so that it becomes her name; then interpreting "roses" as a possessive, singing "roses" but thinking "Rose's." "For me" is repeated six times, each time with mounting urgency, until the bitterness has been purged away. The last "for me," which brings Rose's aria to an end, is an explosion of ego, seconded by a flourish from the orchestra.

Rosalind begged LeRoy to let her perform the climactic "for me," but he refused, perhaps realizing that she could not give it the power it needed. But then, no one could—except Merman. There have always been rumors that Rosalind's voice was blended with Kirk's in certain songs or in sections of them. Anyone familiar with Kirk's voice from the original cast recordings of *Allegro* and *Kate* could hear it in "Small World" and earlier in "Some People," although parts of the latter may have been a mix of their voices. Rosalind acted Rose to perfection, but she could not sing everything unaided. In the language of corporate America, Lisa Kirk was Rosalind's vocal resource person.

In *Banquet*, Rosalind makes no mention of Kirk: "That's Roz, and nobody else, as Rose on the soundtrack," Rosalind insisted. Blau, however, noted that Rosalind was satisfied with Kirk's contribution. Kirk's timbre suited the character of Rose, as Rosalind delineated her; and on the few occasions when Rosalind's voice was heard alone, there was hardly any discrepancy. Kirk's selection was understandable; she was never a belter like Merman. Rather, she had a smoky, intimate voice; even her climactic "for me" did not reverberate like Merman's. But then, Merman was unique.

In 2003 Warner Bros. Records released a *Gypsy* soundtrack with outtakes of the numbers that Rosalind had recorded but were never used. To insiders, the outtakes were not a revelation. At some point in the late 1960s, Merman got hold of the tapes, which she considered her vindication for losing the part she had created. Understandably, she delighted in Rosalind's desperate attempts to scale the same vocal heights that she had reached so effortlessly. Leonard Bernstein may have sensed a musicality in Rosalind's voice, but it was not the kind that Jules Styne heard when he was composing the score for *Gypsy*. Rosalind struggled with the music, substituting expressivity for vocalism and dramatizing what should have been sung. If her "Everything's Coming up Roses" had ever reached the screen (which, thankfully, it did not), it would have been more of a monologue than a song; Rosalind pounded away at the lyrics, as if she were battering them into submission, so that one heard the drama behind the words, but never the music that gave them life.

Although Merman and Rosalind had nothing in common vocally, they did dramatically. They shared an emotion that was at the core of the character: anger. Each had her share of sorrow and pain—both emotional and physical. Merman's second husband, the president of Continental Airlines, not only was a philanderer but also had her billed whenever she and her children flew Continental. In *Happy Hunting* (1956), Merman had the most unpleasant stage experience of her career when her leading man, Fernando Lamas, Rosalind's *Girl Rush* co-star, would wipe his mouth after their first-act kiss to express his opinion of both Merman and the show. When Merman sang, "Everything's coming up roses this time *for me*" at the end of "Rose's Turn," it was as if she were burying the past and planting flowers on its grave.

For Rosalind, the song was an affirmation of life. Unlike Merman (at least in 1962), Rosalind was a cancer patient, who would never know the joy of being cancer free. Before *Gypsy* began filming, Orry-Kelly had to design dresses for Rosalind that had unusually large sleeves to conceal the edema in her arms after the lymph nodes had been removed. Her close friend, designer Jimmy Galanos, did the same for her personal wardrobe. Rosalind had become so inured to pain that at the end of "Some People," when Rose is supposed to put on her hat and jam the hatpin into it, she did it so forcefully that she pierced her skull. Although Rosalind realized what she had done, she was such a pro that she waited for director Mervyn LeRoy to call "Cut!" before attending to the wound.

LeRoy was of little help to the leads. When Rosalind realized he was out of his element, she decided to shape the film along the lines of the original without usurping LeRoy's authority. In the musical, Mama Rose— or, more accurately, Merman—eclipsed everyone, except the trio of strippers who stopped the show with "You Gotta Have a Gimmick." Supposedly, both Natalie Wood (Louise/Gypsy) and Malden (Herbie) were well aware of Rosalind's tendency to dominate a scene. But that was not so much Rosalind as her character. Although Wood's biographer has implied that the confrontation between Louise and Rose was an "over the top contest," the film suggests otherwise. There is a real confrontation: first, rife with anger and recrimination, in Louise's dressing room, as mother and daughter trade barbs; then, on an empty stage, where Rose's bitterness intensifies ("I was born too soon and started too late"), culminating in "Rose's Turn," an unabashedly self-serving catalog of wrongs that grows into a song of the self.

The basic difference between Merman's and Rosalind's Mama Rose was the level of anger that each registered in "Rose's Turn." Merman erupted, first mimicking Gypsy by doing a few bumps and grinds, then launching into her litany of complaints, and finally demanding the spotlight for herself. Rosalind played with the lyrics, which, if delivered with a vengeance, would reduce Rose to a vulgarian ("Some people got it and make it pay / Some people can't even give it away"). Despite her gyrations, which were relatively genteel, Rosalind's Rose was still a lady, albeit with a raucous side. Once Rose admits that she had a dream but it was for June, her concession to altruism is over. She lashes out at Gypsy: "And if it wasn't for me / Then where would you be / Miss Gypsy Rose Lee?" At that point, Rosalind did not explode, like Merman; she made the lyrics more reflective than derisive, partly because neither she nor Lisa Kirk could reproduce Merman's musical rage, but also because Rosalind's Rose was as disillusioned as she was angry. If asked whether she resented the turn her health had taken, Rosalind would naturally have said, "Yes," then adding, "That's show business." That is the same response that Rose gives to Gypsy, when Gypsy admits that her mother could have been a star if she had had someone to do for her what she did for her daughters.

Gypsy was Rosalind's victory, however short-lived, over a number of obstacles (vocal inadequacies, health problems, Merman's shadow) that would have overwhelmed a performer of lesser talent and faith. Sharing that victory was Natalie Wood, who smoothly negotiated Gypsy's transformation from an awkward neophyte, who pulled down a shoulder strap and peeled off a glove, to an assured stripper, who removed less than her rivals but left the audience wanting more. Natalie projected the sly sensuousness of the real Gypsy Rose Lee, but at the same time gave the character a tough facade to conceal her insecurity. And the reconciliation of mother and daughter at the end was unusually moving, which was not the case on stage. Rosalind and Natalie truly respected each other, and their eyes showed it. If Natalie had any reservations about her director or her co-star, she did not reveal it. Unfortunately, neither Rosalind nor Natalie was nominated for an Oscar, although, just in terms of acting, each was outstanding. And, one suspects, Rosalind knew it. As for being bypassed at nominations time, Rosalind/Rose would have shrugged and said, "That's show business."

CHAPTER 10

Mother Mame

Ten years after her film debut, Rosalind—then the screen's definitive career woman—took on her first mother role. The film was *Roughly Speaking* (1945), in which her character was a combination mother-entrepreneur, who went from one business to another and managed to raise five children at the same time, all of whom became patriotic Americans. *Roughly Speaking* prefigured the kind of mothers Rosalind would later portray: women whose children *were* their careers. Actually, Rosalind was at her most maternal in two films that had nothing to do with motherhood: *Sister Kenny*, in which she treated the polio patients as if they were her own children, and *Auntie Mame* (the movie only), where she behaved more like Patrick's mother than his aunt.

While *Auntie Mame* may prove to be her most popular film (or at least the one with which she is identified), it also limited her, just as playing Norman Bates in *Psycho* (1960) limited Anthony Perkins. Audiences seemed to want more of Mame—but Mame the madcap, not Mame the mentor. The problem was the roles, which came increasingly from the theater. Except for the two *Angels* films, *The Trouble with Angels* (1966) and *Where Angels Go . . . Trouble Follows* (1968), all of Rosalind's 1960s films derived from the theater, suggesting that, until she could return to Broadway, stage adaptations would have to suffice.

After *Auntie Mame*, Rosalind played a succession of mothers in film versions of three successful Broadway plays, *A Majority of One*, *Five Finger*

213

Exercise, and *Gypsy*; one off-Broadway hit, *Oh, Dad, Poor, Dad, Mama's Hung You in the Closet and I'm Feeling So Sad*; and one Broadway failure, *A Very Rich Woman*, retitled *Rosie!* for the screen. These were roles created by actresses with totally different performance styles, none of which matched Rosalind's: Gertrude Berg, radio and television's Molly Goldberg (*Majority*); Jessica Tandy, the original Blanche du Bois in Tennessee Williams's *A Streetcar Named Desire* (*Five Finger Exercise*); Ethel Merman, whose voice conductor Arturo Toscanini compared to a musical instrument (*Gypsy*); Jo van Fleet, who could combine Method acting with bravura when necessary (*Oh, Dad*); and Ruth Gordon (*Rich Woman*), the loveable eccentric who, in her prime, had even done Chekhov's *The Three Sisters* with Katharine Cornell and Judith Anderson in a production now considered legendary.

Although *A Majority of One* was released first, the movie version of *Five Finger Exercise*, Peter Shaffer's psychological drama about a German tutor's effect on a British family, had been planned as a vehicle for Rosalind shortly after the play opened on Broadway in December 1959. That the play enjoyed a run of 337 performances was something of an achievement for a five-character chamber drama, in which a four-member household, whose emotional needs are hidden behind a decorous facade, is augmented by a newcomer—a tutor, who becomes their pet, confidant, and, finally, scapegoat. Although Frederick co-produced the play on Broadway in conjunction with the Playwrights' Company, the film version was made through an arrangement between his own production company, Sonnis, and Columbia Pictures, which distributed it. The film might have replicated the original's contrapuntal structure, had the characters not been Americanized. The names were retained, except for the son's, and the plot remained relatively intact. However, the tension that mounted steadily on the stage, as the tutor's presence caused each family member to confront his or her private self, dissipated on the screen, with domestic wrangling and posturing replacing Shaffer's calibrated cycle of confession and betrayal.

Equally damaging was the change of setting—from Suffolk, England, to Carmel, California, where Stanley and Louise Harrington, a self-made furniture manufacturer (Jack Hawkins) and his culture maven wife (Rosalind), have taken a summer place that looks more like a mansion than the usual rental. Determined to enroll Pamela, their teenage daughter, in a private school, Louise hires a German tutor, Walter Langer (Maximillian Schell), to give her French lessons. (Why the tutor refuses to teach his native language is one of several revelations.) In Walter, Louise finds relief from her husband's provincialism; in Louise, Walter discovers a maternalism he has never known, unaware that the warmth she dispenses so freely turns to coldness when she is challenged. Walter's intimation that her son, Phillip (named Clive in the original), is unhappy becomes the equivalent of the tragic error. When Louise insists that Walter be dismissed, Stanley concurs, as does his son. Father and son, who previously had been at odds with each other, finally have a common cause. Phillip is threatened by the prospect of a rival for his mother's affection after he finds Walter and Louise in an innocent, albeit compromising, situation; Stanley feels threatened by the same relationship, which Phillip has convinced him is verging on adultery. Even Pamela sours on Walter, who becomes so disillusioned that he attempts suicide.

The oedipal and homoerotic undercurrents in the play barely produced ripples on the screen, where Phillip's attraction to the tutor is reduced to a suggestion that the two of them set out for the Grand Canyon. Shaffer's Clive is more insistent ("Come away with me"), urging Walter to travel with him to western England, which is hardly the Grand Canyon. Furthermore, in the original, Clive's latent homosexuality is apparent even to his father, who is appalled by the "arty tarty" males with whom he consorts. Shaffer also made more of Louise's obsession with the tutor's self-effacement, which makes him "other" in a family of the self-absorbed—and, in Louise's case, the self-dramatizing. And as the other, Walter is no longer welcome when he ceases to be an object of fascination and is perceived as a threat. Fascination then gives way to rejection, prompting Walter's abortive suicide.

The play ended with Clive's imploring God to give him and his family "courage," not specifying for what, although presumably the courage to change. The screenwriters, Frances Goodrich and Albert Hackett, went further in their attempt to reach old-fashioned closure. Once Walter revives, he disappears from the plot, but not before the guilt-ridden Stanley finds him a job. In the fade out, Stanley and Louise close up the summer house, supposedly reconciled, although one doubts for long.

Except for Walter, the other characters suffered from being transplanted. Louise was the chief victim. When Rosalind delivers her first line, "Well, we're here. Our little retreat," we are back with Auntie Mame, or at least her dark side, with Carmel standing in for Beekman Place. In the play, Louise prides herself on being "Parisian"—so much so that she occasionally lapses into French. Thus, Louise's nicknaming Philip *jou jou* (toy) and Walter *hibou* (owl) is a vestige of her French heritage, not a mark of affectation as it is in the film. If Frederick had been willing to gamble on a faithful adaptation of Shaffer's play, the setting could have remained a weekend cottage in Suffolk, as it was in the play. Rosalind could have resurrected her British accent, particularly since her co-star was a Brit himself, Jack Hawkins, who behaved like a minimally educated entrepreneur, but not necessarily an American one. Even the son's name, Clive, could have been retained, with his sexual orientation implied, as Shaffer had intended. By 1962, homosexuality had progressed from the love that dares not speak its name to the love heard sotto voce through subtext and understatement in such films as *Suddenly, Last Summer* (1959), *Victim* (1960), *Advise and Consent* (1960), and *The Children's Hour* (1961). However, the casting of Richard Beymer as the son, with his boy-next-door looks, dispelled any questions about the character's sexuality. Consequently, the Harringtons emerged as a dysfunctional family consisting of a loutish father, a frivolous mother, a conflicted son, and a spoiled daughter. If the tutor escaped the pitfall of stereotypy, it was only because Maximillian Schell invested the character with such humanity that Walter alone seemed real in a house of waxworks. What might have been a critical success with dubious box-office potential became a critical and financial failure.

Just as *Auntie Mame* fared better on the screen than it did on the stage, so did *A Majority of One*. Leonard Spiegelgass's comedy drama opened on

16 February 1959 at the Shubert Theatre, which was usually reserved for musicals and cursed with an upper balcony with a separate entrance and an ascent so steep that it left all but the fittest theatergoers out of breath. In retrospect, the fourteen-hundred-seat Shubert Theatre was a wise choice. The producers, the Theatre Guild and Dore Shary (who also directed), suspected the play would be a hit, as, indeed, it was. *Majority* enjoyed a run of 556 performances, mainly because of the pairing of Gertrude Berg, a radio and television star, and Sir Cedric Hardwicke, a knighted actor with impressive stage and screen credits. To many, Berg was the chief attraction; she had endeared herself to radio audiences for almost twenty years, starting with her series *The Goldbergs*, which went on the air in 1929. Berg played Molly Goldberg, the prototypical Jewish homemaker, who was always gossiping out the window with her neighbor, Mrs. Bloom. Twenty years later, the series moved to television, lasting from 1949 to 1954.

The secondary attraction was Sir Cedric Hardwicke, better known than Berg to moviegoers and theater audiences. Hardwicke was a West End regular and, since 1936, a frequent visitor to Broadway. Although Hardwicke lacked the celebrity of Laurence Olivier and John Gielgud, as well as the range of Ralph Richardson, he compensated by his gentlemanly demeanor, as if he were a cross between a benign headmaster and a sympathetic barrister. Unlike Berg, Hardwicke had also appeared in a number of films, both British (e.g., *The Winslow Boy* [1948], *Nicholas Nickleby* [1947]) and American (*I Remember Mama* [1948], *A Woman's Vengeance* [1947], *Around the World in Eighty Days* [1956], *The Ten Commandments* [1956]). In the 1950s, Hardwicke discovered another medium for his understated style of acting: live television, where his performances in James Thurber's *The Thirteen Clocks* and Shaw's *Caesar and Cleopatra*, among other productions, gave him even greater exposure.

Although Berg had also done live television, her theater credentials were minimal; her play, *Me and Molly* (1948), in which she also starred, was unsuccessful, suggesting that, unlike the Lomans, the Goldbergs were not meant for Broadway. Molly Goldberg was the exception, but only if her

Bronx homemaker—problem solver persona was replaced by one that was less stereotypical, such as a Brooklyn widow courted by a Japanese industrialist. Such was the premise of *A Majority of One*, which opened in the right season. In February 1959, theatergoers had already seen *The World of Suzy Wong*; the Rodgers and Hammerstein musical, *The Flower Drum Song*, was playing across the street at the St. James; a block away at the Music Box was Fay Kanin and Michael Kanin's dramatization of a classic Japanese film, Akira Kurosawa's *Rashomon*. Plays with Asian settings—or, in the case of *The Flower Drum Song*, with Asian characters—were no longer exotic or intimidating.

Fortunately, for the Theatre Guild and Dore Shary, audiences were willing to take a chance on a play that posed a question similar to the one that opened the popular 1940s radio soap, *Our Gal Sunday*: "Can a girl from a mining town in the West find happiness as the wife of a wealthy and titled Englishman?" *Majority* raised a question that had not only cultural but also religious and racial implications: Can Bertha Jacoby (Berg), a Jewish widow from Brooklyn, who holds Japan responsible for her son's death in World War II, become romantically involved with Koichi Asano (Hardwicke), a Japanese manufacturer and widower, who has also lost a son in the war (but who does not bear a grudge against America)?

The answer is a qualified "yes," but only if the playwright can come up with a plausible way for two such dissimilar types to meet, so that their relationship can develop to a point where matrimony is a possibility. Spiegelgass had been a successful screenwriter (*All through the Night* [1942], *The Perfect Marriage* [1946], *So Evil My Love* [1948], *I Was a Male War Bride* [1949], etc.), with occasional forays into television drama, before he tackled the theater. Because he had written a play that was easily convertible to film, *Majority* made such a smooth transition to the screen that the movie version was completed a year after the play ended its New York run on 25 June 1960.

Since Spiegelgass adapted his own play, he had already solved the problem of how a Jew and a Zen Buddhist were able to meet without requiring a suspension of disbelief. Bertha is a widow with a son, who happens to be a foreign service hotshot and has no intention of leaving his mother in

Brooklyn while he and his equally solicitous wife are stationed in Tokyo. Traveling by sea from San Francisco to Yokohama (a mode of travel that conveniently allows a relationship to develop), Bertha encounters Mr. Asano (Hardwicke), and what ordinarily would have been a "meet cute" becomes a "meet rude." Bertha has still not forgotten December 7. Eventually, she thaws, then warms, and a November-December romance blossoms—but does not exactly burgeon.

On stage, neither Berg nor Hardwicke was much of a revelation: She alternated shtick with pathos; he slanted his eyes, bowed respectfully, and delivered his lines as if he were a spokesperson for *Bartlett's Book of Quotations*. What the film version needed—and received—were two character actors: Rosalind and Alec Guinness. Although Hardwicke brought the right amount of *gravitas* to Asano, it came across as aloofness. Then there was the matter of the makeup. When a Western actor plays an Asian, the makeup calls attention to itself, unless the actor can convince the audience to move beyond the externals into the character himself. Unlike Hardwicke, who never lost himself in the role, Guinness made his appearance such a part of Asano that his makeup was as natural as Rosalind's Yiddish inflections. Neither had an easy time; Guinness had to internalize the emotions of a man whose culture does not allow him to express them directly, causing him to suppress what a Westerner might reveal without regard for propriety. For Asano, propriety is all; it is up to a Westerner, like Bertha or her insensitive son, to translate facial expressions, gestures, and, above all, posture into American English so that rigidity becomes decorum; measured speech, carefully weighed words; and deep feeling, emotionally shaded understatement.

What Rosalind accomplished was no less impressive. Not only did she master the accent with its musical lilt and upward inflections that turned declarative sentences into questions; but there were also the mannerisms: the wave of the hand to dismiss the irrelevant; the shrug, followed by the throwing of a sweater over the shoulders after an argument, as if to ward off a chill.

The Bertha-Asano relationship took on far greater depth on the screen than it did on the stage. The settings, although studio-bound (but visually authentic), helped, but more than the externals was the empathy Rosalind and Guinness felt for their characters and the respect that they had for each other as actors. Unlike Hardwicke, who seemed to be playing straight man to Berg, Guinness did not so much play to Rosalind as play off her. Hers was clearly the showier part, particularly in the scene when she seeks out Asano at his home and has her first taste of saki—one of several tastes—and becomes high but never inebriated.

Rosalind and Guinness seem so perfect for each other that one almost forgets the characters' religious differences. Bertha's son and daughter-in-law, however, do not. For all their liberal posturing, they balk at the idea of an interracial marriage—or, to be more specific, remarriage. Eventually, Bertha comes to the same conclusion, but for different reasons. Hers are more religious than cultural; she is a Jew, and Asano is not. Under the circumstances, conversion on either's part is out of the question. But moviegoers, who believe the bluebird of happiness alights on the windowsill after a storm, were not entirely disappointed. When Asano announces that he has been made a delegate to the United Nations and will thus be spending considerable amounts of time in New York, Bertha starts planning their Thanksgiving dinner. In the fade out, the two of them sit down to a Sabbath meal that she has prepared. Rosalind and Guinness kept the final scene from turning treacly by maintaining their characters' dignity; from Bertha's point of view, this is a Friday evening ritual; from Asano's, it is dinner with a woman to whom he had earlier proposed marriage in as delicate a way as his station allowed. As they toast each other, the camera discreetly pulls back from two people about to embark on what Rick Blaine at the end of *Casablanca* called "the beginning of a beautiful friendship." Although some moviegoers might have hoped for more than friendship; and others, that the racial and religious barriers would fall like the walls of Jericho in *It Happened One Night*, the open-ended fadeout allows equal time for optimists and pessimists.

A Majority of One allowed Rosalind a reprieve from Mame, with whom Bertha Jacoby had nothing in common. There was a bit of Mame in Mama Rose, although one suspects that if Mame Dennis had ever met Rose Hovick, she would have considered Rose the antithesis of herself and fled. Mame was a nurturer, not a manipulator. Mame was also Rosalind's *bête noire*. Rosalind could distinguish between Mame's relationship with her nephew and Rose's with her daughter; she could convert Mame's knack for reinventing herself into Rose's reimaging of Louise. She could even don a Jewish accent to play Bertha Jacoby in *A Majority of One*. But in *Oh, Dad*, Rosalind was faced with a character who was an amalgam of Mame and Rose: the fabulously wealthy Madame Rosepettle, who travels around the world with her son and a coffin containing the stuffed corpse of her husband.

On reading the script, Rosalind assumed *Oh, Dad* was a comedy. Originally, Arthur Kopit's play was a dark comedy. However, by the time *Oh, Dad* reached the screen, the darkness and comedic qualities had disappeared, and Madame Rosepettle's sinister grandeur had devolved into grotesqueness. Rosalind had to draw on every trick she knew to keep the character from turning into a Charles Addams type, like Lily Munster in *The Munsters*, or worse, a human gargoyle.

Barbara Harris reprised her stage role of the would-be seducer of Madame Rosepettle's son (Robert Morse, in the part created by Austin Pendleton). But neither Morse nor Harris had a chance to demonstrate his or her range, which in Harris's case went from deadpan to droll. Kopit's play implied a connection between totalitarianism and oedipalism with Madame Rosepettle as the *mater terribilis* who forbids her son to answer the phone, feeds him an unchanging diet of hamburgers three times a day, and makes him so completely dependent on her that he cannot function on his own. What was subtle on the stage became exaggerated on the screen. The political subtext disappeared in a sideshow disguised as haute couture with Rosalind in unbecoming wigs of various colors (black, blonde, red, blue), one more garish than the other. The nadir was Rosalind in a multicolored outfit and a floppy pink hat that made her look like a harlequin. Equally lamentable was the decision to punctuate the action with iris shots of Jonathan Winters as Dad, delivering witless commentary from the other world.

If Rosalind thought *Oh, Dad* would be a good vehicle for her, she may not have realized that Madame Rosepettle was a transmogrified Auntie Mame. Or if she did, she may have thought that the character would at least resonate with audiences who remembered *Auntie Mame*; the others might come for Robert Morse, who, as Willy Loman would have said, was "known but not well known," or for Winters, who was very well known from his CBS television show, *The Jonathan Winters Show*, which ran from 1967 to 1969.

A far better choice was the screen version of Ruth Gordon's play, *A Very Rich Woman*, based on French playwright Philippe Heriat's *La Jollie des familles*. Gordon's adaptation, directed by her husband, Garson Kanin, opened on Broadway at the end of September 1965 for a run of only twenty-eight performances. Like *Oh, Dad, Rich Woman* was a dark comedy, with an emphasis on comedy, about a wealthy woman whose two daughters believe that their mother's idiosyncrasies, such as standing on her head in front of a beauty salon, calls for institutionalizing. Naturally, the mother outwits the daughters, who are more interested in her money than in her mental health.

Gordon, who specialized in eccentrics (and won an Oscar for playing one in *Rosemary's Baby* [1969]), starred in her own adaptation, garnering respectable reviews for her performance but not for the play. Despite its failure, Ross Hunter, Universal's premier producer, bought the rights. Hunter, whose Universal films (e.g., *Magnificent Obsession* [1954], *All That Heaven Allows* [1955], *Imitation of Life* [1959], *Pillow Talk* [1960]) reflected a style that was all but disappearing from a Hollywood on the eve of corporatization, was always looking for vehicles for stars of a certain age—such as Jane Wyman, Robert Stack, Lauren Bacall, Barbara Stanwyck, Agnes Moorehead, Lana Turner, Doris Day, and his favorite, Virginia Grey—in which they could either be billed above the title or, in Grey's case, below it as a member of the supporting cast. Ross Hunter was old Hollywood's salvation—for a time, at least. He also provided Rosalind with a role that did her justice.

Hunter spared no expense for *Rosie!* (1968), as the film was entitled. Samuel Taylor, an accomplished playwright and screenwriter, did the adaptation. Two of his plays had already been filmed under Billy Wilder's direction: *Sabrina Fair* as *Sabrina* (1954) and *A Touch of Spring* as *Avanti!* (1972). A third, *The Pleasure of His Company*, did not undergo a title change for the screen, nor was the drawing-room wit lost in transit when the film version arrived in 1962.

In *Rosie!* Rosalind donned her Mame persona, but this time without the gothic trappings. She played the title character, Rosie Lord, a wealthy senior citizen (but not looking it) who has a warmer relationship with her granddaughter (played winningly by a mature Sandra Dee) than she does with her daughters (Audrey Meadows and Vanessa Brown, the latter underplaying the role to elicit some sympathy from the audience), who use their mother's unconventional behavior as a pretext to commit her to a sanitarium so they can control her finances.

Except for a few scenes, *Mame* did not demand much of Rosalind as a dramatic actress; *Rosie!* did, notably in the harrowing sequence in which she is kidnapped and taken to an institution, where she is drugged, stripped of her clothes, dressed in what is euphemistically called a "hospital gown," and confined to a cell-like room. When Rosie becomes conscious, her immediate concern is, naturally, for her clothes. Rosalind conveyed the indignity that any woman, senior citizen or otherwise, would feel on awakening in institutional garb. Her eyes, always expressive and now darting in panic from side to side, intensified her helplessness. Rosie succeeds in bonding with a black nurse, beautifully played by Juanita Moore, who finally understands her plight and does not stand in the way of her rescue by her granddaughter and the young attorney (James Farentino), who becomes the equivalent of Mame's Patrick. If Rosalind's film career had ended with *Rosie!* she would at least have left the screen in a stylish Ross Hunter production. But swan songs are rarely what they should be, and Rosalind's would be no different.

At the beginning of 1965, Rosalind expected to return to Broadway in a musical about the life of the great designer Coco Chanel. Until *Coco* was ready—or, if that failed to materialize, then a musical based on the life of evangelist Aimee Semple McPherson—Rosalind was open to movie offers. William Frye, a former agent and television producer whom Rosalind knew from *Four Star Playhouse*, of which he was executive producer, brought her attention to a novel by Jane Trahey, *Life with Mother Superior* (1962). In fact, the working titles of the film version were "Life with Mother Superior" and "Mother Superior," implying that the film would center around the title character.

Rosalind was eager to appear as a different type of "mother." Before beginning *Oh, Dad* and after completing *Rosie!* Rosalind took a hiatus from stage adaptations to play Reverend Mother in *The Trouble with Angels* (1966). Reverend Mother is the head of the mythical St. Francis Academy, a Catholic boarding school for girls in Pennsylvania. If it is true that Frye originally envisioned Greta Garbo in the part (which might have worked if Reverend Mother were a mystic), Rosalind, then nearing sixty, was the only holdover from old Hollywood able to breathe some credibility into the role of a woman who had once been apprenticed to a leading Parisian dress designer and might have become another Coco Chanel, if she had not chosen a life in religion instead.

Of the various actresses who played nuns on the screen—e.g., Ingrid Bergman in *The Bells of St. Mary's* (1945), Deborah Kerr in *Black Narcissus* (1947), Loretta Young in *Come to the Stable* (1949), Audrey Hepburn in *The Nun's Story* (1959)—Rosalind's Mother Superior ranks with Audrey Hepburn's Sister Luke as among the most authentic.

Although Rosalind told columnist Hedda Hopper that she prepared for the role by reading the lives of the saints, she really did not have to do much research to play Reverend Mother. From grade school to college, her teachers were nuns. She understood their ways, which ran the gamut from saintliness to pragmatism and beyond, to the far side of sanctity, where gentle manipulation (always for a good cause) and worldliness (sometimes unavoidable) remained in reserve. Their ways were hers—a deep spirituality often masked by a façade that suggested otherwise. Rosalind knew that, whatever their flaws, the women who taught her believed in their vocation. And these were the nuns she wanted to see portrayed on the screen, as distinct from the dour disciplinarians who rapped knuckles with rulers and banished cutups to the corner or sat them on a chair with a dunce cap.

Reverend Mother, with a fifteen-decade rosary hanging down the side of her habit, is the embodiment of traditional Catholicism. She seems completely indifferent to—or chooses to ignore—the reforms initiated by the Second Vatican Council, which included a new look for nuns (plain dresses and short veils, or even business suits). The only indication that *Trouble* was a 1960s release was the animated main title, imitative of Blake Edwards's *The Pink Panther* (1964), with its cartoonlike representations of Rosalind and her "angels"—specifically, the Hayley Mills character, Mary Clancy, portrayed as the student from hell with a shock of red hair and bent on havoc. In fact, the film makes no reference to anything that can place it within a specific time period, including allusions to Kim Novak and Rock Hudson, who became stars in the 1950s. But that may have been the point: the film is not so much about life in a convent school at a particular time as it is about the maturation of two mischief-makers into responsible young women, one of whom embraces the religious life that initially seemed so alien to her. The kind of transformation that Mary and Rachel Devery (June Harding) experience is not limited to any era—although it would have been more plausible in the 1950s, when religious vocations were more plentiful than they were a decade later.

Rosalind looked the perfect nun. If she ever became one, she would have been an amalgam of Mame Dennis and Elizabeth Kenny. Perhaps the habit flattered her body with its fluidity, and the makeup gave her face a translucence. But just as makeup does not impart saintliness, neither does the uniform make the soldier—or the habit, the nun. Rosalind *is* Mother Superior; she moves with a stateliness and reserve necessary when dealing with adolescents, revealing her true self to her closest friend, Sister Liguori. In her scenes with Sister Liguori, Reverend Mother, whose name in religion we never know, reveals herself as a woman trying to run a boarding school with a defective heating system that can only be replaced with prize money from a band contest, which, given the intercessional power of nuns and a donation of provocative uniforms, St. Francis wins.

Despite the importance of Reverend Mother's role, the character does not dominate the plot; she is a player in a contest of wills between

Mary, a rebel with "scathingly brilliant ideas," and her sidekick, Rachel, who, as Reverend Mother observes, is only a follower, not a leader. When Mary and Rachel are not breaking rules by smoking in the lavatory (and later in the basement, where the smoke brings out the fire brigade), they are putting bubble-bath crystals in the nuns' sugar bowl and leading tours of the off-limits cloister.

As mirror images, Reverend Mother and Mary are fascinated by each other. Although Reverend Mother has every reason to expel Mary, she avoids doing so because, as she admits to Sister Liguori (compassionately played by Marge Redmond), she and Mary have a common bond: pride, which neither can—nor should—conquer. Pride may have been one of the seven deadly sins in the Middle Ages, but without it no head of a religious order could minister to the needs of her community, much less act in loco parentis for the adolescents under her charge. If Reverend Mother seems imperious at times, it is part of the job description. And if Mary refuses to obey orders that impinge upon her personal freedom, it is part of her nature. Reverend Mother must make an effort to understand Mary—and vice versa.

Mary's curiosity about the nuns at St. Francis, particularly Reverend Mother, prompts her to investigate their quarters. She is amazed at Reverend Mother's room, which resembles a monk's cell. After observing Reverend Mother saying her rosary by a statue of the Virgin and placing bread crusts on the shoulder of a statue of St. Francis, Mary begins to realize that spirituality is not reflected in halos and nimbuses, but in actions too commonplace to be noticed—except by one who is searching for some deeper meaning in the ordinary, as Mary clearly is.

Although Mary is reluctant to visit a retirement community at Christmastime and indicates this by her disdain for the elderly ("I hope I die young and very wealthy"), she is touched by the way Reverend Mother consoles one of the residents, who complains that her children no longer visit her during the holidays. At a Christmas vigil, Mary spies the nuns at chapel, where their joyful singing profoundly affects her. When Mary finds Reverend Mother adding the finishing touches to a dress that Rachel had started but could not complete, the two have their first nonconfrontational conversation as Reverend Mother describes her background: born Madeleine Rouche to a Parisian mother and orphaned after her parents died in the flu epidemic of 1918, she was sent back to Paris where she was apprenticed to a famous couturiere. Exposure to the fashion world convinced her that she, too, could be a famous dress designer. "How could you give it up?" Mary asks, incredulously. "I found something better," Reverend Mother replies with great sincerity.

When Reverend Mother informs the students of Sister Liguori's death, she does not register the slightest emotion, causing Mary to wonder if the religious life desensitizes those who embrace it. She soon learns otherwise when she comes upon Reverend Mother in the chapel, kneeling at the casket with her arms stretched around it, as if embracing what lay within. Mary finally understands that, to Reverend Mother, grief is a private matter; and an announcement of a death, a public one. On each occasion, Mary is gradually moving closer to a decision that she reveals on graduation day: her wish to become a nun, much to the dismay of Rachel, who eventually accepts her friend's choice.

The Trouble with Angels is a film of set pieces in need of a director with a unifying vision to impart cohesiveness to a string of vignettes, framed within the perennial clash between the nonconformist and the traditionalist. Apart from the antics of Mary and Rachel, there are such episodes as the bra-buying outing where the girls revel in the profusion of colorful lingerie until Reverend Mother arrives and, holding up a plain white bra, tells the salesperson, "Two dozen." There is also the unmotivated arrival of the new dance instructor, played by Gypsy Rose Lee, who is wasted in her two scenes, one of which has her entering in a shocking pink dress and a butterfly hat; the other, instructing students to envision themselves as willows. Gypsy's presence would only have meant something to those who remembered her as America's premier stripteaser, whose mother Rosalind portrayed in *Gypsy*. If Gypsy Rose Lee took the thankless part as a favor to Rosalind, or if her presence was intended as *hommage* to the 1962 film, she was really cutting-room-floor material. As it was, the film ran for 112 minutes, 10 of which could easily have been eliminated.

It was the performances of Rosalind and Hayley Mills and the invaluable direction of Ida Lupino that held *Trouble* together and kept it from splintering off into mini-narratives. In addition to being a superb actress, Lupino emerged at the end of the 1940s as the only female director, in a male-dominated business, capable of making small, carefully observed films about subjects that the major studios generally avoided (illegitimacy [*Not Wanted*, 1949], polio [*Never Fear*, 1949], rape [*Outrage*, 1950], a mother's exploitation of her tennis pro daughter [*Hard, Fast, and Beautiful*, 1951], bigamy [*The Bigamist*, 1952, in which she also co-starred], etc.). Lupino knew she could not give *Trouble* classic narrative form, but she could establish a rhythm that would give it the equivalent. She sensed the spiritual aura of St. Mary's Home for Children in Pennsylvania, which doubled as St. Francis Academy. Interspersed throughout the film were scenes in which the camera roamed the grounds like a first-time visitor, stopping occasionally at a pond adorned with water lilies or at a statue of a saint, until another episode was ready to unfold. Once Lupino realized the transfiguring effect the nun's habit had on Rosalind, who seemed born to it, shots of Reverend Mother became iconic images—Reverend Mother amid a shower of autumn leaves or against a wintery landscape. To heighten her sense of loss at the death of Sister Liguori, Lupino framed the shot of Reverend Mother embracing the coffin, her head pressed against it, so that the camera could pull back to show the crucifix that had been placed on it. The camera stayed for a moment on the crucifix, as the central image of Christianity became a symbolic reminder of human suffering.

Those who wondered what kind of a nun Mary Clancy became found their answer in the sequel, *Where Angels Go . . . Trouble Follows* (1968), in which Sister George (Stella Stevens), a product of the Second Vatican Council that ushered in a series of changes that shocked traditionalists, squares off with Reverend Mother (Rosalind again), who initially acts as if nothing has happened—either in the Vatican or in America—since the

Eisenhower years. Just as the original was a coming-of-age film, the sequel is a road movie, as a contingent of nuns and students from St. Francis travels from Pennsylvania to California for a peace rally in the same school bus that whistle-blowing Sister Clarissa (the superb character actress Mary Wickes) drove in the first film.

"Peace rally" underscores the difference between the two films. Although *Where Angels Go* makes no specific reference to the changes within the Catholic Church, the Vietnam War, sit-ins, teach-ins, and student demonstrations, 1968 audiences would at least have understood that no group of students and teachers (much less nuns) would be trekking cross country to a peace rally unless there was a war on. Naturally, the war is never mentioned; the only one being waged is that between Sister George and Reverend Mother. Sister George is the new breed of nun: pro-student but prone to anger, especially when the group keeps getting lost because of Sister Clarissa's faulty sense of direction.

Eventually, the tension building up between Sister George and Reverend Mother peaks; when it does, it takes the form of a confrontation between the old order and the new. Reverend Mother, looking older but still clinging to her position of authority, expects obedience from the youngest member of the community; the progressive Sister George cannot follow orders that trouble her conscience, one of which is Reverend Mother's decision to allow Sister Clarissa to map out the route and do the driving rather than risk hurting her feelings by chartering a bus.

Just as Mary learned to appreciate Reverend Mother's wisdom—and Reverend Mother, Mary's unbending nature—so does Sister George. Conversely, Reverend Mother realizes that the changes ushered in by the Second Vatican Council—mass (even folk style) in the vernacular, relaxed rules of dress, social activism, and a renewed sense of mission—cannot be implemented by her generation, but by the Sister Georges, who, unfortunately, will be fewer in number than the Reverend Mothers.

Where Angels Go, although somewhat shorter than *Trouble*, really needed a director like Ida Lupino to give it some kind of focus. To be fair to director James Nielson, once the film became a Pennsylvania-California bus trip, fragmentation was necessary, as is always the case when people are on the road, whether in *The Grapes of Wrath* (1940) or *About Schmidt* (2003). *Where Angels Go* is a series of stopovers—some intentional, such as a night at a boys' school, where innocence triumphs, and a visit to an Indian reservation; and others, the result of chance, such as an encounter with menacing bikers with whom Sister George "communicates," getting them to repair the bus as well as avoiding the proverbial fate worse than death, and the group's stumbling onto the set of a western, where Reverend Mother communicates in a different way with the director (Milton Berle), who wears an eye patch in imitation of John Ford and makes it possible for them to make the rally. Sister George and Reverend Mother practice the art of communication in their own way, each with her own age group. And each gets results, as nuns usually do.

While *Trouble*, a far better film, lacked a 1960s sensibility, *Where Angels Go* had a superabundance of it. The film was pure sixties: tolerance, activism, renewal, commitment, all of which had been grafted onto the script, as if to take the original out of a time warp and into the present, where it became the "before" to the sequel's "after." Yet, in every respect, *Where Angels Go* is inferior to *Trouble*. The sequel has voiceover narration by Reverend Mother; each sequence begins and ends with an iris as if the film were a cartoon. The technique may have seemed hip (although it was really retrograde), but in the late 1960s it was part of the Day-Glo and pop-art look of the period.

Although the peace rally was the film's point of departure, it is never shown, perhaps because it was never intended as anything other than, literally, a point of departure. All we know about the rally comes from Reverend Mother's final voiceover, assuring us that it was an "eye-opener" and the prelude to many changes, including "habits"—the cue for freeze-frames of the nuns in their new attire, including Reverend Mother and Sister George, former adversaries and now allies, ready to bring the Catholic Church into the new age. Rosalind's heart was in the Catholicism of her youth. Besides, she had more important concerns than religious reform as she entered the last decade of her life.

CHAPTER 11

Trusting Him

Professionally, the early 1960s augured well for Rosalind. Despite her failure to win the Oscar for *Auntie Mame*, her name still resonated with moviegoers and exhibitors; *A Majority of One* and *Gypsy* both opened at Radio City Music Hall, "the Showcase of the Nation." To coincide with *Gypsy*'s release, Rosalind's alma mater, the American Academy of Dramatic Arts, sponsored a dinner dance in her honor at the Americana—then one of New York's newest hotels and now a memory—on Sunday evening, 18 November 1962. Senator Jacob K. Javits presented Rosalind with the Academy's seventh annual achievement award: a Steuben glass crystal urn inscribed with the Academy's seal. It was a gala affair, inexpensive by contemporary standards (thirty-five dollars). The invitations, with Al Hirschfeld's caricature of Rosalind as Auntie Mame, became collectors' items.

Since 1955, Rosalind had been hoping to star in *Coco*, a stage musical about Gabrielle "Coco" Chanel. For a lavish but undistinguished (and probably unrevivable) musical, *Coco* had a long gestation period. Eventually, it arrived on Broadway in December 1969 but with Katharine Hepburn, not Rosalind, in the title role. Meanwhile, in 1965 Rosalind found a script that afforded her the opportunity to play a different type of mother. One has only to study her face in *The Trouble with Angels* to see her identification with the character of Reverend Mother. If Rosalind were a nun in charge of a convent school, she would have been Reverend Mother: witty, slyly manipulative, wary of displaying emotion unless alone, but always at the service of her wards, hoping they understood her ways, as she did theirs (but never admitting it).

A few months before *Trouble* began shooting, Rosalind received a call from the former Anne Rogan, whom she met in her freshman year at Marymount College forty years earlier and coached privately when they were appearing in a play about St. Francis Xavier, in which Rosalind had the lead and Anne had a walk-on. Anne, now Mother Superior Marie Joseph, a member of the order of the Sacred Heart of Mary, wondered if Rosalind could attend a fund-raiser for the completion of Marymount Catholic, a girls' high school in a St. Louis suburb. Rosalind had a better idea. She convinced her friend that *Trouble*, given its setting, would be the ideal fund-raiser and asked her to postpone the event until the movie was finished. With some wheeling and dealing on Rosalind's part, Columbia agreed to hold the world premiere of *Trouble* in St. Louis, with the proceeds going to Marymount Catholic. The premiere took place on 30 March 1966 at the Fox Theater in St. Louis, followed by a reception with Rosalind, Hayley Mills, Mary Wickes (a St. Louis native, who was warmly received), and producer William Frye. Unlike the *The Girl Rush* debacle in Waterbury a decade earlier, the St. Louis opening came off smoothly.

The same cannot be said for the rest of 1966, except for Rosalind and Frederick's twenty-fifth wedding anniversary celebration. Rosalind had already experienced two personal tragedies: her brother John died in 1961, her sister, Clara, two years later. In 1966, Rosalind's cancer recurred, requiring a second mastectomy. Still, Rosalind believed she could return to Broadway in *Coco*, a goal she had set for herself even when she was appearing in *Auntie Mame*. In fact, less than five months into the run of *Auntie Mame*, the *Hollywood Reporter* announced on 8 March 1957 that Rosalind would be receiving the final script of *Coco* the next day. As it happened, the next day turned out to be the next decade. By 1966, Alan Jay Lerner had written a first-draft treatment of the book along with the lyrics. Agreements had been reached with Coco Chanel's representatives. Finding the right composer was more difficult. Frederick originally favored Frederick Loewe, Lerner's collaborator on such classics as *Brigadoon*, *Paint Your Wagon*, *My Fair Lady*, and *Camelot*. Since Broadway no longer held any appeal for Loewe, Lerner approached Richard Rodgers, who, although still active, showed no interest in the subject matter. Lerner then thought of André Previn, at the time a budding composer-conductor eager to try a Broadway musical. Everything seemed in place: Lerner would write the book and the lyrics; and Previn, the score. Supposedly, Rosalind would star. But in October 1966, Rosalind was more excited about her twenty-fifth anniversary celebration, courtesy of Frank Sinatra.

Relationships in Hollywood, like those in most businesses, are based on expediency or mutual affection—and sometimes on a combination of both. With Rosalind and Sinatra, it was mutual affection; at least, that is how it started. By the time of Rosalind's death, it was devotion on her part, and genuine love on his. Although they never worked together, each was aware of the other since the late 1930s. Asked what Sinatra's appeal was to his mother, Lance Brisson replied, "F-U-N," emphasizing each letter as if "fun" explained it away. Fun was certainly part of Sinatra's appeal. He would think nothing of calling Lance, suggesting that they fly down to Las Vegas for the evening and return the following day.

In addition to being "fun," Sinatra also pursued the good life, as did Rosalind, whose perception of that life was markedly different from his. To her, Beverly Hills was an address, and Hollywood, a job; Las Vegas meant gaming tables and shows. Sinatra felt similarly about Beverly Hills and Hollywood, but not Vegas, which meant women and the mob—and for a time a showcase for his talent. Rosalind accepted affluence as a by-product of success, although she would have admitted that talent, luck, and hard work can account for only so much; as a Catholic, she would have found something lacking in that success formula: grace, that unanticipated form of divine assistance that can do anything from ennobling a simple action to turning the ordinary into the rare. Agnostics would have substituted genius for grace, and aestheticians would have attributed a dazzling performance to the transformative power of art. But Rosalind knew her catechism. She also knew that she experienced international fame and God's grace, not separately but in combination.

Rosalind and Sinatra enjoyed a common bond, but it was neither Hollywood nor Las Vegas. As Kay Francis once observed, "'Roz is *in* Hollywood, but she's not *of* it.'" Sinatra was *of* Hollywood; in fact, he was *of* whatever he did—movies, concerts, recordings, all of which were an extension of himself. Remaining on the periphery was not Sinatra's style. The trajectories of their careers were also different. Rosalind's peaked early with *Craig's Wife; The Women*, in which she nearly eclipsed the star; the screwball classic *His Girl Friday;* and three Oscar nominations in five years during the 1940s, while Sinatra was at MGM toiling in the shadows of performers with larger-than-life personas, such as Gene Kelly (*Anchors Aweigh* [1945], *Take Me Out to the Ball Game* [1949], *On the Town* [1949]), Betty Garrett (*On the Town, Ball Game*), and Jimmy Durante (*It Happened in Brooklyn* [1947]). It was only after Sinatra left MGM that he revealed a limited talent as an actor that major directors were able to exploit. When he received an Oscar for *From Here to Eternity* (1953), it was because director Fred Zinnemann enabled him to locate Maggio's bantamweight cockiness within himself, as did Joseph L. Mankiewicz in *Guys and Dolls* (1955) and, to some extent, Otto Preminger in *The Man with the Golden Arm* (1955), although another performer, the underrated Eleanor Parker, was more impressive in that film. As an icon, tarnished one year, burnished the next, Sinatra remained in the spotlight, occasionally being cast in such films as *Some Came Running* (1958) and *The Manchurian Candidate* (1962), which actually required some degree of acting. Unlike Rosalind, he was not a natural actor; he was a crooner who developed into an interpretative artist, able to apply his art to lyrics or dialogue.

To some extent, Rosalind and Sinatra had Catholicism in common, which affected each of them differently. Although Sinatra had been an altar boy, he never experienced Rosalind's devotion to her faith, which she never used to promote her career. Rosalind was an actress and a Catholic, not a Catholic actress. As a female in pre–World War I Waterbury, she could never have been a "server," to use the gender-neutral term for altar boy. But to paraphrase Mama Rose, if Rosalind could have, she would have. And she would have upstaged the celebrant. Sinatra was a Catholic who, like his coreligionist Bing Crosby, achieved a level of celebrity that made religion irrelevant, except when it came in handy—for example, in 1976 when Sinatra and Barbara Marx were planning to marry. The only way they could be married in the Catholic Church, as Marx intimated, would be if Sinatra got his 1939 marriage to Nancy Barbato, his first wife, annulled. A 1979 photo of Sinatra receiving communion confirmed the annulment, even though his daughter, Nancy, the recording artist and performer, called it a "sham."

What Rosalind and Sinatra truly had in common was mutual respect. Rosalind had a sense of loyalty that was unusual in an industry known for Schadenfreude and backbiting. She inspired in Sinatra the same kind of deference she received from Harry Cohn, who was not unlike Sinatra. Each was a notorious lothario, capable of vacillating between magnanimity and ruthlessness. Each divided women into two categories: ladies and dames. Rosalind belonged to the former. She had frequently been in Cohn's office, which, despite its deceptive whiteness that gave it a beatific look, was far from hallowed ground; it was used for business transactions as well as for assignations with starlets, who would be rewarded with perfume or nylons. Yet Cohn's reputation as a womanizer did not stop Rosalind from regarding him as a man of great taste, which he was when it came to scripts and stars. That Rosalind attended his funeral in 1958, which was held on the Columbia lot, was her way of paying respect to a man who provided her with her first leading role and the film that brought her her first Oscar nomination.

Rosalind also knew about Cary Grant's alleged bisexuality, although it never troubled her. To her, Grant was the best man at her wedding, a dear friend, and a colleague with whom she co-starred only once—much to her regret. In the Cary Grant Collection at the Fairbanks Center for Motion Picture Study in Los Angeles, there is an undated letter from Rosalind to Grant in which she wrote, "Next to Freddie I adore you." Then she added,

"Besides, I don't really want that thing without you." The "thing" was the Oscar, which eluded both of them, although Grant eventually received an honorary one in 1969. The letter was probably written in the 1940s, when both were nominated: Grant for *Penny Serenade* (1941) and *None but the Lonely Heart* (1944); Rosalind for *My Sister Eileen* (1942), *Sister Kenny* (1946), and *Mourning Becomes Electra* (1947). Most likely, she was referring to Grant's losing to Bing Crosby for *Going My Way* (1944), although Grant's performance in *None but the Lonely Heart* was more impressive, but less heralded.

Whatever the occasion of Rosalind's note, Grant immediately wired back, confessing that her words meant "so much . . . on Saturday afternoon, and so much more at midnight." Their friendship continued until her death. Grant sent Rosalind fruit and champagne on special occasions, and sometimes just as a sign of affection. When Rosalind was critically ill in early November 1976, Grant sent her a floral arrangement that pleased her enormously. On 10 November, she wrote him: "I do feel I have made a little progress. In any event, it will be a longer recuperative period that I had originally expected." On 27 November 1976, Grant placed an order with Birkholm's Solvang Danish Bakery for the pastries that Rosalind liked. Rosalind never had the chance to enjoy them; she died the next morning.

With Sinatra, it was the same combination of affection and respect. As an actress, she was first drawn to his performance style, particularly his ability to interpret lyrics, as if they were a form of narrative, like dialogue. She introduced Lance to Sinatra's recordings, calling his attention to the way Sinatra wove a story from the lyrics, giving them musical life as if he were a balladeer. Rosalind was not the only one to be impressed by Sinatra's technique. Maria Callas and Placido Domingo, among many others, felt similarly. Ol' Blue Eyes, the chairman of the board, leader of the rat pack—this was the Sinatra Rosalind knew from the press, but not the Sinatra she knew personally.

In one of his "Stories from Vegas," Ed Walters recalled the time in the early 1970s when Rosalind and Frederick were playing twenty-one in one of the casinos on the Strip. When Rosalind mentioned to Walters that she was going to Caesar's Palace to see Sinatra (who stopped appearing at the Sands after Howard Hughes bought it in 1967), one of the players asked her, in effect, if Sinatra was worth seeing. Rosalind at first ignored the question, and when the player repeated it, she rose majestically and replied, "Frank Sinatra is the singularly greatest talent I have seen in my lifetime. And sweetie, I've been around." In a short time, Rosalind attracted onlookers, including a newly married couple. When Rosalind suggested that the couple make it a point to catch Sinatra's show, the bride replied that it was too expensive. Rosalind had an answer: They could attend as her guests. The entire room then broke into applause. But there was a condition: Should the couple ever have an argument that could lead to a rash decision, they first had to listen to a Sinatra record. When the husband asked for a specific title, Rosalind replied that it did not matter, since some of his records celebrate the glory of love, while others bemoan its loss. Then it was time to see "the Man."

Sinatra became her special charge. Eight years older than he (but never admitting it), Rosalind was combination big sister/mother surrogate/admirer/best friend, who remained aloof from his dark side that had its own spectrum, with its limited range from jet black to gray. To her, he was Francis. Although Rosalind was aware of the mob affiliations and the women, she also knew there was an artist within "the Man," who would leave a greater legacy than herself. Rosalind never worried about the wags who clucked their tongues about her consorting with a performer, whose appearance as the stage manager in the 1955 musical version of Thornton Wilder's *Our Town* on NBC television sent some members of the clergy into a state of high dudgeon when Sinatra's character officiates at a wedding. Apparently, the aggrieved did not realize that in *Our Town* the stage manager also doubles as the minister at the wedding of Emily and George, played by Eva Marie Saint and Paul Newman—both looking radiantly prelapsarian, as opposed to Sinatra, who looked jaded despite his ministerial attire. The juxtaposition of experience and innocence—not to mention Sinatra's delivery of the show's best-remembered Sammy Cahn and James van Heusen song, "Love and Marriage," a subject on which the egregiously offended felt Sinatra should not be speaking—provided the self-righteous with further ammunition, some even making a horrendous pun on the first syllable of his surname.

As a practicing Catholic, Rosalind may have heard one of the "Sin in Sinatra" sermons that were current at the time, but paid as little attention to it as she did to the nonbinding Legion of Decency pledge that good Catholics were expected to take when it was administered at Sunday mass in December. The Legion had nothing to do with the religion she loved, especially since it originally condemned two of her films and classified many of her others as morally objectionable in part. Nor was the Sinatra denounced from the pulpit her Francis.

At the first of Sinatra's many farewells, which was a benefit for the Motion Picture and Television Relief Fund on 13 June 1971, Gregory Peck, the men's chairman of the gala, introduced Rosalind, the women's chairman, by saying, "You have given to life far more than you have taken from it." Rosalind, resplendent in a rhinestone-studded white crepe gown, then introduced Sinatra. Convinced that this was indeed his farewell to show business, she became so emotional that she could barely finish her brief but eloquent tribute: "He's worked long and hard for us with his head and his voice and especially his heart. But it's time to put back the Kleenex and stifle the sob, for we still have the man, we still have the blue eyes, those wonderful blue eyes, that smile. For one last time we have the man, the greatest entertainer of the twentieth century." Sinatra performed several of his signature songs, ending with "Angel Eyes," timing his exit from the stage with the last verse, "Excuse me while I disappear."

One of Sinatra's biographers, Kitty Kelley, has suggested that he tried to develop associations with "respectable" Hollywood couples—such as Claudette Colbert and her husband, Dr. Joel Pressman; producer William Goetz and his wife, Edie; and, of course, Rosalind and Frederick—to improve his image. The truth is that Rosalind and Frederick knew Sinatra at least since 1940, when he was a vocalist with Tommy Dorsey's orchestra.

Sinatra had no need to court Rosalind and Frederick, only to enjoy their company, as they did his, whether it was a weekend in Palm Springs or a cruise on a chartered yacht. But their presence did nothing to wrap Sinatra in robes of respectability, although it may have gotten him a line or two in somebody's column.

Rosalind, on the other hand, was a friend, not a news item. She accompanied Frank when he visited his mother in Hoboken, New Jersey, where she and Frederick also attended a party celebrating Sinatra's marriage to Mia Farrow. If Sinatra provided Rosalind and Frederick with an unforgettable twenty-fifth anniversary, he did it out of love for a couple who welcomed him unconditionally into their lives.

It is impossible to know how much Sinatra knew about Rosalind's health in 1966. Even if he knew nothing about the second mastectomy, he would have gone through with his plan to honor a couple whose mutual love and fidelity he admired, and probably envied. In October 1966, Sinatra was on his third—and short-lived (1966–68)—marriage. His newest wife was Mia Farrow, who helped him organize the affair. The anniversary celebration was a Frank Sinatra production, orchestrated by the Man himself, which ensured its success. Rosalind also helped, but only with a faux program of events that included a gym class. Since October 25 fell on a Tuesday in 1966, Sinatra arranged for an October 21–23 weekend.

Originally, Frederick was considering a silver wedding anniversary in Copenhagen, until Rosalind realized, to paraphrase Cole Porter, that it was the wrong time and the wrong place. The women would never look their best in a city where daylight ended in mid-afternoon, and the weather was not conducive to glamour. At that point, Sinatra intervened. He worked out a deal with Jack Entratter, entertainment director of the Sands Hotel in Las Vegas, so that the Brissons and their guests would spend the weekend of 21 October there.

It was a formidable guest list. The few who declined gave reasons: William Powell (health), Yul Brynner (on location), Kirk Douglas (same), Jack Valenti (business). The attendees included Lance; Frederick's mother,

Cleo; Pat Kennedy Lawford; Dean Martin; Josh and Nedda Logan; Cary Grant and Dyan Cannon; James and Gloria Stewart; Claudette Colbert and Dr. Joel Pressman; and Roddy McDowall, whose self-effacing manner made him the ideal guest for any occasion.

The weekend began with cocktails at the Brissons on Friday evening, 21 October. The drinks were plentiful both at 706 North Beverly Drive and on the special bus that brought the guests to the airport, where they boarded a chartered plane to Las Vegas at 10:00 PM. Although the trip took about half an hour, there was no shortage of the amenities, including cocktails and caviar. Immediately on arrival, the group proceeded to Villa d'Este for an Italian supper, after which some watched television, while others gambled. And that was just Friday.

Saturday afternoon was golf, or whatever. Dinner began at 9:45 PM in a flower-filled room with an eight-piece orchestra. The guests received silver cigarette boxes inscribed, "25th Anniversary. Roz and Freddie." In honor of Frederick's heritage, there was an Aquavit toast, followed by a gourmet dinner—red and white wines, champagne, beef and veal dishes. Rosalind wore a crystal-beaded white gown, created by James Galanos, her favorite designer. On such occasions, speeches are de rigueur. Rosalind knew she would be expected to say something; meanwhile, she and Claudette Colbert reminisced about the only time they worked together in *Under Two Flags*. Then came the tributes. First was Lance, who was initially nervous, but impressive. Rosalind was even more nervous, but, when her turn came, she noted that spending twenty-five years with someone may seem a long time, but not if it is with someone you love. At that moment, Auntie Mame had disappeared into the studio vaults until she was ready for recycling on VHS and DVD. That night it was just the Brissons and their friends.

The celebration ended around 2:00 AM, although for some of the party it went on until dawn, when it was time for breakfast. Rosalind retired around 4:00 AM. The next day was Sunday, which meant Mass. That evening marked the climax of an unforgettable weekend. Sinatra staged a gala with a Hawaiian motif, complete with a waterfall. Around 11:00 PM, the group jetted back to Los Angeles. Nedda Logan spoke for everyone when she said, "I want to freeze this night in my mind forever." Rosalind did not know that their thirty-fifth wedding anniversary would be a much simpler affair or that it would be their last.

Meanwhile, it was back to work. For Rosalind, it was the sequel to *Angels, Where Angels Go . . . Trouble Follows* and *Rosie!* For Frederick, it was *Coco*.

Rosalind assumed she would be starring in *Coco*, as did some of the press. On 8 March 1967, Jack Bradford in the *Hollywood Reporter* wrote that Rosalind would be receiving the final script of *Coco* the next day. However, Dorothy Manners, writing in the *Los Angeles Examiner* also on 8 March, claimed that Rosalind had turned down the part and that Frederick was considering Julie Christie or Melina Mercouri. Neither Bradford nor Manners knew that on 8 March Alan Jay Lerner came to the conclusion that Rosalind was wrong for *Coco*, even though he was supposed to have written the book and lyrics with her in mind. Lerner revealed his doubts in a handwritten note to an unknown source, clearly not Rosalind, in which he also admitted that directors Mike Nichols and John Schlesinger agreed with him. Whether Rosalind sensed Lerner's ambivalence about her and said as much to Frederick, who then informed Manners, is impossible to know. It was clearly a case of mixed signals.

In a few months, the scenario changed:

France Soir (20 June 1967): Rosalind will do *Coco* and has Chanel's blessing.

Women's Wear Daily (18 July 1967): Rosalind is vacillating, despite the encouragement of Frederick and Chanel.

New York Times (27 September 1967): Rosalind will do *Coco*.

The *Times* was unaware of the letter that Lerner had written to Frederick two weeks earlier, on 13 September 1967, in which he unequivocally stated, "This is definitely not for Roz and Roz is definitely not for it." Lerner was right. His Coco was a formidable creature, craving love but not knowing how to give or receive it. The show needed a bravura performance, not a sympathetic one. Unlike Mama Rose, Coco Chanel enjoyed international fame. Coco's eleven o'clock number, "Always Madmoiselle," begins on a note of self-pity, as she laments never having the chance to reveal the love she has within her—none of which is evident in the show. But after two and a half hours, it would not have mattered what Coco said. Lerner wisely knew that at the end of an evening of self-dramatization (as well as self-promotion), Coco has to bring the audience, if not to their feet, at least to a realization that, as Sinatra would have put it, she does things her way: "Who the devil cares / what a woman wears? / Doesn't mean a stitch / ending up a witch / in a golden shell. / One is as one does / and by God it was / Life was as it had to be. / It was not too bad to be / Always mademoiselle. / Right or wrong, I'm glad to be / Gabrielle Chanel!"

Coco was not a Rosalind Russell vehicle; nothing suited her from the score to the book and the lyrics. "The gay, uninhibited, irresistible zest that Roz uses instead of a voice would be so out of character that she and the songs would be fighting each other," Lerner wrote Frederick. Previn's music and Lerner's lyrics were intended for an actress who could sing or, lacking a trained voice, declaim. A non-singing actress, particularly one who had done the classics, could substitute an exaggerated rhythm for the melodic line, much as Robert Preston did in *The Music Man*, so that the result was somewhere between speech-song and rap. Previn's score is sufficiently musical so that a trained singer can perform the numbers as written, as songs to be sung; a non-singer, as texts to be interpreted dramatically. To Lerner and Previn, there was only one non-singing actress who could both attract audiences and convince them that they were watching a musical despite her nonmusical instincts: Katharine Hepburn.

Frederick replied to Lerner a week later, challenging his assertion that Rosalind lacked "emotional brittleness" and questioning Hepburn's "singing voice," which Lerner implied she possessed. Actually, Hepburn never had a singing voice. She started taking voice lessons before rehearsals for *Coco* began and continued with them throughout the run of the show. Hepburn knew that she could perform the role by substituting musical inflection for song. She succeeded; the numbers sounded as if they came from the far side of music, but were rhythmic enough to pass for singing.

"The matter is closed," Frederick wired Lerner on 1 October 1967. Perhaps the unkindest cut of all came when Chanel gave several interviews in which she commented that Hepburn was the only actress slated for the part who looked like her. Chanel was right. Hepburn not only looked like Chanel, but acted like her: imperious, self-absorbed, and unregenerate. That was also Katharine Hepburn, whose Chanel was a composite of Hepburn's Terry Randall (*Stage Door*), Tracy Lord (*The Philadelphia Story*), and Eleanor of Aquitaine (*A Lion in Winter*). Rosalind may have worn Chanel creations, but she was no more Coco Chanel than Katharine Hepburn was Auntie Mame.

Eager to make amends, Lerner wrote Rosalind at the end of October 1967, indicating that he would be in Los Angeles for the premiere of the movie version of *Camelot* and hoped to clear up the "terrible misunderstanding." "Misunderstanding" was the wrong word. Frederick expected Lerner and Previn to come up with a Rosalind Russell musical. Instead, they came up with a Katharine Hepburn one. Even if Previn and Lerner had emulated Leonard Bernstein, Betty Comden, and Adolph Green and fashioned a musical geared to Rosalind's talents, it is hard to imagine its being a hit. Rosalind may have worn Chanels, but she was not Chanel.

Rosalind's response to a setback was always a return to work. That had been her survival scenario since her first nervous breakdown in 1944, which was followed by *She Wouldn't Say Yes* and *Roughly Speaking* (both 1945). It was a brief convalescence. She knew that nervous exhaustion was no excuse for shirking one's obligations; hospitalization was followed by a short recovery period and a return to the sound stage. Nor did Rosalind have any qualms about her breakdowns appearing in the trades or in the columns. After Rosalind finished making *Sister Kenny* (1946), she was hospitalized for a second time, as Louella Parsons reported in the *Los Angeles Examiner*. Again, recovery was rapid; in March 1947, two of her films were in release: *The Guilt of Janet Ames* and *Mourning Becomes Electra*.

Even in 1965, she had no intention of remaining idle until *Coco* was ready. After the location filming of *The Trouble with Angels* was completed in March 1965, Rosalind headed over to Paramount for *Oh, Dad, Poor Dad*, which was finished in late July. She then returned to Columbia to complete *Angels*, which finished shooting the following October and opened in March 1966. *Oh, Dad* was released in February 1967; *Rosie!* in November 1967; and *Where Angels Go . . . Trouble Follows*, in April 1968. Thus, between 1966 and 1968, four Rosalind Russell films were in theaters.

While Rosalind was making *Where Angels Go* in 1967, she was still expecting to star in *Coco*, which was scheduled for a late 1969 opening. When Alan J. Lerner ruled otherwise, Frederick felt obliged to come up with a film for Rosalind to compensate, if possible, for losing *Coco*. In 1966 Frederick purchased the rights to a novel that he envisioned as a future vehicle for Rosalind. However, he realized he could not wait until he launched *Coco* to put it in production. Rosalind needed a film *now*, and Frederick intended to provide her with one, even if he had to produce it himself— which he did. The result was *Mrs. Pollifax—Spy* (1971), which turned out to be her final film (but not her last performance).

Inspired by *Auntie Mame*, author Dorothy Gilman created her own madcap, Emily Pollifax, a New Jersey widow who fulfills a long-cherished dream of becoming a CIA operative. The first of the Pollifax series, which eventually numbered thirteen, was *The Unexpected Mrs. Pollifax* (1966), the novel that Frederick had optioned and that became the basis of *Mrs. Pollifax— Spy*. Among the Frederick Brisson Papers in the New York Public Library of the Performing Arts is a first-draft screenplay of *Mrs. Pollifax—Spy*, written in the traditional format, with changes of setting clearly indicated and action sequences vividly described. However, one important detail is missing: the author's name on the title page. The final screenplay, to which the first draft bears some resemblance, is credited to "C. A. McKnight," Rosalind's nom de plume. Rosalind's involvement in the first draft may have consisted of establishing the plot points and crafting the dialogue, but the structure points to a professional screenwriter capable of creating both dialogue-driven sequences and purely visual ones, the latter requiring imaginative writing to bring them to life on the printed page, which is certainly the case here. Although Rosalind was a member of the Authors' League of America, the New York Dramatists' Guild, and the Screenwriters' Guild of America and, by 1969, had written more articles than most movie stars of her generation, her writing never revealed the sense of place and the feeling for language evident in the first-draft screenplay.

The draft opens with a prologue in a Costa Rica village. The dialogue is minimal, and what little there is involves a vital piece of microfilm that must be kept from falling into the wrong hands. The microfilm subplot resurfaces, but not immediately. The juxtaposition of the violent prologue—in which a shack is burned down and Tirpak, the possessor of the microfilm, is murdered—and the opening scene—in a doctor's office, where Emily Pollifax, a widow with grown children, discloses her lifelong dream of being a spy—is characteristic of the way the script was originally conceived, menace alternating with madcap. Danger is always in the background, ready to subvert the antic, but never overshadow it. And Mrs. Pollifax may be in the tradition of the zany, but she does not wear the motley on her brain.

With the help of an influential senator, Mrs. Pollifax obtains an interview with the CIA director, blithely admitting that, at her age, she is "expendable" and therefore would be the ideal agent. Mrs. Pollifax becomes a CIA courier, instructed to fly to Mexico City and visit a bookstore where *A Tale of Two Cities* should be on display in the window. However, if it is not, she must not enter the store; if it is, she should ask for it, commenting to the owner, "I think Madame DeFarge is gruesome, don't you?" Noticing that the novel is not in the window, Mrs. Pollifax is about to leave when the "owner" invites her into the store. Unaware that he is also working for the CIA, Mrs. Pollifax, a novice at subtext, does not understand that the absence of the novel in the display window is code for a change of plan. The owner asks cryptically if she enjoys playing cards. Discovering that she does, he recommends *77 Ways to*

Play Solitaire, which she purchases. As she is about to leave, he offers her a package of playing cards gratis. Puzzled by the gift and curious about its significance, she returns the next day, only to find someone else who identifies himself as the owner, as distinct from the "cousin" who had waited on her the previous day. Seeing the novel in the window and assuming that the so-called owner is her contact, Mrs. Pollifax asks the same question about Madame DeFarge and receives a knowing look. When offered a cup of tea, Mrs. Pollifax graciously accepts, unaware that it is drugged and that she will wake up on a jet headed for Albania, handcuffed to a man who turns out to be Farrell, another operative.

The first draft was aimed at an audience with a Cold War mentality that would understand references to Castro's Cuba and Stalinist Albania. The man who gives Mrs. Pollifax the deck of cards is killed by Maoists, who have a secret airfield in Mexico. Farrell, an ex-Marine, describes himself as a former supporter of Castro, until the Cuban leader turned dictator and transformed the island into a socialist state. The presence of Chinese soldiers on the Albania-bound jet makes sense only if one realizes that Albania was allied with Communist China. Somewhat frightened, but a true survivor, Mrs. Pollifax charms an Albanian colonel, who loans her a book about his country; removes a bullet from Farrell's leg after he is shot while trying to escape; and massages the aching back of a general, who, in gratitude, hosts a Christmas party, complete with a tree that Mrs. Pollifax decorates with the playing cards that the Mexican operative had given her, among which she discovers the strip of microfilm that was supposed to have been placed in the copy of *A Tale of Two Cities*.

The tree stand serves as Farrell's crutch when the two plan their escape, which, despite a number of close calls, succeeds. Once Mrs. Pollifax is back in New Jersey, her neighbor, whom she had always addressed as "Mrs. Hart," asks to be called by her first name, Grace. When Mrs. Pollifax agrees, Grace replies, "And what should I call you?" Mrs. Pollifax's answer was to have been the fadeout line: "Duchess." That was the sobriquet that Farrell gave her immediately after they met and that he used during their captivity. "Duchess" was Rosalind's inspiration; it was the nickname Rosalind bestowed on her beloved sister, Clara.

The first-draft screenplay was a template for the final one, which is inferior to it. There is no Costa Rica prologue, no scene in the doctor's office, and no incongruous juxtapositions. Instead, after a cleverly designed main title, in which an animated Rosalind, in black hat and cape, slinks her way through the credits to Lalo Schifrin's sinuous music, the film begins with Mrs. Pollifax volunteering her services to the CIA. The Mexico City assignment is unchanged, though, for some reason, Mrs. Pollifax is given drugged coffee rather than tea.

The most significant changes were the transformation of a Cold War narrative into a joint paean to the CIA and America, the two apparently being inseparable, and the reduction of the historical backdrop, against which the action was originally set, to easily understood visuals and references. Mrs. Pollifax alludes to the "difficult times"—presumably, the Vietnam war, the Soviet threat, guerrilla warfare in Latin America—as one of her reasons for wanting to join the CIA. Tirpak, the operative in the first-draft prologue, is now a name bandied about by CIA officials as they puzzle over his whereabouts, wondering if he is in Nicaragua or Guatemala. In the Mexico City sequence, there is a flash-cut of a murder. However, unless one realizes that the murdered man is Tirpak, and that the flash-cut may have been part of the discarded prologue, the references to Nicaragua and Guatemala are meaningless. C. A. McKnight may have known that both countries were threatened by left-wing insurgencies—the Sandinistas in Nicaragua, Marxist revolutionaries in Guatemala—but one wonders how many moviegoers did in 1971. Guatemala was a special case. In 1954, the CIA, fearful that the lawfully elected president of Guatemala, Jacobo Arbenz Guzmán, was a socialist (or worse, a communist, particularly after he tried to nationalize the United Fruit Company), staged a coup, forcing him to flee and replacing his government with a right-wing dictatorship.

Since C. A. McKnight is given sole credit for the final screenplay, it must have been Rosalind's idea to reduce the number of contemporary references to ones that were self-evident. For example, when Mrs. Pollifax asks Farrell if he thinks they are on their way to Cuba, Farrell replies in the negative, adding that he once ran guns for Castro. Shocked, Mrs. Pollifax retorts, "Don't you know whose side you're on?" Gone are the lines about Farrell's support of Castro after the overthrow of the Fulgencio Battista regime in 1959 and his growing disenchantment with Castro once he turned dictator and started courting the Soviet Union. Since Farrell (winningly played by Darren McGavin) does not explain himself, he seems more of a mercenary than a patriot.

The Albania sequence is the least reductive in the film. Albania was the most xenophobic of the Eastern bloc nations and, in the 1960s, more Stalinist than the Soviet Union. The cars fly red flags; Mrs. Pollifax and Farrell are forced to wear Maoist regulation attire—brown cap, shirt, and pants—as if they were workers in the People's Republic of China, Albania's only ally. These were fine touches, whether Rosalind's or those of director Leslie Martinson. Even those who had no idea where Albania is would assume that Mrs. Pollifax and Farrell were in a Communist country. To engender some sympathy for the Albanian people, Mrs. Pollifax is given a scene in which she expresses her admiration for them, but then points to the picture on the wall of their president, whom she denounces as an oppressor. It is hard to believe that most audiences would have known that the president was Enver Hoxha, who declared Albania an atheist state and outlawed organized religion. But even if they didn't, they would have understood that Mrs. Pollifax was able to separate the people from their ruler and the police state he created.

The escape from Albania—by donkey, foot, car, and water—is also impressive. Rosalind and/or Martinson were obviously admirers of Hitchcock's *North by Northwest* (1959). Just as Roger Thornhill (Cary Grant) and Eve Kendall (Eva Marie Saint) slide down Mount Rushmore in *North by Northwest*, Mrs. Pollifax and Farrell work their way down a cliff—hands clasped at one point like those of Hitchcock's characters. Nor is it accidental that the two race through a cornfield to elude the enemy, as Thornhill did in *North by Northwest* when he realized that the plane he assumed was a crop duster was firing at him.

Mrs. Pollifax—Spy was far from an embarrassment; it was, however, a classic case of missed opportunities. Had Rosalind followed the first-draft screenplay, the film would have ended more engagingly than it did. Once Rosalind decided to eliminate the character of Mrs. Hart, "Duchess" could not be the last line. In fact, "Duchess" no longer figured in the dialogue; Farrell refers to his fellow captive only as Mrs. Pollifax. Instead, the film ends with Mrs. Pollifax and Farrell at CIA headquarters, where they are commended for their work and given trench coats, the iconic attire of secret agents, as tokens of gratitude. Farrell helps Mrs. Pollifax put on hers, and she helps him with his. Then the two walk out together, presumably about to embark on a beautiful relationship, which, given the disparity in their ages (McGavin was fifteen years younger than Rosalind), would have to be friendship.

By late fall 1969, the filming was over; at the time, Rosalind had no idea that the West Coast and London premieres of *Mrs. Pollifax—Spy* would be benefits for the Arthritis Foundation of America and the Kennedy Institute of Rheumatology, respectively. All she knew was that the shoot was an ordeal, particularly going on location to Wyoming's Grand Tetons, which doubled as Albania. Never one to express discomfort, Rosalind attributed her health problems to the elements. She soon discovered that her swollen hands had nothing to do with a cold climate and a high altitude. It was rheumatoid arthritis.

Two mastectomies and now another affliction. The diagnosis coincided with the opening of *Coco*; still, Rosalind played the dutiful wife, accompanying Frederick to the 18 December premiere at the Mark Hellinger, even though she had great difficulty buttoning up the back of her dress before they left for the theater. Opening night was the usual round of bussing and embracing. Then Rosalind's treatments began, which included gold injections and steroids. Rosalind joked about the injections, claiming to have the most expensive backside in America. The steroids were another matter; they robbed her face of its angular beauty. Designer clothes could minimize the weight gain from the cortisone, but no amount of makeup could sculpt a face subjected to medication that was never intended to beautify.

After *Mrs. Pollifax—Spy* opened to reviews ranging from lukewarm to hostile, Rosalind realized there would not be another movie on the horizon—or at least not one that would be released theatrically. And returning to Broadway was out of the question. But there was always television, which Rosalind embraced in its infancy, when she appeared in a live version of *Never Wave at a WAC* in 1951, before it was filmed.

ABC's sixty-minute Movie of the Week was shorter than the kind to which Rosalind was accustomed, but it was a movie nonetheless—and one that would reach a much larger audience than *Mrs. Pollifax—Spy*. On 8 November 1972, *The Crooked Hearts* aired on ABC, with Rosalind as a con artist masquerading as a wealthy widow and planning to swindle Douglas Fairbanks, whom she meets at a Lonely Hearts Club, not realizing that he has similar plans for her. Their machinations are complicated by the presence of a serial killer who is stalking Rosalind. The reviews were positive, but by late 1972 it would not have mattered. Rosalind's body was at odds with her performing self. There were still media events—personal appearances and awards ceremonies that only required a stylish entrance and a short speech. And stylish she was, despite the new body she had acquired. Other stars would have shunned the spotlight if they found themselves round-faced and shapeless, but Rosalind embraced it, as if professing her refusal to yield to the illness that had transmogrified her.

In August 1972, President Richard Nixon appointed Rosalind to the National Council of the Arts for a six-year term, ending September 1976, which turned out to be two months before her death. Given her deteriorating health, she attended whatever events she could, such as Oscar night, 27 March 1973, when Frank Sinatra presented her with the Jean Hersholt Humanitarian Award. Rosalind used the occasion to acknowledge that the industry had changed since she started in it four decades ago. However, she also expressed her disapproval of films that exceed the boundaries of good taste, noting that she had no interest in anyone's sex life except her own.

That September, when she was in New York with Frederick, she stepped in a pothole on Madison Avenue, ending up in Lenox Hill Hospital with cuts on her arms and legs. Nothing was broken, but, to use a phrase Rosalind would have understood, it was a preview of coming attractions. Three months later, citing reasons of health, she declined an invitation to the Women's Press Club luncheon, where she was scheduled to receive the Louella Parsons Award for representing Hollywood at its best, even though she would never make another movie.

There may not have been any more movie roles, but there was one in real life that was perfect casting: arthritis activist. Since no one would be writing parts for an arthritic actress on cortisone, Rosalind decided to create her own starring vehicle that she could adapt to whatever group she was addressing. When she was not being hospitalized for stomach blockages, she was out campaigning for arthritis research. It was her final role, but it was in her own script.

From 1974 to 1976, she served as one of eighteen members on the National Commission on Arthritis and Related Musculoskeletal Diseases; her work on the commission led to federally funded national arthritis centers, one of which was posthumously designated by Congress to bear her name: the Rosalind Russell Research Center for Arthritis at the University of California in San Francisco, founded in 1978.

In *Dark Victory*, Judith Traherne, a role Rosalind coveted, knows her death from brain cancer is imminent when she suddenly loses her sight. Refusing to keep her husband at her side when he is expected at an important medical conference, she conceals her blindness from him, reminding him pointedly, but subtly, that love outlasts death: "That's our victory. Our victory over the dark. And it's a victory because we're not afraid."

By accepting death, Judith triumphed over it; by publicizing her arthritis, Rosalind scored a similar victory: she enlisted the support of the federal government in her crusade against the disease that turned her body against her. That satisfaction more than compensated for the Oscar she never received.

Rather than answer questions about her health, no matter how well-intentioned they were, Rosalind would reply with a poem she had written:

There is nothing whatever the matter with me.
I'm just as healthy as I can be.
Well, I do have arthritis in both my knees.
And when I talk, I talk with a wheeze.
My pulse is weak, and my blood is thin
But I'm really well . . . for the shape I'm in.
Now the moral is, as the tale we unfold,
That for you and me, who are growing old,
It is better to say, "I'm fine," with a grin
Than to tell everyone of the shape that we're in.

Despite her health, 1974 turned out to be a satisfying year. Author-publicist John Springer began capitalizing on the growing interest in the stars of Hollywood's Golden Age by sponsoring "An Evening with . . ." programs, featuring film clips and a question and answer session. His success with "An Evening with Bette Davis" prompted him to arrange a similar program with Rosalind at New York's Town Hall on 23 September 1974. Rosalind was not an arbitrary choice. Springer knew that six months earlier, on 31 March 1974, Rosalind had been feted at the Los Angeles International Film Exposition (FILMEX). Roddy McDowall acted as moderator; Rosalind, wearing white gloves and a peppermint-striped jacket with white slacks, was every inch the star—and acted it.

The Town Hall tribute was so successful that it went on tour. A few weeks later, on 5 October, ANTA (American National Theatre and Academy) West in Los Angeles sponsored "An Evening with Roz" at James Sweeney's Bel Air estate, where Rosalind held forth in a hand-embroidered white lace pajama suit. She and Edie (formerly Edith) Adams, who had now reconciled, performed "Ohio," their duet from *Wonderful Town*.

From 3 to 8 December 1974, she starred in "A Tribute to Rosalind Russell: The Career of an American Woman" at Washington, D.C.'s historic Ford Theatre. Rosalind was resplendent in a brown and black Galanos coat dress, silk scarf, Chanel pumps, and a diamond necklace and earrings. The program consisted of two hours of clips from *The Women*, *The Citadel*, *Sister Kenny*, *Picnic*, and *Gypsy*, plus excerpts from a kinescope of the television production of *Wonderful Town*. Afterwards, Rosalind did twenty minutes of questions and answers. The inevitable question about her favorite film received a two-word answer: *Sister Kenny*. In view of her condition, Rosalind probably believed *Sister Kenny* was her favorite, although her fans would have felt differently. However, few of them knew that, like the polio victims in the film, Rosalind was hoping for a miracle, which, unfortunately, was not forthcoming.

Still, the tour continued: Santa Barbara, in April 1975; Toledo, Ohio, in October. A month before her Santa Barbara engagement, Rosalind experienced one of the most fulfilling moments of her ever-shortening life: on Sunday, 15 March 1975, she attended her son's wedding to Patricia Morrow at the Church of St. Charles Borromeo in North Hollywood. At the time, Lance was the deputy to the Los Angeles county supervisor. Patricia had been a regular on the television series *Peyton Place*, in which she played Rita Jacks Harrington from 1965 until the series ended in 1969. Acting, however, was not a career that interested Patricia, although in 1972 she briefly returned to television to reprise her original role when *Peyton Place* was revived as a daytime serial, *Return to Peyton Place*. Patricia, whose father was an attorney, decided to pursue a similar career path by enrolling at California's Glendale College of Law, but with a goal that was radically different from her father's: she planned to use her degree to help the underprivileged. Because both Lance and Patricia were a socially committed couple, they seemed ideally suited to each other. However, the marriage ended in divorce within less than a decade.

A month after the wedding, Rosalind was hospitalized with pneumonia, spending ten days at Cedars Sinai Medical Center and recovering in time for her Santa Barbara appearance. Suspecting that Rosalind's days were numbered, Frederick booked a two-week cruise (8–21 July 1975) that brought them to Amsterdam, Hamburg, Leningrad, Stockholm, and Copenhagen, where they visited Carl Brisson's grave. Coincidentally, one of the films shown on the cruise was *Auntie Mame*. One would like to think that when the passengers discovered the star was on board, they would have reacted like adoring fans. If they had, Rosalind would have been gracious, even though she must have sensed it was her last cruise.

A few months after the cruise, Rosalind experienced kidney failure, from which she was not expected to recover. For five months, she was on dialysis and fed intravenously. That was 1975.

Nineteen seventy-six was the beginning of the end. After Rosalind was diagnosed with rheumatoid arthritis, she found even greater solace in Catholicism than she did when she was well. A frequent flyer, Rosalind always carried her rosary, fingering the beads to give her strength. In 1971, Rosalind did not need a publication in, of all places, *Our Sunday Visitor*, a Catholic weekly. Still, she felt compelled to remind readers how a medal of St. Joseph Cupertino saved the life of a flyer during World War II. Rosalind had originally intended the medal for Frederick, until she felt impelled—for reasons that she alone would have understood but could only explain by the phrase "God's grace"—to offer it to one of Frederick's friends, Colonel Adamson. When Adamson's plane crashed, he spent twenty-two days at sea, holding onto the medal as if it were a life jacket and believing that he would be rescued. He was.

It is hard to know what prompted Rosalind to write a World War II vignette two decades after the war ended. Perhaps, in 1971, Rosalind had not given up on miracles. Five years later, she still believed in miracles, but not for herself. But she never despaired, as she revealed in a poem she wrote near the end of her life:

> Trust Him, when darkest thoughts assail thee.
> Trust Him, when thy faith is small.
> Trust Him, when to simply trust Him
> Is the hardest thing of all.

She had every reason not to trust Him after August 1976. The cortisone had made her bones so brittle that she required a right hip replacement. During the three weeks she spent at the UCLA Medical Center, she received between four hundred and five hundred letters a day from well-wishers. The operation was successful, but it was no cure for the cancer that had now metastasized. She and Frederick knew it was only a matter of time. Lance did, too. Regardless, Rosalind was determined to die at home.

She must have suspected the inevitable that August. At a party given in her honor by James and Gloria Stewart, Rosalind, wearing an eye-catching Galanos dress that could not camouflage the ravages of her cancer, thanked everyone for their love and concern. She then compared life to a rope that is "tied with lots of knots, and it goes straight up. I have been climbing that rope, and each knot I come to is one of you. And then I climb to the next. And to the next. I'm still holding on." It was typical of Rosalind to compare life to a rope, rather than, say, a ladder. Rope-climbing is more arduous. Instead of ascending to the future by stepping on the rungs of the past, the climber moves up a rope knotted with clusters of friendships until he or she reaches the top, where no further knotting is possible. For Rosalind, the climb ended three months after the Stewarts' party.

In 1976, Thanksgiving fell on 25 November. Ordinarily, Rosalind enjoyed Thanksgiving dinner, but this time she preferred to remain in her room. Realizing that it was no longer a matter of time but of days, Lance phoned his father, who was in New York, urging him to return immediately. Frederick flew back to Los Angeles and was able to spend Saturday with her. Early on Sunday morning, 28 November, Rosalind fell into a coma; death came around 10:00 AM. At her bedside were Frederick, Lance and Patricia, and Rosalind's confessor, Father Robert Curtis, with whom she developed a close relationship during her last years. Their conversations must have touched on death, and it may have been a combination of her deep faith and his spiritual guidance that allowed her to experience, as Father Curtis phrased it, a "death textured with peace."

That Tuesday at 7:30 PM there was a rosary service for her at the Church of the Good Shepherd in Beverly Hills, where she had been a parishioner for many years. James Stewart and Gregory Peck attended. The funeral mass took place the next day at 11:00 AM. Peck delivered a eulogy that encapsulated Rosalind's essence: "Glamour, beauty, excitement, purpose, wit, gaiety, drama, entertainment, social commitment, song and dance. All together, Rosalind Russell." Peck was followed by Stewart, whose tribute was characteristically low-key until the end: "Thank you, God, for giving her to us. Take care of her. . . . [We] sent you our best this time." Sinatra, who was also buried from the Church of the Good Shepherd two decades later, was uncharacteristically emotional. With voice cracking, he concluded by saying, "I will always love Rosalind Russell Brisson."

Internment followed at Holy Cross Cemetery in Culver City, California, where MGM, her home studio for seven years, was then located. For one who had suffered so much during the last decade of her life, it was only fitting that towering over her grave was a striking representation of the crucifixion. It was also a marker; visitors had only to locate section M in the cemetery and approach in the direction of the cross.

On 6 February 1977, Frederick arranged a tribute to Rosalind at New York's Shubert Theatre, where clips from some of her films were shown. Shortly thereafter, Rosalind's autobiography appeared, but not with the imprint of the publisher that had commissioned it. At the time of her death, Rosalind had been working with Chris Chase on a 120,000-word autobiography, for which G. P. Putnam's Sons had paid her an advance of twenty-five thousand dollars, with November 1976 as delivery date. Since death pays no attention to deadlines, except its own, Frederick was two months late in submitting the manuscript—not an inordinate delay in trade publishing. Putnam rejected the manuscript, which was not only 45,000 words short of the specified length but also lacking in form. Putnam was right on both counts. Had Rosalind been in better health, she could have written *Banquet* without the aid of Chase. Frederick anticipated Putnam's reaction; he then turned to Random House, which published *Banquet* in 1977. Presumably, Frederick returned the advance, especially after Putnam discovered that he had received one from Random House.

Banquet is not the standard Hollywood autobiography, in which love affairs are catalogued, and lovers critiqued. It is scandal- and orgy-free, as one would expect from a practicing Catholic. Rosalind devoted an inordinate amount of space to her Waterbury years, and far too little to her work in stock companies, where she obviously acquired the skills that brought her to Hollywood. Fans, on the other hand, wanted more about the films, some of which were not even mentioned. *Craig's Wife*'s director, Dorothy Arzner, never even made the index.

Although Sinatra receives an entire chapter, some of the creative men and women with whom Rosalind worked emerge as little more than names. Ida Lupino receives one mention, and not even in conjunction with *The Trouble with Angels*, which, if it continues to enjoy an afterlife on cable and DVD, is partly due to Lupino; she imparted form to what would otherwise have been another coming-of-age film by integrating the lives of the students in a convent school with those of their teachers, but always keeping Rosalind's character, Mother Superior, at the center of the action—not an easy task.

Still, *Life Is a Banquet* is breezy, anecdotal, and, at the end, profound, as Rosalind, on the brink of death, speaks eloquently about God's brightness, in which one would like to believe she was bathed as she passed into eternity that Sunday morning.

On 4 May 1978, a year and a half after Rosalind's death, Frederick married the Belgian-born Arlette Josephson. Frederick was then sixty-five; Arlette, thirty-eight and the mother of a sixteen-year-old son, John.

The wedding took place in London, where Arlette's brother-in-law, Sir Kenneth Cork, was lord mayor in 1978. The reception was held at Claridge's, a five-star hotel in Mayfair, and the couple honeymooned in Paris. If it seemed odd that Frederick—who regularly visited Rosalind's grave, speaking to her as if she were present, like Captain Nathan Brittles (John Wayne) in John Ford's *She Wore a Yellow Ribbon* (1949)—married so soon, Lance believed it was his father's inability to function on his own. Frederick was used to having his meals prepared and his laundry done. He was so accustomed to depending on cooks, maid service, and restaurants, not to mention Rosalind, that what others would have regarded as life's necessities, he considered the amenities. If Frederick expected Arlette to provide them, he was mistaken.

At the time of the wedding, little was known about Arlette, except that she was the consultant for a communications company and maintained an Upper East Side apartment. But as Arlette Brisson and later as vice president of Public Relations for Tiffany's, she became part of the New York social scene, attending premieres, receptions, supper dances, and dinner parties. She was quoted in the *New York Times* on topics ranging from handling impertinent questions to remarriage.

Arlette and Rosalind had little in common. Arlette had the icy beauty of a continental movie star, an impersonal allure that was all the more mysterious because it seemed so impenetrable. Rosalind's beauty had a spiritual dimension that high fashion could only enhance but never conceal. There was a persona, as one would expect from a Hollywood star; but there was no facade. What Arlette and Rosalind did have in common, however, was a preference for James Galanos's creations. But what Galanos designed for Arlette—for example, a low-cut, bare-backed evening gown—was a far cry from the way he dressed Rosalind.

Frederick's marriage to Rosalind lasted thirty-five years; his marriage to Arlette, five. Realizing that she was competing with both Rosalind's memory and her husband's second love, the theater, Arlette insisted on a separation. Arlette may have been no substitute for Rosalind, but Broadway was no consolation to Frederick either. Unable to understand the success of rock musicals such as *Hair* and *Jesus Christ Superstar*—the latter striking him as blasphemous—or that his type of play had become outmoded, he went ahead and produced James Prideaux's comedy, *Mixed Couples*. Frederick tried to interest every major Hollywood studio to come on board as a general or limited partner, hoping that at least one of them would sign on for the movie version as well. The studios were not interested. Despite the presence of Geraldine Page, Julie Harris, and Rip Torn in the cast, *Mixed Couples* barely lasted a week—from 28 December 1980 to 3 January 1981.

Frederick had great plans, none of which materialized: a new comedy by Leonard Gershe, author of the highly successful *Butterflies Are Free*; a musical about Theodore Roosevelt and his daughter, Alice Roosevelt Longworth, with Robert Preston as the president; a London production of *Coco* with Lauren Bacall; a non-musical movie of *Coco*. His last stage production, *Dance a Little Closer*, opened and closed at the Minskoff Theater on the same night: 11 May 1983.

Dance a Little Closer was typical of Frederick's taste in musicals at a time when taste did not matter. It was based on Robert E. Sherwood's antiwar play, *Idiot's Delight* (1936), filmed in 1939 with Clark Gable and Norma Shearer. The book and lyrics were by Alan J. Lerner, who had done the same for *Coco*; the music, by Charles Strouse (*Bye Bye Birdie, Golden Boy, Annie*). The stars were Len Cariou, fresh from his success in Stephen Sondheim's *Sweeney Todd*, and Liz Robertson, Lerner's wife, in the Gable and Shearer roles. In the reviews, Strouse and Lerner did not come off badly, nor did Liz Robertson, but the general consensus was that *Dance a Little Closer* was not even a *succès d'estime*. For Lerner, it was the end of a brilliant career. For Frederick, it was the end of a long relationship with the theater, the medium he loved above all others.

A year later, on Monday, 8 October 1984, Frederick died of a stroke at New York Hospital–Cornell Medical Center at the age of seventy-one. His obituary appeared three days later in the *New York Times*, a week later in the *Los Angeles Times*. Legally, Arlette was Frederick's widow, but not necessarily his heir. Within two weeks, Lance lodged a suit against Arlette, challenging her rights to his father's estate. Two years later, a settlement was reached to Lance's satisfaction.

Meanwhile, it was dispossession time. Before he died, Frederick gave Sotheby's Rosalind's gold cigarette case and lighter, the latter a gift from Sinatra, both of which were auctioned shortly after Frederick's death. He had already donated much of Rosalind's wardrobe, assessed at $171,800—and designed by, among others, Orry Kelly, Balienciaga, Chanel, Travis Banton, and Galanos—to a number of institutions, including the Smithsonian, the

Philadelphia Museum of Art, the Fine Arts Museum of San Francisco, and New York's Metropolitan Museum of Art.

Rosalind's and Frederick's personal effects—including jewelry, scripts, celebrity-autographed photos, and letters from presidents—were auctioned at Christie's East Galleries in New York on 17 December 1984. In November 1986, there was an announcement in the trades that Lance and his ex-wife, Patricia Morrow, would be producing a television documentary about Rosalind, narrated by Patricia, with proceeds going to the Rosalind Russell Research Center in San Francisco. It never materialized. Even if there is never a documentary, Rosalind is well represented on film and at the center that bears her name.

After Rosalind opened in *Wonderful Town*, Tom Lewis, Loretta Young's husband, congratulated her on her triumph: "Success can be a prayer of many kinds. . . . It can inspire others to want to do—the right and good and generous things—as you always do."

It may seem strange that Lewis equated success with prayer, rather than attributing it to the result of prayer. Rosalind, however, would have understood. To her, prayer was a matter of cause and effect, but not in the usual sense of success as the answer to a prayer. Rather, success is a prayer in itself—a prayer that blesses those who have been touched by it, making them the better for it. Rosalind would have put success in the same category as knowledge, which she never considered an end in itself, but only a means to an end, such as self-improvement. But even that would not have been enough: Self-improvement should eventually lead to the improvement of others. For Rosalind, success was not a career that spanned four decades, but one that enabled her to embrace humanitarian causes, which she probably would have espoused anyway, even if she never became a star. Whether or not Rosalind had ever read Benjamin Franklin's *Autobiography*, she would have subscribed to his belief that "the most acceptable service to God is doing good to man."

Throughout her life Rosalind did more than her share of good, even though, to every generation, she will always be Auntie Mame. Yet Mame was far from an Ayn Rand egoist; she was willing to bid on property in Connecticut to establish a home for Jewish refugee children, striking a blow in her own way to Aryan supremacy.

No doubt, Mame's "life is a banquet" philosophy will be applied retroactively to Rosalind, whose life was not so much a banquet as a dinner party, carefully arranged and elegantly prepared, that began with grace before meals, the traditional expression of gratitude for such bounty. And Rosalind would have been the first to say that it was not the hostess to whom the guests were indebted, but the one who made it possible for her to extend such largesse to others.

Life may have been a banquet for Auntie Mame, but Rosalind Russell's heart kept open house.

MAJOR RADIO APPEARANCES

Lux Radio Theatre

Stage Door†	20 February 1939
My Favorite Wife*†	9 December 1940
Craig's Wife*†	12 May 1941
My Sister Eileen*†	5 July 1943
Flight for Freedom*†	20 September 1943
Roughly Speaking*	8 October 1945
What a Woman!*†	14 March 1949
Mildred Pierce*†	6 June 1949

* Available in Special Collections, Fairbanks Center for Motion Picture Study FCMPS.
† Available though Old Time Radio (http://www.ORCAT.com/luxradio.htm).

Screen Director's Playhouse

Hired Wife	6 February 1949 and 12 April 1951
A Foreign Affair	6 March 1949
This Thing Called Love	10 February 1950
She Wouldn't Say Yes	2 June 1950
Take a Letter, Darling	1 February 1951

All are available through http://www.audio_classics.com.

MAJOR TELEVISION APPEARANCES

Never Wave at a WAC   Schlitz Playhouse of Stars, CBS, 19 October 1951

The Night Goes On   General Electric Theatre, CBS, 18 March 1956

Wonderful Town*   CBS-TV, 30 November 1958

The Wonderful World of Entertainment*   Ford Startime, NBC, 6 October 1959 (Rosalind and Arthur O'Connell reenacted the proposal scene from *Picnic*, and Rosalind spoofed her "boss lady" movies.)

The Crooked Hearts   TV movie, ABC, 8 November 1972

* Available at the Museum of Television and Radio, New York and Beverly Hills.

FILMOGRAPHY

Metro-Goldwyn-Mayer

Evelyn Prentice   (William K. Howard, 1934)
Forsaking All Others   (W. S. VanDyke II, 1934)
West Point of the Air   (Richard Rosson, 1935)
Reckless   (Victor Fleming, 1935)
Casino Murder Case   (Edward L. Marin, 1935)
The Night Is Young   (Dudley Murphy, 1935)
China Seas   (Tay Garnett, 1935)
Rendezvous   (William K. Howard, 1935)
Trouble for Two   (J. Walter Ruben, 1936)
Night Must Fall   (Richard Thorpe, 1937)
Live, Love, and Learn   (George Fitzmaurice, 1937)
Man-Proof   (Richard Thorpe, 1938)
The Citadel   (King Vidor, 1938)
Fast and Loose   (Edward L. Marin, 1939)
The Women   (George Cukor, 1939)
They Met in Bombay   (Clarence Brown, 1941)
The Feminine Touch   (W. S. VanDyke II, 1941)
Design for Scandal   (Norman Taurog, 1941)

Paramount

The President Vanishes   (William Wellman, 1934)
Take a Letter, Darling   (Mitchell Leisen, 1942)
The Girl Rush   (Robert Pirosh, 1955)
Oh, Dad, Poor Dad, Mamma's Hung You in the Closet and I'm Feeling So Sad   (Richard Quine, 1967)

264

Twentieth Century–Fox

It Had to Happen   (Roy DelRuth, 1936)
Under Two Flags   (Frank Lloyd, 1936)

Warner Bros.

Four's a Crowd   (Michael Curtiz, 1938)
No Time for Comedy   (William Keighley, 1940)
Roughly Speaking   (Michael Curtiz, 1945)
Auntie Mame   (Morton DaCosta, 1958)
A Majority of One   (Mervyn LeRoy, 1961)
Gypsy   (Mervyn LeRoy, 1962)

Columbia

Craig's Wife   (Dorothy Arzner, 1936)
His Girl Friday   (Howard Hawks, 1940)
This Thing Called Love   (Alexander Hall, 1941)
My Sister Eileen   (Alexander Hall, 1942)
What a Woman!   (Irving Cummings, 1943)
She Wouldn't Say Yes   (Alexander Hall, 1945)
The Guilt of Janet Ames   (Henry Levin, 1947)
Tell It to the Judge   (Norman Foster, 1949)
A Woman of Distinction   (Edward Buzzell, 1950)
Picnic   (Joshua Logan, 1955)
Five Finger Exercise   (Daniel Mann, 1962)
The Trouble with Angels   (Ida Lupino, 1966)
Where Angels Go . . . Trouble Follows   (James Neilson, 1968)

Universal

Hired Wife   (William A. Seiter, 1940)
Rosie!   (David Lowell Rich, 1967)

RKO

Flight for Freedom   (Lothar Mendes, 1943)
Sister Kenny   (Dudley Nichols, 1946)
Mourning Becomes Electra   (Dudley Nichols, 1947)
The Velvet Touch   (John Gage, 1948)
Never Wave at a WAC   (Norman Z. McLeod, 1952)

United Artists

Mrs. Pollifax—Spy   (Leslie Martinson, 1971)

SOURCE NOTES

The following archives were used in researching this book (the abbreviations are used in the notes):

Cinema/TV Collection, University of Southern California
Louella Parsons Collection	LPC-USC
Neal Graham Collection	NGC-USC
Jack L. Warner Collection	JLWC-USC
King Vidor Collection	KVC-USC

Margaret Herrick Library at the Fairbanks Center for Motion Picture Study
Cary Grant Collection	CGC-FCMPS
George Cukor Collection	GCC-FCMPS
Gladys Hall Collection	GHC-FCMPS
Hedda Hopper Collection	HHC-FCMPS
Lux Radio Theatre Collection	LRTC-FCMPS

Motion Picture Association of America, Production Code Administration PCA-FCMPS

National Legion of Decency   NLD-FCMPS

Marymount College of Fordham University
Rosalind Russell File	RRF-MC

New York Public Library for the Performing Arts
Frederick Brisson Papers	FBP-NYPLPA

University of California at Los Angeles, Arts Library Special Collections
Rosalind Russell Papers	RRP-UCLASC

Chapter 1: The Gal from Waterbury

Biographical information derives from Rosalind's posthumously published autobiography, *Life Is a Banquet*, written with Chris Chase (New York: Random House, 1977), hereafter abbreviated as *Banquet*; the three-part series, "The Kind of Gal I Am," *Saturday Evening Post*, 29 September 1962, 26–30; 6 October, 36–44; 13 October, 72–75, abbreviated as "Kind of Gal"; correspondence from, and phone conversations with, present and former Waterburians identified in the text; material from Waterbury's Silas Bronson Library, including a copy of Rosalind's birth certificate; and Rosalind's file at Marymount College of Fordham University, Tarrytown, New York.

Quotations

8   "What a gal!": phone interview with Lou Gallulo, 16 April 2003.
10   "Nobody locked their doors": Peg Ruhlman, letter to author, 6 July 2003.
11   "The courage of this great lady": RRP-UCLA, Collection 183, 21.
12   "Do you know": phone interview with Rev. Thomas F. Bennett, 16 April 2003.
12   "Stop slouching": Ruhlman, 6 July 2003.
13   "the vocal chords of a frog": Rosalind Russell, "Kind of Gal," 13 October 1962, 27.
14   "To the above mentioned": Caroline Somers Hoyt, "Rosalind Russell's Strange Inheritance," *Movie Mirror*, April 1938, 56.
15   "where she dabbled in literature": *Contemporary Biography* (1943) (New York: H. W. Wilson, 1944).
15   "I regret very much" and "making a little progress": RRF-MC.

Chapter 2: Riding the Broadway-Hollywood Local

I am indebted to Ms. Betty Lawson, archivist and director of External and Alumni Affairs at the American Academy of Dramatic Arts (AADA) for allowing me access to AADA's Rosalind Russell file, which includes her audition report and student identification card, both of which are discussed in this chapter. I have based most of my information about Rosalind's stock company work from uncatalogued scrapbooks in RRP-UCLA, which Julie Graham, arts librarian for Special Collections at UCLA, made available to me.

Quotations

18   "Have you ever missed out": Helen Hover, "Popping the Question to Rosalind Russell," *Hollywood*, June 1942, 29.
19   "fantastic": Rosemary Jackson, "From Willow Street to Boston, It Was a 'Banquet,'" *Waterbury-Republican*, 11 November 1977, 14.
20   "Suppose we now skip lightly": "Kind of Gal," 6 October 1962, 41.

Chapter 3: The Lady and the Lion

The sources are mostly Rosalind's MGM films and loan-outs (1934–41) with dialogue taken from the movies themselves. King Vidor's preferences for the female lead in *The Citadel*, none of which included Rosalind, are in the form of casting suggestions in KVC-USC, Box 30.4.

The origins of the visually complex MGM logo are explained in Peter Hay's *MGM: When the Lion Roars* (Atlanta: Turner Publishing, 1991), 312; and Charles Higham's *Merchant of Dreams: Louis B. Mayer, MGM, and the Secret Hollywood* (New York: Dell/Laurel, 1993), 77.

Chapter 4: The Lady and the Mogul

Rosalind relates her encounter with Harry Cohn in *Banquet*, 110–111. Cohn's office is described by Bernard F. Dick, *The Merchant Prince of Poverty Row: Harry Cohn of Columbia Pictures* (Lexington: University Press of Kentucky, 1993), 72–73.

The details of Rosalind's Columbia contract can be found in RRP-UCLA, Box 24.

The two most useful discussions of *His Girl Friday* appear in Gerald Mast, *Howard Hawks, Storyteller* (New York: Oxford University Press, 1982), 208–242; and Todd McCarthy, *Howard Hawks: The Grey Fox of Hollywood* (New York: Grove, 1997), 278–287.

On the influence of the Legion of Decency in the 1940s, see James M. Skinner, *The Cross and the Cinema: The Legion of Decency and the National Catholic Office for Motion Pictures* (Westport, CT: Praeger, 1993).

Quotations

70   "innate taste": *Banquet*, 110.
71   "the Ambrose lighthouse": "Kind of Gal," 29 September 1962, 26.
72   "a hundred dollars a day": *Banquet*, 122.
77   "travesty of marriage," "enormous protest": Breen to Cohn, 29 December 1936, *This Thing Called Love* file, PCA-FCMPS.
79   "Christian concept of marriage," "in accordance with your request": NLDF-FCMPS, folder 8.
87   "delivers a screaming message": LRTC-FCMPS.
88   "suicide of the leading character": NLDF-FCMPS, folder 8.
96   "Rosalind's ability to play a career woman": RRP-UCLA, Box 27.

Chapter 5: Losing to Loretta

The text of *Mourning Becomes Electra* is the one in *Three Plays of Eugene O'Neill: Desire under the Elms, Strange Interlude*, and *Mourning Becomes Electra* (New York: Vintage, 1958), 223–376.

Oscar night, 28 March 1948, is vividly evoked in Mason Wiley and Damien Bona, *Inside Oscar: The Unofficial History of the Academy Awards*, ed. Gail McColl (New York: Ballantine, 1987), 179.

Quotations

111   "O Shenandoah": *Mourning*, 228.
116–17   "My dear 'Lavinia'": FBP-NYPLPA, Box 7, folder 9.

Chapter 6: Becoming Rosalind Russell Brisson

Biographical information about Frederick Brisson and his family derives from FBP-NYPLPA, Box 46, folders 18, 22, and 25. Jennifer Booth, assistant general secretary of the Rossalian Club, has verified for me Frederick's dates of attendance (1928–29) at the Rossall School, then called Rossall College. David Chierichetti has documented the production history of Carl Brisson's American film debut, *Murder at the Vanities*, in *Hollywood Director: The Career of Mitchell Leisen* (New York: Curtis, 1973), 76–83.

Charles Higham and Roy Mosley, *Cary Grant: The Lonely Heart* (New York: Harcourt, 1989), 28, 85, have shown how the lives of Frederick, Cary Grant, and talent agent Frank W. Vincent intersected, resulting in life-long friendships.

Rosalind described her wedding in "Cary Grant, the Magnificent," *Movieland*, May 1948, 88.

In an e-mail (15 June 2004) Lance Brisson explained his parents' selection of his given name.

Drafts of Rosalind's attempts at writing for the stage ("Little Mac") and the screen ("You Can't Judge a Lady" and "Teach Me to Love") can be found in RRP-UCLA, Boxes 5 and 63 ("Little Mac"), 9 ("You Can't Judge a Lady"), and 53 and 64 ("Teach Me to Love").

Quotations

122   "scenes . . . which show," "indecent or undue exposure": Robert Stanley, *The Celluloid Empire: A History of the American Motion Picture Industry* (New York: Hastings House, 1978), 277, 278.

131 "I shall adjust my career," "and if I have a child": Gladys Hall, "Rosalind Russell's Treasure Hunt Marriage," GHC-FCMPS, folder 415.

134 "Rosalind Russell's Modern Manor": *Modern Screen*, October 1945, 60–61.

135 "Towering surf": *Los Angeles Times*, 21 July 1964, RRP-UCLA, Box 10.

139 "I enjoyed making": LPC-USC, Box 6:5.

Chapter 7: A Return to the Roots

The text of *Bell, Book and Candle* is the one in *John Gassner's Best American Plays*, 3rd series, 1945–51 (New York: Crown, 1952), 593–626. Details of the *Bell, Book and Candle* tour come from RRP-UCLA, Box 31. Claudia Cassidy's review of *Bell, Book and Candle* appeared in the *Chicago Tribune*, 26 February 1952, part 3, 1.

The genesis of *Wonderful Town*, including the initial involvement of Arnold B. Horwitt and LeRoy Anderson, can be found on http://www.users.globalnet.co.uk/ ~mcgoni/wonderful_town.html, accessed 14 October 2004. The *Wonderful Town* lyrics cited in this chapter have been transcribed from the 6 April 1953 original cast recording, reissued on CD (MCA10-10050) as part of MCA's Broadway Gold Classics.

Betty Comden shared her memories of *Wonderful Town* with me in a 10 April 2003 phone interview.

In his autobiography, *Mr. Abbott* (New York: Random House, 1963), 248, George Abbott explains how Frederick joined the producing team of *The Pajama Game*.

Quotations

151 "I learned more": Shirley Hertz, as quoted by Mervyn Rothstein in "A Life in the Theatre," *Playbill*, August 2004, 50.

157 "I am not going": "Kind of Gal," 29 September 1962, 28.

157 "Have you made up your mind?": phone interview with Betty Comden, 10 April 2003.

161 "She was a lady": George Gaynes, e-mail to author, 10 September 2003.

161 "It's something like": Edie Adams and Robert Windeler, *Sing a Pretty Song . . .: The "Offbeat" Life of Edie Adams, including the Ernie Kovacs Years* (New York: William Morrow, 1990), 245.

Chapter 8: The Last of Boss Lady

The various drafts of *The Girl Rush* mentioned in this chapter exist in RRP-UCLA, Box 4. Ms. Rosemary Franzen, archivist of St. Margaret's–McTernan in Waterbury, confirmed the sale of the Russell home on Country Club Road to St. Margaret's, which subsequently merged with the McTernan School. Dialogue from *Picnic* is taken directly from the film.

Quotations

170   "manage a few tears": Cukor to Allenberg, 19 May 1954, GCC-FCMPS, William Morris Agency, folder 841.

173   "for sending [Rosalind] to us," "the purpose of this letter": Fryer to Hopper, 31 December 1952, HHC-FCMPS, #3189.

173   "the very best": Brisson to Hopper, 19 November 1954, HHC-FCMPS, #3189.

175   "ghastly": Transcript of tape interview with Pete Martin, May 1962, RRP-UCLA, Box 59, reel 6.

Chapter 9: Auntie Roz and Mama Rose

References to Patrick Dennis's novel, *Auntie Mame: An Irreverent Escapade* (1955), are from the 2001 Broadway Books edition. The various versions of the novel—film, Broadway musical, and film of the musical—are described in Richard Tyler Jordan, *But Darling, I'm Your Auntie Mame* (New York: Kensington, 2004). On the disputed role of Craig Rice in the writing of Gypsy Rose Lee's *The G-String Murders*, see Jeffrey A. Marks, *Who Was That Lady: Craig Rice, the Queen of Screwball Mystery* (Summit, MO: Delphi Books, 2001), 24.

The various suggestions for Rosalind's voice double for *Gypsy* appear in a memo from agent Leonard Hirscham to Mervyn LeRoy, 2 March 1962, JLWC-USC, Box 24.

While there are differences of opinion about Rosalind's working relationship with Natalie Wood during the filming of *Gypsy*, I am inclined toward Karl Malden's version, which he recounted to his friend, biographer Donald Spoto (e-mail from Spoto to author, 20 May 2003), that acting with Rosalind was "an enormous joy" and that "the circumstances of making the picture were hugely satisfying for everyone." Malden corroborated the story that Rosalind accidentally pierced her skull with a hat pin at the climax of "Some People." He also told Spoto that there was talk at Warner's of hiring Patricia Morison to supply the high notes for Rosalind, an idea that Rosalind herself vetoed.

Quotations

180   "You are my one and only": Joyce Haber, "From Stage to Screen—Brisson Success Formula," *Los Angeles Times*, Calendar, 22 April 1973, 13.

184   "shit": phone interview with Lawrence Roman, 2 September 2004.

185   "Look, I hate to tell": Lawrence Roman, *Under the Yum-Yum Tree*, act 1, scene 2 (New York: Dramatists Play Service, 1961), 28.

189, 190   "Only about twenty," "I have known": Dennis, *Auntie Mame*, 180, 216–217.

205   "He could get things done": phone interview with Lawrence Roman, 2 September 2004.

206   "beautiful symbol . . . You are very special": Rosalind to Jack Warner, 5 November 1956, JLWC-USC, Box 66:50 (Folder "R").

206   "It seems that . . . ": Rosalind to Jack Warner (undated, circa June 1959), JLWC-USC, Box 70 (Folder "Q/R," 1959).

208   "I certainly compare": quoted in Ethel Merman, *Merman: An Autobiography*, with George Eells (New York: Simon & Schuster, 1978), 216.

208   "Everyone knows": *Banquet*, 201.

209   "no limit": Blau to Pete Knecht, 17 April 1962, JLWC-USC, Box 24, 3.

209   "That's Roz": *Banquet*, 201.

211   "over the top contest": Gavin Lambert, *Natalie Wood: A Life* (New York: Knopf, 2004), 184.

Chapter 10: Mother Mame

Rosalind's statement that she was preparing for the role of Reverend Mother in *The Trouble with Angels* by reading Butler's *Lives of the Saints* was reported in Hedda Hopper's 26 September 1965 column, NGC-USC. Dialogue is quoted directly from the films discussed in this chapter.

Chapter 11: Trusting Him

Rosalind's idea of turning *The Trouble with Angels* premiere into a fund-raiser for Marymount Catholic High School is corroborated by newspaper clippings in RRF-MC.

Details of the controversy over Rosalind's starring in *Coco* are taken from correspondence and press clippings in FBP-NYPLPA, Box 5, folders 11 and 12.

The first-draft screenplay of *Mrs. Pollifax—Spy* can be found in FBP-NYPLPA, Box 19.

Rosalind's "The Story of a Medal" appeared in *Our Sunday Visitor*, 22 August 1971, 5.

The texts of the eulogies at Rosalind's funeral mass can be found in RRP-UCLA, Box 22; see also "My Wife, Roz," 234. I am grateful to Lance Brisson for describing his mother's last day of life for me. Details about *Banquet*'s publication problems, Frederick's remarriage, and his contested will come from material in the Frederick Brisson Clippings File, FCMPS.

Arlette Brisson is quoted in Enid Nemy, "New Yorkers, etc.," *New York Times*, 14 April 1982, C14; and Enid Nemy, "'What? Me Marry?' Widows Say No." *New York Times*, 18 June 1992, C1.

Quotations

233   "F-U-N": personal interview with author, 31 May 2004.

234   "Roz is *in* Hollywood": *Banquet*, 241.

235   "sham": J. Randy Taraborelli, *Sinatra: Behind the Legend* (Secaucus, NJ: Carol, 1977), 30.

236   "I do feel": CGC-FCMPS.

237   "Frank Sinatra is": Ed Walters, "Songs by Sinatra: Stories from Vegas," www.songs-bysinatra./com/stories/stories26html-5k, accessed 4 September 2004.

238   "You have given . . . greatest entertainer of the twentieth century": Michael Freeland, *All the Way: A Biography of Frank Sinatra* (London: Weidenfeld and Nicholson, 1997), 354.

238   "respectable": Kitty Kelley, *His Way: The Unauthorized Biography of Frank Sinatra* (New York: Bantam, 1986), 346.

241   "I want to freeze": Rosalind Russell, "Frank Sinatra's $25,000 Weekend," *Ladies Home Journal*, January 1967, 115.

241   "This is definitely not for Roz": Lerner to Frederick, 13 September 1967, FBP-NYPLPA, Box 5, folder 11.

242   "Who the devil cares": *Coco* CD (MCAD-11682), MCA Records, 1970.

242   "the gay, uninhibited, irresistible zest": Lerner to Frederick, 13 September 1967, FBP-NYPLPA, Box 5, folder 11.

242   "emotional brittleness," "singing voice": Frederick to Previn, 18 September 1967, FBP-NYPLPA, Box 5, folder 11.

243   "the matter is closed": Frederick to Previn, 1 October 1967, FBP-NYPLPA, Box 5, folder 12.

243   "terrible misunderstanding": Previn to Rosalind, 30 October 1967, FBP-NYPLPA, Box 5, folder 12.

252   "There is nothing": RRP-UCLA, Box 22; also "My Wife, Roz," 232.

254   "Trust Him": RRP-UCLA, Box 22; "My Wife, Roz," 234; *Challenger*, Newsletter of the Arthritis Foundation, #8, 1977, 4.

255   "tied with lots of knots": William Frye, "The Wizard of Roz," *Vanity Fair*, April 2002, 285.

255   "death textured with peace": "My Wife, Roz," 194.

260   "Success can be a prayer": Tom Lewis to Rosalind Russell, FBP-NYPLPA, Box 7, folder 9.

SELECT BIBLIOGRAPHY

Agan, Patrick. "Rosalind Russell: Life Was a Banquet until the End." *Hollywood Studio Magazine* (February 1984): 8–12.

Bowers, Ronald. "New York's Rosalind Russell Festival." *Films in Review* (November 1974): 572–573.

Brisson, Frederick. "My Wife, Roz." *McCall's* (April 1977): 194+.

Carson, James. "The Rosalind Russell Road to Successville." *Modern Screen* (April 1940): 28+.

———. "Time Out for Comedy." *Modern Screen* (September 1940): 22+.

Dick, Bernard F. *The Merchant Prince of Poverty Row: Harry Cohn of Columbia Pictures.* Lexington: University Press of Kentucky, 1993.

Hall, Gladys. "Rosalind Russell's Treasure Hunt Marriage." *Silver Screen* (March 1942): 22+.

Hoyt, Caroline Sommers. "Rosalind Russell's Strange Inheritance." *Movie Mirror* (April 1938): 56+.

———. "Roz Lives Alone—and Hates It!" *Modern Screen* (June 1939): 38+.

Kilgallen, Dorothy. "That Complainin' Roz." *Modern Screen* (April 1937): 59+.

Parrish, James R., and Ronald L. Bowers. *The MGM Stock Company: The Golden Era.* New York: Bonanza Books, 1972.

Ringgold, Gene. "The Rosalind Russell Story." *Films in Review* (December 1970): 585–610.

Russell, Rosalind. "Cary Grant, the Magnificent." *Movieland* (May 1948): 44+.

———. "The Kind of Gal I Am." *Saturday Evening Post,* 29 September 1962, 26–30; 6 October 1962, 36–44; 13 October 1962, 72–75.

———. "Frank Sinatra's $25,000 Weekend." *Ladies Home Journal* (January 1967): 48+.

———. "The Story of a Medal." *Our Sunday Visitor,* 22 August 1975, 5.

Russell, Rosalind, and Chris Chase. *Life Is a Banquet.* New York: Random House, 1977.

Zeitlin, Ida. "Object—Gayety?" *Modern Screen* (May 1941): 28+.

INDEX

289